FEEDING
THE FUTURE

ALSO PART OF THE INGENUITY PROJECT

Fueling the Future

FEEDING
THE FUTURE
FROM FAT TO FAMINE
HOW TO SOLVE THE WORLD'S FOOD CRISES

EDITED BY
ANDREW HEINTZMAN AND EVAN SOLOMON

ANANSI

Published in 2004 by
House of Anansi Press Inc.
110 Spadina Avenue, Suite 801
Toronto, ON, M5V 2K4
Tel. 416.363.4343
Fax 416.363.1017
www.anansi.ca

Distributed in Canada by
Publishers Group Canada
250A Carlton Street
Toronto, ON, M5A 2L1
Tel. 416.934.9900
Toll free order numbers:
Tel. 800.663.5714
Fax 800.565.3770

08 07 06 05 04 FP 1 2 3 4 5

House of Anansi Press is committed to protecting our natural environment. As part of our efforts, this book is printed on Rolland recycled paper: it contains 100% post-consumer recycled fibres, is acid-free, and is processed chlorine-free.

Library and Archives Canada Cataloguing in Publication Data

Feeding the future : from fat to famine, how to solve the world's food crises /
Andrew Heintzman and Evan Solomon, editors.
Includes bibliographical references.
ISBN 0-88784-186-4
1. Food supply. 2. Famines — Prevention. 3. Agricultural innovations.
I. Heintzman, Andrew, 1967– II. Solomon, Evan, 1968–
HD9000.5.F443 2004   363.8 C2004-906605-6

Jacket and text design: Bill Douglas at The Bang
Page composition: PageWave Graphics Inc.

Canada Council
for the Arts

Conseil des Arts
du Canada

ONTARIO ARTS COUNCIL
CONSEIL DES ARTS DE L'ONTARIO

We acknowledge for their financial support of our publishing program the Canada Council for the Arts, the Ontario Arts Council, and the Government of Canada through the Book Publishing Industry Development Program (BPIDP).

Printed and bound in Canada

For those who in a world of plenty are still going hungry;
and for those who are trying to feed them.

And also for our children: Molly, Maizie, Theodore,
and the recently arrived Gideon.

CONTENTS

FOREWORD

WHEN YOU LOOK calmly and rationally at the world's food system today, there are many reasons to feel depressed. Everywhere, farmers are being driven off the land. Agribusiness companies wield more power than at any other time in history. The supermarkets have more power. Wal-Mart has more power, squeezing producers harder and paying employees even less than many supermarkets do. The same fast-food chains sell the same food worldwide. Soda companies aggressively target children in schools. Meatpacking companies mistreat their livestock, overuse antibiotics and growth hormones, abuse their workers, pollute rivers and streams, sell meat tainted with fecal material and harmful bacteria. Farm-raised salmon are often contaminated with pesticide residues, while wild salmon are vanishing from the seas. And then there's mad cow disease, avian flu, and genetically modified foods. The wealthy, industrialized nations dump subsidized grain on the poorer, less developed ones, destroying fragile rural economies and creating famines. Modern industrialized agriculture depends upon cheap petroleum, and we're running out of that. A clear look at what's happening today is bound to overwhelm you with doom and gloom.

Some of the best things in life, however, have nothing to do with cool, calm reason. To make real change, you need other qualities, like anger, passion, and that most illogical human trait:

hope. Things are bad, all right — but things didn't have to turn out this way. The more time I spend investigating how we produce and distribute our food, the more I realize that none of these problems was inevitable. Today's food system was not the inescapable result of free market forces, natural law, technological advance, or the triumph of modernity. Indeed, the "free market" had little to do with determining how and why certain foods are now produced. For years the American fast food industry has benefited from government subsidies, government-funded road construction (so essential for all those drive-throughs), and minimum wage policies that keep labour costs low. Right now in the United States more then half the money earned by corn farmers comes directly from taxpayers. This cheap, subsidized corn becomes cheap animal feed, lowering the cost of meat. And there's nothing inevitable about how the U.S. Congress frames its farm bills. Every year the large agribusiness firms and corporate farmers get what they want, family farmers get squeezed, and ordinary consumers pay the bill.

About a dozen agribusiness companies now control most of the food that Americans eat. And the powerful oligopolies that dominate nearly every commodity market are a violation of free market principles, not their fulfillment. If America's antitrust laws were enforced today the way they were fifty years ago, during the administration of President Dwight D. Eisenhower, most of our leading agribusiness companies would be dismantled. Eisenhower, hardly a left-wing activist, strongly believed in the importance of competition — and during his first year in office boldly launched an antitrust campaign against the nation's five biggest oil companies. For the past twenty-five years, government policy has encouraged unprecedented centralization and consolidation. In 1970, the four largest meatpacking companies controlled about 20 percent of the American beef market. Today the four largest control more than 80 percent. Tyson Foods — the largest producer of both chicken and beef — is now the biggest meatpacking company the world has ever seen. Its market power has huge implications for farmers, ranchers, workers, and consumers — in the United States and Canada. Fate and the free market were not the guiding forces that brought us unchecked corporate power. Every step of the way, important choices were made by politicians, chief executives, and unwitting consumers. Different choices can still be made.

In 1959, the year I was born, people of colour in much of the United States were forbidden to use the same public toilets as white people or to sleep at the same hotels. The Soviet Union oppressed its own citizens and ruled half of Europe. Blacks in South Africa were treated like serfs. In 1959, if you'd predicted that Nelson Mandela would one day be elected president of a free, multiracial South Africa, people would have said you were out of your mind. In my lifetime, I've seen segregation, the Berlin Wall, and apartheid vanish from the Earth. So I refuse to believe that the way we feed ourselves today must endure forever. Our current system won't last because it can't last. It is not sustainable. This centralized, industrialized agricultural system has been in place for just a few decades — and look at the destruction it has already caused. Look at the harm it has inflicted upon consumers, livestock, and the environment. In the final analysis, our fast, cheap food costs too much.

Yet amid the daily litany of depressing headlines, there are reasons to be cheerful. People who are well-informed about food issues — largely members of the educated, upper middle class — are changing their eating habits. They are buying organic, free-range, locally produced foods. They are rejecting fast food and supporting the Slow Food movement. They don't want anything to do with the highly processed, freeze-dried, chemical-laden foods that most people still consume. This is hardly a widespread revolution — but it could be the start of one. Change has to begin somewhere, and, like the abolition movement of the nineteenth century and the civil rights movement of the twentieth, the drive to get rid of bad food has begun mainly among the wealthy and well-educated. As awareness of the problem spreads, so will anger and disgust. Some day government policy will stop subsidizing the wrong foods and make healthy food affordable for the poor.

In Germany mad cow disease opened people's eyes. You could hardly find a nation more dedicated to reason, more obsessed with efficiency, technology, and the cool ethos of the engineer. Yet the German response to mad cow disease rejected all of that. After years of distortions and cover-ups by German agricultural officials, Renate Kuenast, a member of the Green Party, became minister of Agriculture, Nutrition, and Consumer Protection in 2001. "Things will no longer be the way they are," Kuenast declared, introducing a fundamentally new approach to food policy. The German government is now officially committed to the de-industrialization of agriculture. It vows to make 20 percent of German farmland organic within a decade. It has enacted the world's first animal bill of rights. If Germany can head down this path, so can the rest of the world.

The essays in this book suggest new agricultural technologies and new business models. Some may prove important; others, a complete waste of time. You may agree with some of the arguments made in these pages, and vehemently disagree with others. All of them, however, present us with the opportunity to make choices.

How we get our food today is by no means the only way to get it. Uniformity and conformity, a blind faith in science, a narrow measure of profit and loss, a demand for total, absolute control — these are the central values of the current food system. A new one will emerge from an opposing set. The change won't just happen, though. People will have to make it happen. Passionate anger at the way things are must replace the sense of doom and gloom. Championing the right foods, instead of the wrong ones, won't require martyrdom or violent uprising. But it will need activists to oppose the reigning food giants in the courts, the legislatures, the schools, and the realm of public opinion. Consumers can play an important role, too, just by buying foods that have been produced the right way, by supporting local farmers and ranchers. That won't take much sacrifice. To paraphrase the great Alice Waters: this revolution tastes good.

— Eric Schlosser

INTRODUCTION

TO FULLY COMPREHEND the shocking paradoxes of the modern history of food, you have to go back to April 22, 1915, at 5 p.m., when a mysterious yellow-green cloud blows over the muddy fields of Belgium, near the town of Ypres. The cloud is eight kilometres (five miles) wide and smells vaguely of pineapple and pepper. From their trenches, thousands of French and Algerian soldiers watch nervously as it moves towards them. They've seen gas attacks before. Back in August of 1914, when the war was barely a month old, the French themselves used tearing agents to temporarily blind and disable German troops. But this is clearly different. This cloud is heavier, clinging low to the ground as it would smother the soldiers like a pillow. And then there's that strange smell, reminding some men of how long it's been since they've had a good meal. What's going on?

A few hundred yards away, in the German trenches, a bald man with a small mustache and pince-nez glasses paces excitedly. Though he's in uniform, the man is actually a scientist. On his orders, a specially trained unit of German soldiers has just released 5,200 cylinders or 168 tonnes of chlorine gas into the air. If the wind direction holds and the chlorine cloud — his cloud! — does its job, this man believes the war will be won. Then the name Fritz Haber will be known to all Germans. He will be a hero.

As a scientist, Haber well knows the effects of his new weapon. When chlorine gas comes into contact with moisture — say the moisture in the eyes and lungs of the enemy soldiers across no-man's land — it transforms into the deadly chemical called hydrochloric acid. Haber knows the French and Algerians will feel a sudden, terrible stinging in their eyes, followed by choking nausea. And then they will die of asphyxiation. It's a simple matter of science.

The French commanders don't understand this kind of chemistry. Believing the cloud is another German ruse meant to camouflage an imminent attack, they order their troops to "stand to" in readiness. It's a fatal error. Within hours, over 5,000 soldiers are dead and 15,000 others are terribly wounded. The rest of the troops abandon their position and flee. A six-kilometre (four-mile) hole opens up in the line. For Fritz Haber it is a major triumph.

The Germans commanders, however, do not take immediate advantage of the open ground. They fear gassing themselves with Haber's weapon, so they wait. When they finally advance two days later, they're met with fierce resistance from Canadian brigades who rush in to plug the hole. Haber gasses the Canadians too.

Fritz Haber's moment of glory does not last long. Within days, the British and French respond with their own deadly chemicals, and the age of gas warfare begins. Both sides quickly develop protective gear rendering Haber's theories about the power of gas — shall we say — overly optimistic. Like all new inventions, this one has unanticipated consequences, as Haber soon discovers.

Two days after that first attack, Haber's wife Clara is despondent. Also a brilliant chemist, Clara knows her husband is using his genius in unethical ways. She's done all she can to try to stop him, but Fritz never listens to her. He's obsessed with glory. And now, with the gassings at the front, he has implicated her in what she believes is a crime against humanity. There is only one option left, a final way to protest her husband's work. Taking a pistol from a drawer, Clara Haber puts it to her chest and shoots herself through the heart.

What does the story of Fritz Haber have to do with modern food? Everything, actually. Years before he launched that murderous gas attack, Haber pioneered one of the twentieth century's most important inventions, arguably more influential than Thomas Edison's light bulb or the Wright brothers' plane. Fritz Haber discovered how to make artificial fertilizer.

If artificial fertilizer doesn't sound as revolutionary as, say, the light bulb, it's because Haber's invention remains hidden behind the growth of the modern world, whereas Edison's illuminates it. But it's hard to overestimate the importance of Haber's work. Almost everything we eat today — from the corn that feeds our cattle to the fruits we grow — comes from artificially made nitrogen-based fertilizers created from Fritz Haber's life-saving process.

And life saving it's proven to be. Fertilizer is made of ammonia and nitrogenous compounds, and, as scientists in Haber's day realized, Mother Nature doesn't make nearly enough of it to feed the world's population. Without access to more fertilizer, scientists predicted mass global starvation. At the time, the largest natural source of fertilizer happened to be located along a 350-kilometre (220-mile) stretch of the Chilean and Peruvian coast, where huge deposits of guano or bird droppings were discovered in the form of saltpetre. Guano was considered so valuable that in 1856 the United States actually passed the Guano Island Act, enabling any U.S. citizen to seize guano deposits in the name of the United States of America:

> Whenever any citizen of the United States discovers a deposit of guano on any island, rock, or key . . . the same, such island, rock, or key may, at the discretion of the President, be considered as appertaining to the United States.

Wars were fought over guano the way wars today are fought over oil. Between 1879 and 1884, the so-called "Nitrate War" raged in South America, driven by Great Britain's desire to control Chile's saltpetre mines. In winning that war, the British also scooped huge chunks of valuable coastal land from countries like Bolivia, which remains landlocked to this day. In 1907, when a Chilean movement arose to unionize the brutal saltpetre industry, Great Britain and the United States refused to see their cheap fertilizer source jeopardized by disgruntled workers. They promptly supplied weapons to the local military who massacred 2,500 workers in the town of Iquique. So it's not an exaggeration to say that one hundred years ago, bird shit was gold worth killing for, and the gold was disappearing fast.

One year after the saltpetre massacres in Chile, Fritz Haber found a way around the looming food crisis. By mixing hydrogen and nitrogen gas in a high-pressure tank and then heating it to over 500°C, Haber discovered that he could produce small amounts of ammonia, the base ingredient for fertilizer. Haber quickly informed the German chemical giant Badische Anilin und Soda Fabrik (BASF) of his discovery, and they were so amazed that they bought the patent. They asked their own scientist, Carl Bosch, to make Haber's method commercially viable, and in 1913 Bosch did just that. Soon the so-called Haber-Bosch method for synthesizing massive amounts of ammonia transformed the world.

All of which explains why in 1918, *after* he had been called a criminal by the Allies for his use of chlorine gas, Fritz Haber was awarded the Nobel Prize for Chemistry. Some scientists protested the honour, but most of the community conveniently forgot about Haber's tainted past and celebrated his great break-through. "Improved nitrogen fertilization of the soil," Haber wrote in his Nobel Prize lecture, "brings new nutritive riches to mankind and the chemical industry comes to the aid of the farmer who, in the good earth, changes stones into bread."

If "changes stones into bread" is typical of Haber's hyperbolic self-regard, it is not so inaccurate. As Vaclav Smil argues in his seminal book *Enriching the Earth: Fritz Haber, Carl Bosch, and the Transformation of World Food Production*, "The single most important change affecting the world's population — its expansion from 1.6 billion people in 1900 to today's 6 billion — would not have been possible without the synthesis of ammonia." Today the world produces over 130 million tonnes of ammonia, most of it used for fertilizer. "Without this [Haber-Bosch process]" Smil writes, "about two-fifths of the world's population would not be around — and our dependence will only increase as the global count moves from 6 to 9 or 10 billion people." As Smil likes to say, we can live without computers, cars, light bulbs, and planes, but we cannot live without food. And much of the world eats because of Fritz Haber.

Few people embody the Janus face of scientific progress better than Fritz Haber. On one side he smiles at the great promise of discoveries like synthesizing ammonia, and on the other side he frowns at the great peril of chlorine gas as a weapon. Like Haber's, however, all our inventions have a dark and a light side. Nothing illustrates that better than the modern story of nitrogen. Much of the 100 million tonnes of synthetic nitrogen fertilizer we use today to grow our crops ends up in our environment, where it causes serious pollution. Nitrogen run-off from farmers' fields ends up in our lakes and oceans, causing an explosive growths of algae called eutrophication. Mid-western runoff emptying into the Gulf of Mexico from the Mississippi River has created a 20,000-square-kilometre (8,000-square-mile) area known as the dead zone. The nitrogen has caused so much algal growth that it's stopped the sunlight from penetrating to the bottom of the sea, killing a multi-million-dollar fish and shrimp industry.[1]

Haber's life continued to embrace this great paradox. In the 1920s, Haber ran Germany's greatest science lab where he developed a remarkably effective pesticide called Zyklon B. His career might have gone on for years, but in 1933 Adolf Hitler rose to power and purged Germany of all Jewish scientists. Though a zealous German patriot and a convert to Christianity, Fritz Haber was born a Jew. Forced to flee to Switzerland, Haber died on January 29, 1934, at the age of 65, rejected by the country he tried so hard to serve. Zyklon B, Haber's insecticide, would be the chemical used in the gas chambers of Nazi Germany's death camps.

Is Haber a hero or a villain? He's both, of course, which is why he is such a fascinating symbol for our discussion about the future of food and the role that science plays in it. In the age of genetically altered foods, fast food, and mass famines, Haber's life stands as a warning to those who would use science to solve the food problem. As Haber's own son Ludwig wrote, "In Haber the German High Command found a brilliant mind and an extremely energetic organizer, determined, and also quite unscrupulous." Today we also have brilliant, energetic, and determined minds. Some offer unscrupulous solutions, others more sustainable ones. Which will we choose? How can we avoid the unanticipated consequences of our actions, and correct the mistakes of the past? How can we know that the artificial fertilizers of today will not turn into the chlorine gasses of tomorrow? When it comes to food, these questions go right to the gut.

THE INGENUITY PROJECT YEAR 2: FROM ENERGY TO FOOD

Food lies at the crossroads where global issues meet personal choice, where we all quite literally taste the world around us. Every bite of food connects us, however unconsciously, to systems and debates about fat and famine, mad cows and GMOs, global trade regulations and subsidies, pesticides and collapsing fish stocks. In the face of these grand issues, it sometimes seems as if nothing can be done. It's all too big, too complicated, too inevitable. That's wrong.

Three years ago, we established The Ingenuity Project to attempt to move beyond this paralysis. We wanted a deeper understanding of the most intractable challenges facing our world — to discover practical solutions. We call these practical solutions ingenuity, a term popularized by a fine Canadian thinker, writer, and friend, Thomas Homer-Dixon. In his best-selling book *The Ingenuity Gap*, he defines ingenuity in two ways. Firstly, technical ingenuity: the inventions and technologies that help us solve problems. Secondly, social ingenuity: the institutions, laws, and relationships that we use to solve our problems. When we can no longer supply enough ingenuity to solve our problems, Homer-Dixon says we have an ingenuity gap. He concludes that societies too often turn to technical ingenuity when social ingenuity is really needed to solve their problems. Our mandate is to apply both technical and social ingenuity to big problems, and to do so in a language people can understand.

Last year we applied this mandate to the problem of energy. In *Fueling the Future: How the Battle Over Energy Is Changing Everything* we asked the question "How can we build a sustainable, plentiful energy future for everyone, without over-taxing the environment, our health, and future generations?" As can be expected from such a challenging question, the answers were not simple. No one solution can solve all of our energy woes. Rather, in canvassing some of the best and brightest minds from around the world, we found a myriad of solutions: greater efficiencies in our energy system; new technologies like fuel cells, and wind and solar power; smarter ways to design our houses and buildings; different means to minimize pollution through processes like carbon sequestration. By combining the effects of all of these good ideas, and by looking for ways to integrate them, we discovered an ingenuity array that can indeed provide a more sustainable and effective energy system.

Even more important than the specific answers, however,

was the process of asking the questions. Asking questions forced us to look at the social structures around us, to find out how they determine our behaviour and what other options we have. Suddenly, the big obstacles we saw in front of us gave way to opportunities for change, revitalizing our faith in the power of citizenship, consumers, and pragmatism.

Food is intimately connected to energy and so it is the logical next step for The Ingenuity Project. After all, food is the body's energy. The astounding ability of plants to convert the Sun's energy into food through photosynthesis is at the root of all life. All food and all energy trace their origins back to the same ultimate source: the Sun. The connection between energy and food is also apparent in our western economies, but of course in a very different way as our sprawling food networks have become rapacious energy consumers.

In a brilliant *Atlantic Monthly* article, "The Oil We Eat: Following the Food Chain Back to Iraq," Richard Manning argues that for every calorie of food-energy we produce, "the food-processing industry in the United States uses about ten calories of fossil-fuel energy." And that's just the energy required to produce the food; it does *not* include the fuel used to transport the food. When you consider the trucks, trains, ships, and planes required for worldwide distribution to ensure that we get our fruits and vegetables year-round, the coolers and freezers needed to keep the "cold chain" functioning and our food unspoiled, it is clear that the logistics of our food system are startlingly energy intensive and complicated. The implications of these inefficiencies are shocking: according to Manning, if everyone in the world consumed food the way that North Americans do, all known fossil-fuel reserves will be used up in seven to ten years.

The connection between food and energy goes even deeper, and is perhaps best exemplified by the horrible famine in Ethiopia. Like much of the developing world, Ethiopia was a virtual breeding ground of famine, afflicted by a perfect storm of war, overpopulation, and drought. In 1984, pictures of children with bloated bellies, children too frail and tired even to chase away the flies collecting at corners of their mouths, haunted us all. At the time we were told that political upheavals in the country caused the famine.

But there was another factor in the 1984 Ethiopian famine, and the five other famines that have since occurred there, a rarely mentioned factor: deforestation. For most Ethiopians, the major — often the only — energy source is fire. As the population has grown, the land has been cleared of trees to provide energy for heat and for cooking. Deforestation caused soil erosion, which in turn resulted in the loss of agricultural lands. To make matters worse, global warming has led to more frequent droughts. This has created a vicious cycle that has made the country ever more vulnerable to famine. And it underlines, in a singularly devastating way, the intricate connection between energy and food.

Like energy, the food industry is a complex web that we consumers encounter daily in many different forms; but it is also hard for the average person to fully grasp and understand. Like energy, some of our food problems have to do not with having too little but with having too much, or not the right kind of food in the right place and time. After tens of thousands of years of struggling to avoid famine, most of us in the developed world are now faced with the strange problem of having too much to eat. The food crisis, like the energy crisis, is in fact a variety of totally contradictory crises: the crisis of starvation in Ethiopia and the crisis of obesity in North America.

Thinking about food, we reflect on a myriad contradictory problems. And these complex problems themselves suggest a range of contradictory solutions. The issues are real, and the choices difficult. But the only way forward is to start the journey with some questions, some stories, in the search for ingenuity.

A HISTORY OF FOOD

1.9 MILLION B.C. Our ancestors learn "tuber cooking," which allows them to cook roots and vegetables for eating. This results in a number of changes to human anatomy, including a smaller jaw and tooth size because the tender cooked plants require smaller teeth. Cooking foods makes a larger number of foods available to early humans; this greater nutritional value results in people growing much larger. The broader diet also allows early humans to roam and colonize new locations, and leads to a broader dissemination of the species.

10,000 B.C. Humans learn how to make flatbread by baking flour and water.

3000 B.C. Using yeast and wheat grain, ancient Egyptians master the ability to make raised bread. They also perfect ovens to bake multiple loaves simultaneously. Bread becomes so popular in ancient Egypt that the pyramid workers are often paid in bread rather than currency.

2200 B.C. Chinese emperor Hsia Yu levies a tax on salt, in one of the first known examples of taxation.

2000 B.C. Ancient Egyptians make a candy from a mixture of honey and the sap of the marsh-mallow plant *Althaea officinalis*, which lives by the edges of saltwater marshes and rivers.

500s B.C. Greek mathematician Pythagoras — espousing a philosophy of respect for all living things and the injunction against eating meat — becomes the first known vegetarian, and a touchstone for vegetarians down the ages. He recognizes the health benefits from vegetarian thinking and the moral problems of killing animals. Other Greeks, such as Aristotle and Socrates, seem to share his injunction.

410 A.D. The Visigoth ruler Alaric demands 1,350 kilograms (3,000 pounds) of pepper annually, as a ransom from Rome.

600s A.D. The leek becomes a national symbol of Wales when soldiers use leeks to distinguish themselves in battle from their enemies.

▼ CONTINUED ON PAGE 36

SAVING AGRICULTURE FROM ITSELF

STUART LAIDLAW

THROUGHOUT RURAL MANITOBA there are signs of decay. Abandoned farmhouses. Overgrown railroad tracks running to closed grain elevators. Boarded-up businesses next to tattered, aging stores still open but with few cars parked outside and fewer customers inside. There are signs, too, of what was slowly creeping into the countryside in their place. Hog barns dwarf the family farms of just a decade ago. On the prairie landscape, inland grain terminals rise like mountains along the main trunk lines that left the traditional wooden grain elevators and their spur lines obsolete. Wal-Mart.

But there are also small acts of defiance: new community centres and curling rinks built with local labour and paid for with fundraising by people who believe in the future of their communities. Farmers getting together to talk about building a co-operative slaughterhouse, an alternative to the industrial food complex that has left them wondering if their farms will survive to see another generation. And, perhaps most encouragingly, gatherings of young and old to spend an evening discussing how to change two generations of farming methods for a new way.

In Pilot Mound, Manitoba, strong community-loyalty and a defiant determination to keep farming viable for future generations drew seventy-five people to a night of roast beef, overhead slides, and lectures on how to break out of the industrial food system. Pilot Mound is a typical prairie town: one main street lined with wood-frame, false-front shops, and angle parking. I arrived at the community hall in October 2003, part of a group of three to lead a discussion on alternative agriculture. My job was to talk about establishing closer ties between city and country people in hopes of producing better food and giving farmers a bigger share of the grocery dollar. Fred Kirschenmann, of the University of Iowa's Aldo Leopold Center for Sustainable Agriculture, was also there. He would talk about wheat farmers who had converted their farms into bakeries. Groups of farmers who had established a dairy co-operatives to sell better milk at higher prices — and were making more money than ever before. His mission, in short, was to fill the farmers with belief in the future. Ordained as a minister, Kirschenmann says his true calling has been to convert the 3,000-acre (1,200-hectare) North Dakota farm he inherited to organics, and to spread the word of sustainable agriculture. Rene Van Acker, a professor at the University of Manitoba, had brought both of us to his province for the four-town lecture tour. He was researching the appetite for change in rural Manitoba.

About an hour before our event was to begin, there was no one at the hall. The door was locked; the parking lot was empty. We tried to ignore the sinking feeling that we would be speaking to an empty hall, and went for coffee. The streets, like the community centre, were empty. So, too, was the coffee shop. We made small talk, about families, work, the weather. For as long as possible we put off going back to the centre to see if anybody would show up. When finally we did, we found the kitchen busy with women preparing that night's meal, the tables set, and a lectern in place.

There's no shortage of towns in which to give such a talk. Across North America, industrialized agriculture has caused an unprecedented emptying of our rural areas as farmers are driven from the land to make way for larger operations. Economy of scale has become the driving force of farming. But when farms get big, they do so by forcing others from the industry. In 1950, 38 percent of the population in the developed world lived in the country, according to the United Nations.[1] By 1990, only 8 percent was rural, with predictions of a further drop to 2 percent by 2025 — a level already reached in Canada and the United States. In fact, the U.S.A. now has more inmates in federal penitentiaries than it has farmers.

Such statistics pushed American essayist Wendell Berry to ask, "What are people for?" Berry, like many before and since, draws a straight line between rural depopulation and the companies behind industrialized farming. "The farm-to-city migration has obviously produced advantages for the corporate economy. The absent farmers have had to be replaced by machinery, petroleum, chemicals, credit, and other expensive goods and services from the agribusiness economy, which is not to be confused with the economy of what used to be called farming."[2]

Certainly, people have always moved from the country to the city, but industrial agriculture has sped up the process, leaving small towns unsustainable, without services, schools or businesses. Our rural areas seem destined to be little more than massive industrial parks manufacturing food away from prying eyes. Such a system is not sustainable, environmentally or economically. But it is driving urban consumers to find new sources of food. And it brought seventy-five people out to our lectures in Pilot Mound, and to more to lectures in Dauphin, Riverton, and St. Pierre, to find ways to feed that market. These men and women were raised to believe that theirs was a renewable industry. The truth is, it is not. Not any more.

Through almost all of its 10,000-year history farming was, by definition, renewable. Wherever agriculture began around the world — grain in the Middle East, rice in China and India, corn in Central America, and potatoes in the Andes — it marked an end to the hunter-gatherer life that preceded it. Rather than waiting to see what nature offered, early farmers saved seeds for replanting. Each year's harvest, then, provided not only food for the rest of the year, but also seed for the following year. Manure from domesticated animals fertilized the land. No other industry has matched this level of sustainability, and saving seeds remained the foundation of farming until just the last few generations.

The beginning of the end of this ancient practice — still used widely in developing countries — came in the 1920s when Henry Wallace of Iowa began selling hybrid corn through his Pioneer Hy-Bred Corn Company. Wallace had developed a system of multi-generational crossbreeding that resulted in one, and only one, generation of high-yielding corn. Charles Darwin had explored the notion, which came to be known as "hybrid-vigour," as early as 1877, but it was Wallace who commercialized

NO OTHER INDUSTRY HAS MATCHED THIS LEVEL OF SUSTAINABILITY, AND SAVING SEEDS REMAINED THE FOUNDATION OF FARMING UNTIL JUST THE LAST FEW GENERATIONS.

it, and changed farming forever. Previously, farmers saved part of their corn crop to sow their fields the following spring. Seeds from hybrid corn, however, do not pass their high-yielding qualities to the next generation, forcing farmers to buy new seeds each year. Seed production soon became a thriving industry separate from farming itself. In 1933, only one percent of corn grown in the United States was hybrid. Ten years later, hybrids had captured half the market.[3]

There's good reason for such swift market expansion. Hybrids are a big boost to production, returning in added yield about three dollars to the farmer for every dollar invested in seeds.[4] But a subtle attitude shift had taken place. "Off-farm inputs," introduced to agriculture, opened farmers to a wide array of industrial inputs over the coming years. [5] Tractors replaced horses, leading to yet another input: fuel to run the tractors. With fewer animals on the farm, farmers had less manure to use as fertilizer, and so had to buy nitrogen. They also bought chemicals to kill bugs and weeds.

Before artificial fertilizers were available, farmers had to find other ways to keep their soil productive. Manure helped replenish lost nutrients in the soil, but it was not enough. They also had to rotate crops — every year altering the crop grown in each field so the soil could replenish itself. This also kept bugs and weeds in check. With nitrogen fertilizer, such care was no longer needed. Farmers could grow the same crops in the same fields year after year, and simply apply nitrogen to restore the soil's fertility. This nitrogen fix made monoculture possible, and chemical pesticides necessary as bugs and weeds thrived in the large, uniform fields. Tractors were needed to plow and harvest the vast fields. Early potato harvesters, for instance, could clear a field of at least 80 acres (32 hectares), compared with the maximum of 30 acres (12 hectares) that a family could harvest by hand. Such mechanization soon fed on itself. A machine that can harvest 80 acres needs at least an 80-acre field to produce enough revenue to pay for the machine.

Industrial methods were introduced to farming piece by piece. Yet in the span of just one generation, farmers put the renewable heritage of their land behind and transformed their farms into assemblers of inputs from other industries — seeds from one company sprayed with chemicals from other companies using tractors and fuel from still more companies. Functions once fulfilled by on-farm inputs — animals, manure, and crop rotation — were now tied to off-farm suppliers. Bob Stirling, a rural sociologist at the University of Regina, says the farmer's job evolved from knowing his land and its needs to one of sorting through the marketing pitches of the companies supplying him. "Skill at the work of actually growing something becomes secondary in this new set of practices."[6]

The industrialization of agriculture was so gradual, and so tied to marketing pitches telling farmers how all these new inputs would make them progressive and modern, that its unsustainability would not be revealed for decades. Nitrogen, for instance, proved to be very inefficient. Use of nitrogen fertilizer increased more than tenfold in the last half of the twentieth century as depleted soils on industrial farms demanded ever-more fertilizer to keep producing. As well, only one-third to one-half of the nitrogen applied to a field is actually absorbed by the plants they are meant to help.[7] The rest simply runs off with rainwater into streams and rivers, eventually making its way to our oceans. Along the way, the nitrogen continues to fertilize, speeding up algal growth in waterways. The algae use up all the oxygen, causing hypoxia — a lack of life-sustaining oxygen in the water. Nothing can live in such an environment. Where the Mississippi River empties into the Gulf of Mexico, a 20,000-square-kilometre dead zone continues to grow, fueled by nitrogen running off the farms of the American Midwest. In 1993, floods swelled the Mississippi, and an algal bloom formed in the Gulf of Mexico. The disease-ridden blob soon floated north, killing dolphins, whales, seals, and porpoises as far north as the St. Lawrence Seaway.

Farmers, however, are reluctant to give up nitrogen. For one thing, it's cheap, even with up to two-thirds of the fertilizer being wasted. Government subsidies, which encouraged the chemical-based Green Revolution, give farmers little reason to drop nitrogen use. The National Farmers Union of Canada has tracked the cost of nitrogen, relative to the price paid to farmers for corn and wheat.[8] As the grain-price fluctuates, so too does the price of nitrogen. The result is two-fold: the nitrogen companies capture any benefit that comes with better grain prices; and, by dropping their prices when grain prices fall, ensure that farmers will keep buying their inputs.

Farmers do have alternatives to artificial fertilizers. The most obvious is manure, a natural source of nitrogen. This, in fact, was once the main nitrogen source on farms. It turned a waste from one part of the farm — the livestock's manure — into a valuable input for another, the fields. But few farms today are diversified enough to have the animals needed to produce manure for the fields fertilized. One exception is Canada's dairy farms. They can stay small thanks to supply-management, which ensures farmers get a good price for their milk. The average Canadian dairy farm milks about fifty cows per day. That's small enough that the farmer can also raise most of the crops he needs to feed his cows. The cows then produce two things: milk and manure. The farmer sells the milk and spreads the manure on the land to grow crops, which are then fed back to the cows, and the cycle continues. If all farms could achieve such a balance between crops and livestock — as they once did — there would not be such a need for artificial nitrogen fertilizer.

Other techniques could be used as well. Many come from organic farming, which does not allow farmers to use artificial fertilizers. The main practice of organic farmers is crop rotation. Each crop pulls different nutrients from the soil, so rotating crops allows the soil to replenish itself while still producing food. While some conventional farms rotate three crops through a field, meaning a crop will only be planted in any given field once every three years, organic farmers may rotate five or more crops through their fields — giving their soil an extra chance to replenish itself. Combined rotations of nitrogen-fixing crops such as soybeans, peas and alfalfa, which extract nitrogen from the air and put it in the soil, eliminate the need for artificial nitrogen on organic farms. On conventional farms, crop rotation could reduce nitrogen use to a low enough level that farmers are no longer putting the environment at risk. Such techniques would also necessitate diversifying our farms, and moving away from the monocultures that dominate farming today.

Our farms, however, have become addicted to nitrogen. After decades of monocultures and industrial agriculture, the soil has become so depleted of natural nutrients that it needs the boost offered by chemicals. In the summer of 2001, after visiting an organic farm in Ontario's Wellington County, I stopped by the side of the road to get a closer look at Green Revolution farm.[9] While the soil at the organic farm down the road was rich in

AFTER DECADES OF MONOCULTURES AND INDUSTRIAL AGRICULTURE, THE SOIL HAS BECOME SO DEPLETED OF NATURAL NUTRIENTS THAT IT NEEDS THE BOOST OFFERED BY CHEMICALS.

organic material and moist after a rainfall the night before, the soil at this farm was hard and dry and crumbled into sand. The rain had simply washed off, filling a ditch by the side of the road. In the field, the corn was maturing in full, plump cobs. Only artificial fertilizers could perform such a feat. On this farm, and millions like it, decades of monoculture had robbed the soil of its nutrients so that it now needed regular nitrogen applications to keep productive. Nitrogen also increases soil acidity, which slows biologic activity, hurting the soil's ability to produce food on its own, so even more nitrogen must yet again be applied.[10] The land is, in short, addicted to nitrogen.

And when the soil depends on nitrogen, so too do farmers. The mixed operations of the days before nitrogen offered farmers a chance to offset troubles in one sector — such as low prices — with better conditions in another. But with nitrogen-dependent monoculture, farmers have little such flexibility. Farmers need their crop to do well if they are to stay in business. As farmers took out loans to buy farmland, machinery, chemicals and seeds, farming shifted from being labour-intensive to capital-intensive. This further restricts their flexibility, according to Don Mills, Ontario co-ordinator with the NFU. "They can't cut costs in tough times," he said.[11] "They have regular payments to make."

In such a situation, farmers are less able to take risks. They cannot gamble that their crops won't do well. With loan payments looming, the added cost of spreading nitrogen fertilizer seems a worthwhile investment, even if most of it will run off the field. A 1988 study of Mexico's Yaqui Valley, published in the journal *Science*, found that farmers could boost their profits by 12 to 17 percent by spreading nitrogen only when their wheat was best able to absorb it. This reduced the amount of nitrogen needed from 250 kilograms per hectare (kg/ha) to 180 kg/ha, cutting both farm costs and environmental impact. Armed with these numbers, researchers tried for five years to get more farmers in the Yaqui to cut their nitrogen use, but to little avail. With loans to pay and inputs to buy, farmers were unwilling to risk a new management technique that went against the teachings of the Green Revolution. "Nitrogen is cheap insurance," observed author Richard Manning. "Expecting farmers to respond to market signals now is a bit like expecting an alcoholic to order herbal tea at an open bar. This is the legacy of subsidy. Governments, including Mexico's, got in the business of making nitrogen cheap, and farmers lapped it up."[12] The result has been devastating. An August 2002 study in the journal *Nature* found that 17 percent of the world's farmland had been degraded since 1945 due to Green Revolution farming.[13]

Pesticides and herbicides used to kill insects and weeds have, if anything, made the situation worse. By killing off organic material that might otherwise fertilize the plants, they make nitrogen even more necessary. Like nitrogen, pesticide use increased tenfold in the last half of the last century, and is very inefficient in its application.[14] An Environment Canada study found that less than one percent of the pesticides sprayed on a field actually reach the targeted pests, and that up to 40 percent blows away on the wind as it is sprayed.[15] And, also like nitrogen, pesticides run off the land with the rain. Prince Edward Island experienced a 632-percent increase in pesticide use between 1982 and 2000 as potato production exploded. Province-wide, there have been at least 26 fish-kills since 1994 as pesticides washed into the island's 263 waterways. In one two-week period in the summer of 2002 alone, more than 12,000 fish washed up on the shores of P.E.I.'s streams and rivers.[16]

Every time pesticides flooded into a waterway, inspectors from provincial and federal ministries of the environment and agriculture were dispatched — often on overtime and on weekends. In the few cases where charges were laid, courts were tied up for up to a year sorting through the charges, and penalties were small. Afterward, Environment Canada and the province launched projects to revitalize the damaged streams and rivers. None of this comes cheap. Farmers had to spray their chemicals again, since most of what they had already applied was now damaging the water instead of the land. Such a system of ever-increasing inputs, supported by government subsidies, simply passes its environmental costs on to the rest of society. With governments struggling to keep their budgets balanced, this cannot be sustained.

Industrial agriculture can also damage local economies. Rural communities that accept massive hog barns into their midst, for instance, often do so with visions of jobs and investment coming to their communities. Industrial livestock operations tend to congregate in rural areas desperate for an infusion of cash, a United States Department of Agriculture study found. Modern hog barns were developed in North Carolina just as the tobacco industry fell into decline, and massive poultry barns were first developed in the depressed southern United States. In Canada, Manitoba communities turned to hog farming after wheat was hit by the elimination of a transportation subsidy known as the Crow Rate in the 1990s. The cruel reality for rural communities is that the new industries, rather than rebuilding local economies, slowly eat away at their financial foundations.

Numerous studies in the United States have all come to the same conclusion, that large hog barns drive down property values as neighbours complain about the smell from the barns and water wells are contaminated by manure runoff.[17] In North Carolina, property values dropped 7.1 percent on farms near a hog barn, while property values near barns in Iowa fell up to 40 percent and in Illinois up to 30 percent. All this reduces the taxes the community can collect from adjacent properties, while the barns themselves bring added costs to the community. One rural municipality in Iowa saw its gravel costs rise 40 percent as big trucks serving the hog barns tore up its roads.

Hog barns can hinder other economic development. Environmental problems may deter investment or imperil existing businesses, making the communities even more dependent on the hog barns to survive. "Their only solution is to let in more polluting activities since no other enterprises will consider locating in their area," writes Bill Weida, director of the GRACE Factory Farm Project based in New York.[18] Rather than boosting the local economy, as hoped, the introduction of factory farming can slowly destroy it — just as the fertilizers and pesticides meant to boost the productivity of soil instead slowly degrades it. One study of more than a thousand rural communities found that economic growth in areas without large hog barns was 55 percent higher than in areas with such operations.[19]

Part of the reason is that the barns themselves don't create enough jobs, either directly or indirectly, for the local economy to survive. Only three or four jobs are created for every thousand hogs on a factory farm, compared with 12.6 people needed to raise the same number of animals on traditional farms. That means fewer people earning a living and shopping at local stores. As well, large operations tend to buy their supplies outside the community, while small farms frequent local suppliers, keeping the rural economy alive. In 1994, a University of Minnesota study found that farms with incomes of $100,000 a year bought 90 percent of their inputs locally, while those with sales of $900,000 or more bought only 20 percent locally.[20] This is because large operations are tied to vertically integrated food processors that not only slaughter animals, but also sell farmers feed and dictate the breeds of animals they will raise. With such a top-down system, it is cheaper for the processor to buy feed from a central location rather than at several local operations. While this can be good for the corporate bottom-line, it is bad for rural economies and communities.

With the shift from people to machines — today's farms are much too large to be farmed without massive machines — agriculture has become dependent on cheap fossil fuels to keep operating. The fuel runs the tractors that sow the seeds, spread the chemicals and harvest the crops, the trucks that haul away the produce and the factories that process it into grocery-store products. It is also the basic ingredient in making nitrogen fertilizer. In livestock farming, fossil fuels power the trucks that haul feed to the barns and feedlots where the animals are fattened up, then haul away the animals to slaughter. Getting food to our tables demands an ever-increasing use of fossil fuels both to produce and ship the food, especially when consumers have come to expect fresh fruits and vegetables all year round. In 1940, the average American farm produced 2.3 calories of food energy for every calorie of fossil fuel energy it used.[21] Today, the tables have more than turned, with three calories of fossil fuel needed to produce just one calorie of food.

As Brian Halweil at the environmental think-tank WorldWatch Institute says, the modern food industry "probably wouldn't be feasible without abundant and cheap oil."[22] Breakfast cereal, for instance, requires four calories of fossil fuel energy to make one calorie of food, once the milling, grinding, drying, and baking are taken into account. "A two-pound [one-kilogram] bag of breakfast cereal burns the energy of a half-gallon [two litres] of gasoline in its making," says writer Richard Manning.[23] Livestock farms can be even worse. Beef feedlots, in which cattle are penned shoulder-to-shoulder as food is brought to them, require thirty-five calories of fossil fuel to produce just one calorie of beef. Sixty-eight calories are needed to produce one calorie of pork. Burning fossil fuels so much, of course, creates greenhouse gases and environmental problems that are not borne by the farms or food companies, but are passed on to the rest of society.

It doesn't have to be this way. One of the truly marvellous things about cattle, for instance, is that they can take something we can't eat (grass) and convert it into something we can (beef). The same was once true of pigs, which turned farm waste — slop — into pork. Modern factory farms, however, don't feed animals grass or slop. They feed them corn, because corn fattens them up quicker. More than half of the 10 billion bushels of corn grown in the United States, for instance, is fed to farm animals.[24] In

ONE OF THE TRULY MARVELLOUS THINGS ABOUT CATTLE, FOR INSTANCE, IS THAT THEY CAN TAKE SOMETHING WE CAN'T EAT (GRASS) AND CONVERT IT INTO SOMETHING WE CAN (BEEF).

Mexico, where corn was first domesticated, 45 percent of the crop goes to animals, compared with just 5 percent in 1960.[25] This is an incredibly inefficient use of one of the world's most important crops. Two kilograms of corn are needed to produce one kilogram of chicken, while four kilograms of grain are needed to produce one kilogram of pork. The cattle industry is the most inefficient, requiring eight kilograms of grain to make one kilogram of beef.[26]

All we need to raise cattle is an open field and some sun. But the industrial model of livestock farming (keeping animals penned up and bringing food to them) only works if we feed the animals grains, since grains can be harvested and stored more easily. Those grains require an enormous amount of chemicals and fossil fuels to be grown, harvested and delivered. We have taken a renewable industry and made it dependent on outside inputs. Once all those inputs are counted in, 284 gallons (1,075 litres) of oil have been burned, on average, by the time a steer goes to market. "We have succeeded in industrializing the beef calf, transforming what was once a solar-powered ruminant into the very last thing we need: another fossil-fuel machine," writes Michael Pollan of the *New York Times*.[27]

With the world's population growing rapidly, we can no longer afford such an inefficient system of food production. We need to find more efficient ways of producing food. Today's agricultural system is very good at creating wealth for the companies at the top of the food chain, and at providing cheap food in our grocery stores, but not at creating the food itself or at providing farmers with a living wage.

In fact, Kirschenmann told the farmers on our tour, there is a limit to how much more efficient farms get as they grow. Economies of scale on hog forms, for instance, peak between 800 and 1,200 hogs, while soybeans and corn peak at about 600 acres (240 hectares).[28] After that, economies of scale lose ground to the cost of maintaining huge operations. One North Dakota farm Kirschenmann cited tills 30,000 acres (12,000 hectares). One of its fields is sixty kilometres from the homestead, requiring the farming to travel more than twice that distance just to get back and forth from the field. "It costs more to service that field than the one next to the farm," he said. Such farms rely on cheap fossil fuels, as well as government subsidies that drive down the cost of production, to produce food that is not sustainable either economically or environmentally.

This is what drew the men and women of rural Manitoba to Rene Van Acker's dinner and discussion sessions. The farmers who came out are part of an industrial food system that has detached them from consumers. They are at the bottom of the food supply chain, and paid poorly in keeping with their lowly status. They no longer produce food, but inputs for an industrial food system whose processing plants and profit centres are far away. Even at their local grocery store — Kirschenmann and I browsed through one in Riverton while waiting for the local curling rink to open for our talk one night — most of the food is from far away. This, of course, is not unique to rural Manitoba, though one might reasonably expect a store surrounded by farms to have some fresh, local produce.

Local food simply does not fit with the narrow definition of efficiency used by the grocery-store chains that dominate the retail food sector. For them, it makes more sense to source all their food centrally and then distribute it to their retail outlets, like the one in Riverton. As a result, food grown right outside a rural town is shipped to a central depot, then shipped back to where it came from for sale. Or it might go somewhere else. I once went into a chain grocery store in Parry Sound, Ontario, passing several women selling plump, juicy blueberries by the side of the road. At the store, the only blueberries were Californian. They were cheaper, but not as good, having travelled across the continent to get to me, deteriorating along the way. Such berries are bred more for their ability to withstand shipping than for their taste.

Brian Halweil at the WorldWatch Institute describes the "transcontinental head of lettuce." Such produce, grown in California and flown nearly 5,000 kilometres to his local grocery store in Washington, DC, burns thirty-six times as much fossil fuel energy in transport as it produces in food energy.[29] He cites a study by Kirschenmann's Leopold Centre in 2001 that found that while locally grown food travels at average of 74 kilometres to get to a dinner plate in Iowa, food shipped from outside the area travels an average of 2,577 kilometres. Besides supporting local farmers and providing fresher produce, buying locally was found to be much better for the environment. Local meals used between four and seventeen times less fossil fuels and produced five to seventeen times less carbon dioxide emissions than food bought from outside the area. Numbers like that have convinced many that locally-grown food is the answer. Not only is it better for the environment, but the food is fresher and buying it often means bypassing big chain stores and industrial farms. As well, farmers selling to local niche markets, such as organic, can command premiums from the market that increase their profits, making it easier to stay on smaller farms where industrial methods are not needed. As Manning writes, "Quality is subversive."

Tim Schmucker's Toronto shop sells hormone- and drug-free meat raised by Old Order Mennonite and Amish farmers in southwestern Ontario. He calls himself a "social entrepreneur," driven as much by a desire to do some good as to make a profit. "We're an alternative to the big chains," he says. After years of operating out of the back of his car or from the walk-in fridge at a U-brew beer shop, he and his wife Jacquie opened their own Fresh From The Farm shop in Toronto's Donlands neighbourhood, and tapped into a growing market for alternative foods. The Schmuckers deal with each of their supplying farmers individually. Tim places each order separately, and makes the two-hour drive to each farm every week to get his orders. He has been able to contract for some help to pick up orders, but just keeping his small store stocked has become a weekly logistical challenge, and some weeks he can't get everything his customers want.

He's hardly alone. Tod Murphy runs the Farmers Diner in Barre, Vermont, featuring food raised by local farmers.[30] He set up the restaurant on the small town's main street as a personal commitment, but soon found that customers were eager to support the effort. "I thought most would just see it as a diner, but they see what we're doing," he says. What he's doing is bypassing the industrial food system to buy food that's local, fresh, and sustainably grown. He soon found that it was fairly easy to get local vegetables, though sometimes his menu had to be changed to reflect what was available. Meat, however, was more difficult. He managed to find farmers he could buy from, but processing the meat was another issue. The emergence of large food companies controlling the meat industry — four companies claim three-quarters of the North American meat market — had put small meat processors out of business. Murphy had no one to convert pigs into hams and bacon. And what would a diner be without bacon? So he set up his own, very small, meat processing plant down the road from his diner. "All these food facilities that are so basic to society — the creamery, the local butcher — they're gone. You have to build them yourself." Trying to put his menu together, Murphy, like Schmucker, spends hours every week making deals with individual farmers. By contrast, the manager of a nearby Friendly's chain restaurant fills out one form online and sends it to a regional distribution centre in another state. "It takes me about five minutes," says the manager, who did not want to be named. "And then the big Friendly's truck shows up with everything."[31]

Halweil at the WorldWatch Institute says rebuilding the connection between farmers and local customers is key to establishing a viable alternative to industrial agriculture. "We need to go beyond farmers' markets," he says, and establish local infra-structures that serve more than one shop or restaurant.[32] Customers have gotten used to stores and restaurants that have full shelves and consistent menus. Back in Toronto, Schmucker is working with a few farmers to set up a sales shed where urban buyers can come to bid on fruits, vegetables, and meat once a week. They would leave with orders in hand, helping ensure the steady supply their customers demand. They would still need to get their purchases back to the city, but a sales shed would be much simpler for both the Toronto buyers and the farmers. "We need some convenience, too," says Schmucker.[33]

If the environment and adverse economic impacts are the greatest challenge to the sustainability of industrial agriculture, inconvenience may be the greatest challenge to alternative food systems. It needs to be more convenient for customers, store and restaurant owners, and, perhaps most importantly, for the farmers. They have heard the stories like the ones salting Kirschenmann's talks, but don't know how to make similar steps themselves to get out of the industrial food system. Already heavily capitalized, each year they farm hundreds, or thousands, of acres. Their marketing consists of little more than delivering their produce to the local elevator and taking whatever price has been set at the Chicago Board of Trade that day. "You can't just go to town and exchange all that for less land and smaller machines to serve the sixty people in your area," says Halweil.[34] Some farmers, he said, are simply too big, too industrial, to be turned around now. But they are the minority. Halweil endorses what Kirschenmann has dubbed "taking back the middle" — farmers too big to sell their food at farmers' markets, but who could ensure a steady supply of food to local restaurants and stores. And that means re-establishing local infrastructures such as small slaughterhouses and millers. Not only would that infrastructure ensure the steady supply retailers and their customers need, but it would give farmers somewhere else to sell their food and a way to break out of the industrial food market.

There are a few models to draw on, where local farmers and their customers are working out ways to rebuild that lost infrastructure. In Oregon, ranchers owning a total 250,000 acres (100,000 hectares) formed a group to sell their beef. They stagger production among themselves to ensure a steady supply to their customers, and bypass the big companies controlling the meat industry. "That's really the future of this," says Weida.[35] A similar group is selling meat in Colorado. After mad cow disease was found in Alberta in the spring of 2003, a group of Manitoba farmers who could no longer ship their meat to the United States got together to set up their own small slaughterhouse to serve the local market. In our tour of Manitoba in October of that year, Kirschenmann told the story of Montana grain-farmer Dean Fallboard, who began baking his wheat into bread, then set up a retail bakery, then a deli and a store where customers could grind their own wheat into flour. Out back, his grain elevators gave other local farmers an alternative market, apart from the large grain companies, to sell their wheat.

In some cases, farmers have banded together to build a better life by working collectively. This is basically the old co-operative model that farmers have used for generations to give themselves market clout by acting together rather than bidding against each other to sell to the large corporations that dominate the food industry. But while the co-ops of bygone generations tended to organize around farmers in the same geographic area, modern co-ops often organize across wide geographic areas to corner part of a specific market. Organic Valley Farms, for instance, has 633 farmers in seventeen U.S. states from Maine to California milking 20,475 cows a day. They also produce eggs, juice, cheese, spreads, butters, creams, and meats under the Organic Valley name.

By joining together to sell their products, they can build their brand around the membership and improve the way those farmers are treated. "They want you to know that ever since they started their business, the farmers come first," Kirschenmann said during our presentation in Dauphin.[36] As he spoke, he flashed on an overhead screen graphics from the Organic Valley web site, showing how much the farmers are paid for their milk. In 2003,

WHILE THE CO-OPS OF BYGONE GENERATIONS TENDED TO ORGANIZE AROUND FARMERS IN THE SAME GEOGRAPHIC AREA, MODERN CO-OPS OFTEN ORGANIZE ACROSS WIDE GEOGRAPHIC AREAS TO CORNER PART OF A SPECIFIC MARKET.

co-op farmers received US$20.17 per hundredweight of milk — two-thirds more than conventional farmers in the United States that year.[37] Small wonder farmers with Organic Valley can get by with farms of just thirty-two cows on average — about half the size of an average American dairy farm. In fact, they often lead better lives.

Travis Forgues joined in 1999, investing US$11,000, or 5.5 percent of his expected gross income the first year in Organic Valley. He invested the money up front, but Organic Valley does allow farmers to pay off their investments over several years if need be. Forgues readily admits he was attracted by the money, hoping to profit from the higher prices paid for his milk. "The vast majority, including myself, go into organics as a financial decision. After about a year, it changes," he says.[38] Farmers soon start to embrace the environmental aspect of organic farming, and wouldn't go back to conventional farming, with all its chemicals and artificial fertilizers, even if the prices were better. "People start thinking, 'I don't want my family around those things, I don't want it in the lake.'" For his equity stake in the co-op, Forgues is guaranteed a return of 8 percent a year, but usually gets about 14 percent, on top of the $200,000 a year he gets from milking cows. That's enough to support him, his wife, two daughters, and his parents. He's making more money with fewer cows than his father ever did when Forgues was growing up, and doing it more sustainably. "You won't see us going back," Forgues says. With stable prices offered by the co-op, he can better plan for the future, something farmers in the volatile conventional market can only dream of doing.

In his talks, Kirschenmann told the Manitoba farmers about how the co-op uses the stories of people like Forgues in its marketing. In-store posters feature the farmers' pictures and testimonials. The co-op's web site is geared to customers, with stories of how and why Forgues and other farmers joined the co-op, and with details about their farms, their families and their cows. It tells visitors how the cows are raised, what organic standards mean, and what Organic Valley farmers do to meet and at times even exceed those standards. There is a special kids' section with games and information on where our food comes from, to build on the relationship between farmers and consumers — something that's missing in supermarkets and factory farms. Customers' children can even learn about the farmers' children and their lives. "What they want you to know is that when you buy a quart of Organic Valley milk, you are supporting these farmers, those families and those kids that you visited on their web site," Kirschenmann said. "That's part of their marketing strategy."

The co-op began in 1988 when farmer George Simeon (now Organic Valley's CEO) and seven of his neighbours banded together in Wisconsin. Within four years, its sales had topped US$2 million. Tapping into a market of consumers who want to know that their food is sustainably grown on family farms, Organic Valley has grown to be the largest co-op in the United States, with sales of more than US$150 million per year.

While not all farmers have the entrepreneurial sprit displayed by Organic Valley or Dean Fallboard, they don't need to. Fallboard's 12,000 acres (5,000 hectares) can't keep his bakery — which bakes 10,000 loaves of bread a day — and elevators fully stocked, so he buys from other area farmers looking for ways to leave the commodity market. Organic Valley and other co-ops are constantly looking for new members. In 2003, for instance, Organic Valley added 118 farmers, a 22.9 percent increase over 2002. With that kind of growth, there is plenty of room for farmers who just want to raise their cattle or grow their crops and leave the marketing to someone else. All it takes is one Dean Fallboard or one George Simeon to get things going, and before long hundreds of farmers can turn their backs on industrial agriculture and help build thriving new businesses.

That was the message Kirschenmann and I stressed the night we were speaking in Dauphin, Manitoba, where much of the audience was made up of staff from local economic development offices. Their job is to attract businesses to town to help maintain the local economy. We urged them not to fall into the trap of "smokestack chasing," and instead find ways to help local farmers stay on the land. Encouraging the kind of infrastructure Halweil says is needed for alternative food systems to take hold would also promote shopping in local stores. "The sustainable ag community must build a supply chain," Kirschenmann told them.[39] "Who is in a better position to process and retain the identity of these products than micro food enterprises in our rural communities rather than a huge processing plant that's off someplace outside of our communities?" The key to such enterprises is to avoid competing with the big companies directly. Instead, micro-processors should sell specialty products with smaller markets but larger profit margins. These are markets ignored by the big companies, whose business models are based on uniformity and consistency.

Farmers supplying such enterprises tend to not take government subsidies — they don't need them — and pass on few costs to the rest of society. If they are organic, they do not use nitrogen fertilizer or chemical pesticides that poison surrounding land and waterways. By selling locally and operating smaller farms with smaller machines, they burn fewer fossil fuels. But projects such as Fresh From the Farm and the Farmers Diner have probably gone as far as they can, and risk losing market share if they can't keep up with demand. Like any growing industry, they are at a stage in their development where they need an infusion of cash to maintain their momentum. The problem is, the agriculture industry is not likely to make such an investment. Agribusiness is based on selling inputs to farmers and uniform products to consumers, and this new industry is based on selling fewer inputs and distinctive products.

The best option, then, might be for government to help by redirecting subsidy money away from industrial farming to sustainable farming and infrastructure. Economic development officers could use the money to attract and set up small processing plants and to recruit farmers to supply the enterprise. Farmers themselves could also be helped. A farmer must stop using chemicals for three years before his farm can be certified organic. During those years, production plummets while organic material is built back up in the soil, but the farmer is unable to collect the premium prices offered for certified organic crops. That can make for some difficult years, something few farmers can afford.

Subsidies to get farmers through that difficult transition would be a big help, and be more of an investment than an expense. By helping farmers go organic, governments could limit future expenditures on environmental cleanup and health problems. They could also reduce the risk of cobbling together expensive bailout packages for industrial farmers caught in yet another income crisis. Organic Valley's Forgues likes the idea of governments' helping farmers switch to organic, so co-ops like his can keep up with demand.[40] But he warns against making the switch too easy. A flood of organics would drive down prices and hurt farmers like him who are already in the industry. Assistance that's high enough to tempt farmers, but low enough that they have to be serious about the transition, would likely be the best — and most cost-effective — solution.

Government subsides got the Green Revolution started, and through research grants to our universities have kept it going. It seems only prudent — and fair — to spend some money now to clean up the environmental and social messes that revolution left behind.

A HISTORY OF FOOD (CONTINUED)

1298 | Marco Polo returns from China with news of oriental spices.

1492 | Christopher Columbus's discovery of the Americas reveals a variety of edible fruits and vegetables (such as tomatoes, potatoes, and pineapples) that were unknown to the Europeans.

1497 | Genoese explorer Giovanni Caboto, a.k.a. John Cabot, writes the first known description of the Grand Banks as so "swarming with fish [that they] could be taken not only with a net but in baskets let down with a stone." Just 120 years later the Grand Banks cod fleet will grow to over 1,000 ships.

1505 | The Spanish discover cinnamon growing in its wild state in Ceylon (Sri Lanka). Cinnamon becomes a major component of the spice trade.

1563 | John Hawkins, an English sea captain, introduces the potato to England.

1660s | Uneducated Dutch tradesman Anton van Leeuwenhoek invents the microscope and discovers bacteria and other microscopic parasites.

1773 | In protest against the Tea Act of 1773, American patriots dressed as Indians board ships owned by the East Indian Company and dump numerous bags of tea into the ocean. (This event will later become known as the Boston Tea Party.) This marks the beginning of the hostilities that will lead to the War of Independence between America and Great Britain.

1793 | Yale-educated inventor Eli Whitney invents and patents a device, the Cotton Gin, to remove the seeds from cotton, allowing for the faster processing of cotton and increasing the profitability of cotton farming and harvesting. Despite the great potential benefits of his new machine, Whitney falls victim to his own greed and is unable to profit from his invention. His plan to charge exorbitant sums (as much as two-thirds of the revenues from anyone who uses his machine) backfires when several imitators develop similar machines. Whitney becomes mired in debt trying to protect his patent, and eventually sells the rights to the State of South Carolina.

▼ CONTINUED ON PAGE 70

BETTING THE FARM: FOOD SAFETY AND THE BEEF COMMODITY CHAIN

IAN MacLACHLAN

EDITORS' INTRODUCTION

We're walking with Mayor Don Weisbeck down the main street of Brooks, Alberta. A two-hour drive from Calgary, the town is now home to one of the biggest slaughterhouses in North America, the Lakeside Meat Packing Factory, owned by the American food giant Tyson Foods.

Big beef has brought big changes to Brooks. There are now seventy-three different languages spoken in Brooks, boasts Mayor Weisbeck. Five years ago? One. Now, he says, there are people of every race, colour, and creed. Five years ago? One: white. "The world is here in Brooks, Alberta," he says, smiling expansively.

The world is coming to Brooks, Alberta, because the Lakeside slaughterhouse and processing plant has a virtually insatiable need for employees. According to its website, Lakeside pays new workers $11.75 an hour, rising to $14, far higher wages than the minimum an immigrant without English might expect to make. Not only that, the Lakeside plant hires all year round.

The plant is capable of killing and processing almost two million head of cattle a year. In one eight-hour shift, a worker on the kill floor may slaughter two thousand head of cattle. That's one cow killed every 14.4 seconds. Most of the meat you buy in Canada comes from either the Lakeside plant in Brooks or the Cargill plant in Manitoba. Without the Lakeside plant, there would be no immigrants to Brooks. Without the Lakeside plant, it's fair to say, there might not be a Brooks, Alberta, at all.

But the cost of such industrial practices is huge. One of the reasons the plant in Brooks needs so many new workers is that the job is so brutally hard. The Workers Compensation Board designates working at a slaughterhouse to be one of the top three most dangerous jobs in Canada. In the spring of 2004, over seventy workers, many from Sudan, were fired from the plant when they complained about their working conditions. The firings made headlines around the country, but still the Lakeside management said the workers who protested were in breach of contract. Mayor Don Weisbeck was helpless to do anything.

For all the opportunities huge beef-processing plants like Lakeside create, they are at the centre of controversies related to our food chain. For example, like so many other plants, Lakeside has been forced over the years to recall tons of beef potentially tainted by *E. coli* O157:H7.

Brooks is emblematic of the dark and light of the big beef industry. It is such a crucial and controversial part of our food chain that it bears close and serious examination. But for all the discussion in the media about mad cows, workers' rights, and food-borne illnesses, few of us truly understand the process that takes huge animals and turns them into small, edible packages we buy in our local grocery store. Which is why we've asked Ian MacLachlan, the man who wrote the authoritative book on the meat industry in Canada, *Kill and Chill,* to tell us the inside story of beef. And how to fix the system.

ON MAY 20, 2003, the discovery of a single cow infected with bovine spongiform encephalopathy (BSE) — mad cow disease — from Marwyn Peaster's farm in Peace River, Alberta, heralded an economic catastrophe for Canadian cattle producers. Over thirty-three countries closed their borders to Canadian beef exports. The potential negative impact of a $2.5-billion loss in cattle exports will translate into a $2-billion loss in GDP, a $5.7-billion decline in total output and 75,000 jobs lost.[1] BSE made the front page not because efforts to prevent the entry and transmission of BSE had been too little, too late, and not because of the potential human health risks — but largely because of the enormous disruption caused to Canada's cattle markets and regional economies. In fact, BSE was not diagnosed until over three months after the cow had been condemned as unfit for human consumption and slaughtered. Meanwhile, the carcass had already been rendered into livestock feed.

Consumers have been questioning food safety for over a century. From Upton Sinclair's *The Jungle* in 1906 — an exposé of unsanitary food handling in Chicago's meat packing plants — to Eric Schlosser's *Fast Food Nation* in 2001, the livestock and meat-packing industries have lent themselves to alarming accounts. A century ago, the prevalence of bovine tuberculosis spurred the establishment of government-sanctioned meat inspection, while today meat is associated with a new set of diseases. The fact is, after all the science, all the guidelines and all the exposés, we still do not understand all of the risk factors or how to respond to them. As we'll see later, the risks posed by BSE were mismanaged in the U.K. and Canada's own BSE policies are questionable.

Which explains why, despite all the headlines about BSE or *E. coli* O157:H7, the greatest contemporary challenge faced by the cattle and beef industry, its regulators and public policy makers, is risk management. Consumers rely on their government to oversee farm-to-fork quality assurance programs. These programs span a long commodity chain that is often hidden behind closed doors and divided between federal and provincial jurisdictions. If we as consumers are to understand the risks to beef safety, and, most importantly, understand what ingenuity can be brought to the process to manage these risks, we need to understand the industry itself.

THE CATTLE–BEEF COMMODITY CHAIN

As with all other food, the production of beef is vertically organized into a sequence of activities — the commodity chain — which adds value to basic organic ingredients: grass and cows. The first link in the chain, calf production, is found on specialist farms known as cow-calf operations, and also takes place among other activities on mixed farms. As the gestational foundation of the commodity chain, beef cows are found in every Canadian province. In 2001, 80.7 percent of beef cows originated in Prairie Canada — 43.7 percent from Alberta alone.[2] Dairy cows are concentrated mainly in Quebec and Ontario, and their bull calves are also raised for slaughter.

Within months of birth, calves are dehorned to prevent injury, vaccinated to prevent common bovine diseases, and bull calves are castrated to prevent the development of masculine characteristics. Growth hormones are commonly administered to beef calves, usually as an implant in the outer ear, a body part that never enters the human food chain. Growth hormones help cattle to reach market weight sooner and reduce feed costs by increasing feed efficiency. In North America, it is believed that the concentration of hormones in the beef of treated cattle is

WITHIN MONTHS OF BIRTH, CALVES ARE DEHORNED TO PREVENT INJURY, VACCINATED TO PREVENT COMMON BOVINE DISEASES, AND BULL CALVES ARE CASTRATED TO PREVENT THE DEVELOPMENT OF MASCULINE CHARACTERISTICS.

minute relative to the natural background level of hormones in the human body, and that they pose no health risk to consumers. Nevertheless, the European Union has banned the import of beef produced using growth hormones, effectively shutting Canada out of European beef markets.

Backgrounding, the second phase in cattle production, starts with weaned calves. Standing grass in summer and sun-cured hay in winter provides the nutrients required for them to grow out and build the skeletal frame of mature animals. It is the most land-intensive production phase of the commodity chain, and producers must manage grassland carefully to prevent over-grazing and secure sufficient winter-feed.

Grain feeding, the third phase, finishes animals to slaughter weight — about 1,200 pounds (540 kilograms) for heifers and 1,300 pounds (590 kilograms) for steers. In Ontario and eastern Canada, this is often a small-scale winter enterprise on mixed farms. In Alberta, cattle finishing takes place on specialized feedlots containing 10,000 to 20,000 head, though some are

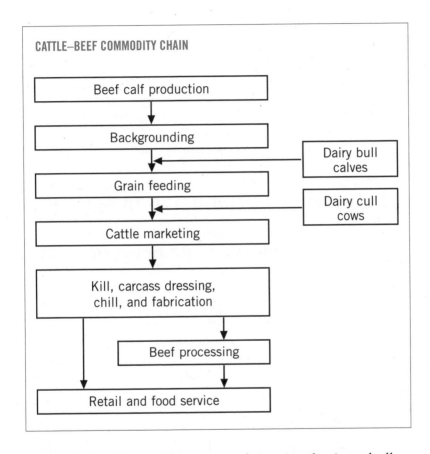

CATTLE—BEEF COMMODITY CHAIN

Beef calf production

Backgrounding

Dairy bull calves

Grain feeding

Dairy cull cows

Cattle marketing

Kill, carcass dressing, chill, and fabrication

Beef processing

Retail and food service

much larger. New arrivals receive a hay ration that is gradually stepped up to about 80 percent grain. In Ontario, the principal grain is corn while Alberta's cooler climate and shorter growing season make barley the feed of choice. Alberta dominates the industry; on January 1, 2003, it accounted for 63.5 percent of Canada's total beef cattle on specialized feeding operations.[3]

Finished cattle are shipped to the packinghouse by livestock trucking firms in cattle-liners, large aluminum semi-trailer trucks. Most cattle are sold direct to the packer. Pricing systems are complex and may be based either on liveweight or carcass weight. Prices are often negotiated as forward delivery contracts for truckload lots, months in advance of delivery.

Slaughter plants receive cattle on a just-in-time basis, seldom holding live animals for more than a few hours, providing time for ante-mortem inspection by a veterinarian. Alberta kill plants tend to specialize in the highest-quality grain-fed steers and heifers. In Quebec, the largest packing plants process spent cows culled from the dairy herd, which are used for ground beef and processed meat products. In older and smaller plants, cattle are stunned unconscious one at a time in a traditional "knocking box." But in most large-scale facilities, there is a continuous-flow style of humane slaughter. Cattle walk calmly into the plant, gradually straddling a conveyor that lifts them gently off the floor. They glide calmly along the moving rail, oblivious to the impending blow from a pneumatically powered stunner that will cause sudden and immediate unconsciousness.[4] The insensible animal is shackled and slowly rises to the bleeding rail for exsanguination. The feet are cut off with powerful hydraulic shears and the carcass is suspended from a gambrel that slides along an overhead rail for removal of the hide and head. The abdominal cavity is opened to remove the viscera, and the carcass is then split into two sides. Conveyor tables carry pans of viscera in synch with the carcass until meat inspectors have examined the critical organs and lymph nodes and are satisfied there is no evidence of disease. Suspect and randomly selected carcasses are subject to in-plant swab tests and laboratory analysis of various tissues to identify antibiotic or hormonal residues and a variety of other contaminants. After final trimming to remove any visible contamination, bruises or lesions, the carcass is transferred to the cooler where Canadian Beef Grading Agency staff assign a carcass quality grade depending on age, meat texture, and marbling. Once again, Alberta dominates, accounting for 68.5 percent of Canada's reported cattle slaughter in 2002.

Large-scale beef dressing lines in state-of-the-art plants are designed to avoid the potential for cross-contamination, which has been recognized as a food safety hazard since the nineteenth century.[5] The "hide-off area" of the kill floor is segregated from the "hide-on area," which is prone to manure splash from dirty hooves and hides. All cutting tools must be immersed in scalding water between each animal on the line. At some workstations, direct contact with blood or viscera is unavoidable. For these workers, there are long rubber aprons and high boots. Between each animal on the line, the worker steps into a clear plastic shower booth equipped with water jets to remove all trace of the previous carcass before the next in line is handled. The largest beef dressing plants are also equipped with massive steam pasteurization chambers that use scalding steam to kill any pathogens inadvertently transferred to the surface of the carcass during processing.

Fabrication or carcass-breaking divides the side of beef into smaller primal cuts (hip, sirloin, short loin, rib and chuck), each of which is subsequently carved into subprimal cuts. The various cuts are sorted into standard lots, vacuum-sealed in plastic film and packed in cartons, labelled to indicate the name of the cut and the source of the beef. Boxed beef is shipped in refrigerated semi-trailer trucks as soon as possible to minimize the time that it must be held in the plant's cold storage warehouse. Much of the output is destined for the distribution centres of supermarket and fast food chains while the reminder is sent to manufacturers for further processing into specialty meat products and individual portion-controlled servings for institutional and commercial kitchens.

As one might expect of an intensely competitive and entre-preneurial industry, the basic commodity chain has many variants. The tendency to specialize in just one link of the chain is offset by the propensity to integrate forwards or backwards, and take some degree of control and profit over adjacent activities. Some parts of the chain have become fully integrated and co-located. For example, cow-calf producers may also background their weaned calves while Lakeside Packers of Brooks, Alberta, operates a feedlot across the highway from its kill plant, providing an in-house source for slaughter cattle.

Like many other resource processing industries, meat packing restructured dramatically in the 1980s and 1990s. Meat packing shifted westward to follow cattle production, which has become strongly concentrated in Alberta. Canada Packers and Swift Canadian, the packinghouse leaders of the mid-twentieth century, gradually withdrew from the production of fresh commodity beef as a new beef processing duopoly emerged:

- Cargill Foods of High River, Alberta, a wholly-owned subsidiary of Minnesota-based Cargill, a global food processor and grain trader.
- Lakeside Packers of Brooks, Alberta, a wholly-owned subsidiary of South Dakota-based Tyson Fresh Meats, the world's largest beef and pork supplier.

These two plants account for 80 percent of Canada's capacity for slaughtering heifers and steers.[6] While the industry leaders have changed, the meat-packing sector retains its high level of market concentration.

As trends in domestic beef consumption became uncoupled from domestic cattle slaughter, exports of boxed beef increased impressively in the 1990s with the United States accounting for 80 percent of beef exports. Canadian beef also made inroads further afield with notable success in Mexican, Japanese, and South Korean markets. Canada's beef competed favourably on quality and price while the government assured consumers that Canada was free of BSE.[7] By 2003, 20–25 percent of the Canadian cattle

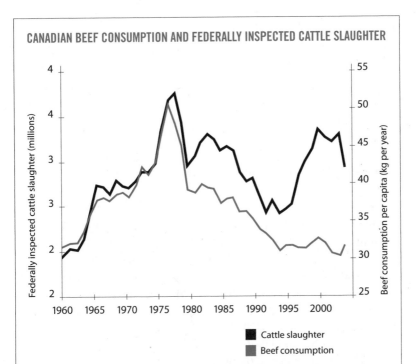

CANADIAN BEEF CONSUMPTION AND FEDERALLY INSPECTED CATTLE SLAUGHTER

Legend:
- ■ Cattle slaughter
- ■ Beef consumption

Source: Agriculture and Agri-Food Canada *Livestock Market Review* (various years) and Statistics Canada Cansim II Series V108859, Table 20011, Apparent per capita food consumption in Canada (1960–2003)

This graph illustrates the divergence and gradual uncoupling of cattle slaughter from domestic beef consumption that began in the early 1990s. During the 1960s Canada's federally inspected cattle slaughter grew rapidly to meet the rising consumption of beef by Canadian consumers. Consumption peaked in 1976 and has since declined almost continuously, as did cattle slaughter until about 1990 when the relationship broke down. Divergence shows that the Canadian cattle and beef commodity chain has become uncoupled from domestic demand while live cattle and boxed beef exports have grown in significance. Canadian consumer preferences were less relevant to an industry that became increasingly reliant on exports.

The year 2003 marks a stunning discontinuity as the series suddenly converge, a perverse outcome of the uncoupling of slaughter from consumption. Slaughter has dropped precipitously as Canada's cattle inventory rose to an all-time high. Consumers responded enthusiastically to lower prices in a spirit of support for cattle producers and increased their beef consumption, highlighting the elasticity of its demand.

sold in a typical week were exported live, on the hoof for slaughter in the United States.[8] Export markets gave leverage to producers when they bargained with Canadian packers but left the producers vulnerable to U.S. trade policy on livestock. The worst-case scenario was realized on May 20, 2003, when a single case of BSE was confirmed and all of Canada's beef and cattle export markets slammed shut within hours.

BOVINE TUBERCULOSIS: THE ENIGMATIC ZOONOSIS

Long before the discovery of BSE, government regulation of cattle imports and the domestic meat supply was influenced by the prevalence of other zoonoses, animal diseases such as tuberculosis that can be transmitted to humans. TB was responsible for an estimated one-third of all deaths from disease in Victorian Britain.[9] It had been recognized as a killer of the urban poor for centuries but its contagious character was not grasped until 1865, and the tuberculosis bacterium was not isolated and identified until 1892. By the time of Britain's first Royal Commission on Tuberculosis in 1895, it was believed that bovine TB posed a threat to humans. But the level of risk and the procedures that should be followed when tuberculosis was detected were unclear and would become increasingly controversial. Could humans contract TB by eating beef from infected animals? What degree of tuberculous infection was tolerable in a beef carcass? If a valuable beef carcass was to be condemned in the interest of public health, should the butcher be compensated by the state? After three "science-based" Royal Commissions, there was still uncertainty. We now know that raw milk, not beef, is the major vector of bovine TB.[10]

By the 1960s, Britain's eradication program had been so effective that Britain's cow-herd was declared tuberculosis-free. However, in the mid-1990s, the incidence of bovine TB began to increase and spread. The cause of this resurgence is unclear but wild badgers are the most likely culprits. The efficacy of badger culling is questionable and hotly contested (Donnelly 2003). Science still cannot provide the certainties that farmers and consumers would like. Britain's experience shows that after decades of claiming that bovine TB was effectively eradicated, it has reappeared with no consensus on the best method to control its spread.

Canada, too, has been attempting to eradicate bovine TB for many decades. But sporadic cases still appear during post-mortem inspection. Infected herds are typically quarantined and the cattle destroyed. While the Riding Mountain area of Manitoba is the only area of Canada *not* considered free of bovine TB, isolated cases are still discovered elsewhere, and in March 2004, bovine TB was discovered near Steinbach, Manitoba, outside of the Riding Mountain Eradication Area. In Canada, cervids, such as elk and mule deer, are the most likely source of infection, but reservoirs of TB may be found in any warm-blooded vertebrate community. It is especially difficult to control, given the spatial extent of Canada's grassland and its availability as cervid habitat. As in Britain, cattle producers have called for an aggressive cull of the elk population, and, as in Britain, the effectiveness of such a cull has been challenged.[11] The dynamics of bovine TB transmission are still poorly understood,[12] but there is considerable evidence of the growing threat to human health posed by multiple-drug resistant strains of the TB bacterium.

POLICY FAILURE: THE CASE OF BSE IN THE UNITED KINGDOM

Given the enigmatic nature of TB after a century of research and concerted efforts to eradicate the disease, it is no surprise that bovine spongiform encephalopathy (BSE) is not completely understood either. The agent that causes BSE is a prion, a self-reproducing proteinaceous infectious particle that did not conform to any of the prevailing models of microbiology when it was hypothesized as the cause of sheep scrapie in 1982. The prion was named and discovered by Dr. Stanley Prusiner who lost his research funding and was in danger of not being awarded tenure at the University of California at San Francisco. Virologists treated his revolutionary hypothesis with enormous skepticism when it was first proposed.[13] Fifteen years later, Dr. Prusiner was awarded the Nobel Prize in Medicine for discovering the prion, which we now know is associated with BSE. The discovery of the prion shows how recent scientific developments shape our understanding of the cause of BSE; it also underscores the contentious nature of scientific progress.

BSE was identified in November 1986 after a cow's abnormal behavioural symptoms were first recorded in December 1984. Britain's Ministry of Agriculture, Food and Fisheries (MAFF) did not know if BSE was transmissible to humans. There was no evidence. While absence of evidence is not evidence of absence, the government assured the British public, repeatedly and authoritatively, that British beef was safe, and that BSE was *not* a danger to human health. The link between BSE and variant Creutzfeldt-Jakob disease (vCJD)[14] was denied for nine years. Meanwhile, a natural experiment was in progress that would last until the incubation period (itself unknown) provided epidemiologists with sufficient data to draw a conclusion. Exponential growth in the number of reported cases of BSE in cattle was undeniable. There was a growing *apprehension* of a link between BSE and vCJD. But without a smoking gun, Britain's MAFF took little heed of the limited bits of evidence that were becoming available. Instead, the primary concern of MAFF was the negative, indeed catastrophic, impact that public knowledge of BSE would have on Britain's cattle and beef exports.[15]

Thus the British public was taken completely by surprise in March 1996 when the government made a stunning volte-face. Ten cases of vCJD in people under the age of forty-two had been confirmed, and while there was still no proof that BSE could be transmitted to humans by eating beef, the most likely explanation

BRITAIN'S CATASTROPHIC EXPERIENCE WITH BSE HAS ERODED PUBLIC TRUST IN THE AGRO-INDUSTRIAL COMMODITY CHAIN THAT CHANNELS THE FOOD SUPPLY TO THE SUPPER TABLE.

was that those cases were linked to exposure to BSE before specified bovine offal products (brain, spinal cord, spleen, thymus, tonsils, and intestines) were banned for human consumption in 1989. Seven days later, the European Union prohibited the export of all live cattle and beef products from the U.K. In an effort to eradicate the disease, Britain belatedly announced that no cattle over the age of thirty months would enter the food or animal feed chains.[16]

By July 30, 2004, a total of 142 deaths had been attributed (definitely or probably) to vCJD in the U.K. Annual vCJD mortality increased rapidly but epidemiological research suggests that Britain's vCJD epidemic is nearing its peak.[17] Only one death has been attributed to vCJD in Canada; it appears likely that the victim contracted the disease during multiple visits to the United Kingdom.[18]

Britain's catastrophic experience with BSE has eroded public trust in the agro-industrial commodity chain that channels the food supply to the supper table. The challenges posed by BSE were not unique — similar dilemmas were raised when the hazards of bovine tuberculosis were first recognized in the nineteenth century. Yet it seems that regulators and policy makers were no better able to manage scientific controversy and technical uncertainty in the 1990s than they were in the 1890s. Science is a process, not a pat answer with a single objective truth. Scientists do not always agree and their findings can be ambiguous or even contradictory. In the case of BSE in Britain, scientific claims-makers divided into in-groups — whose findings were declared credible and politically sound — and out-groups — who advocated precaution, but without access to research material to pursue their unpopular views.[19] Recent calls for policies, which are simply "science-based," do not recognize the complexity, uncertainty and contingency of scientific research, let alone the awesome problem of risk in decision-making. Experience with bovine tuberculosis since the nineteenth century suggests that it may be unwise for policy makers to prevaricate until the scientific process has finally yielded complete and unambiguous answers.[20]

ONE IN A MILLION: CANADA'S NEWEST FOOD-BORNE ZOONOSIS

Eleven months after the detection of BSE in May 2003, the Canadian Senate's Standing Committee on Agriculture and Forestry investigated the situation, "to explore potential solutions, *with the aim of preventing the recurrence of such a disaster*." True to its agricultural mandate, it emphasized the tragic consequences of trade disruption for farm communities, but gave no attention to the challenge of risk management. The committee concluded:

> The reopening of the US border is vital to the industry's survival, and the Committee wants the government to pursue its efforts to convince the United States that it is in the best interests of North America as a whole to show leadership to the rest of the world in resuming trade *based on scientific grounds.*[21]

The Senate Committee heard from "stakeholders from the entire beef chain," including farmers, packers and retailers, the Minister of Agriculture and Agri-Food, bureaucrats from Agriculture and Agri-Food Canada and the Canadian Food Inspection Agency (CFIA), representatives from each prairie province's association of rural municipalities, and the Chief Veterinary Officer for Canada. Of twenty-seven witnesses, only *one* was a veterinarian, and not a single microbiologist, epidemiologist, animal scientist, or food scientist was identified on the witness list. Yet the Senate Committee advocated a resumption of trade *based on scientific grounds!* Like Britain's discredited MAFF, which was later restructured out of existence, the primary concern of the Senate's Standing Committee on Agriculture was the catastrophic impact of BSE, not the risk-management policies that were the ultimate cause of the crisis. Calls for science-based policy require that scientists have a seat at the table. By focusing exclusively on the economic disruption, the Senate missed the opportunity to ask more fundamental questions:
- Why did BSE appear in Canada?
- Why did the discovery of BSE take producers and consumers by surprise?

Until May 2003, the Canadian Food Inspection Agency insisted that Canada was "BSE-free." It was believed that bovine feed ingredients from domestic animals posed "no measurable BSE risk to the health of Canadians."[22] This policy was maintained even though it was well known that hundreds of cattle from BSE-infected countries were imported into Canada between 1979 and 1993, one of which was confirmed to have BSE in 1993. Based on statistical analysis, the mean expected number of cases of BSE among the imported cattle was three, with twenty-four cases as the probable limit.[23] What were the chances that one of these imported BSE-infected animals was slaughtered or died between 1979 and 1997 (before the feed ban), its carcass subsequently rendered to produce animal feed causing another animal to became infected with BSE? The estimated probability of at least one infection of BSE occurring prior to 1997 was calculated to be 0.0073, about seven chances in a thousand.[24] The CFIA concluded that the likelihood of establishment of BSE in cattle in Canada prior to 1997 was negligible. But two cases originating in Canada were discovered in 2003. Either Canadian cattle producers were extremely unlucky or the risk factors are still not understood.

Professor William Leiss, one Canada's foremost experts in the field of risk communication, argues that the estimated probability assessment ignored the consequences — thus it was not measuring risk at all. Risk is properly calculated as the probability times the consequences. Despite the remote probability, the consequences would be catastrophic for the cattle industry. The estimation of risk should be driven by the magnitude of the consequences as much as by the remoteness of the probability. Thus Leiss argues that the risk was far from negligible — indeed, the risk was "intolerable."[25]

Canada can no longer claim to be BSE-free. Health Canada's "precautionary assumption" is that "there may be a low, previously undetected, BSE prevalence in Canada."[26] By contrast, the CFIA declares, "the incidence of BSE in Canada is equivalent to that of a minimal risk country." Based on the Terrestrial Animal Health Code of the acknowledged authority, *l'Office international des epizooties*, the incidence of BSE in Canada is considered to be less than one in a million. Only one case of BSE has been detected during the last twelve-month period in a herd of approximately 5.5 million adult cattle.[27] Nevertheless, based on the recommendations of the international panel that was commissioned to review Canada's response to the discovery of BSE, Food and Drug Regulations were amended to ban the sale or import of specified risk materials (SRM) for food in July 2003, fourteen years after Britain had banned the human consumption of specified bovine offal.[28]

> "I guess any self-respecting rancher would have shot, shovelled and shut up, . . ."
>
> Ralph Klein, Premier of Alberta,
> Western Governors' Association annual meeting
> in Big Sky, Montana, September 14, 2003

To maintain Canada's current international standing as a "minimal risk" country and to stand a chance of restoring export markets for live cattle and beef from animals over thirty months old, the level of BSE testing will have to be greatly increased, especially among the older and higher-risk animals. Producers are reluctant to pay for veterinary treatment when older animals with little market value appear sick, and veterinarians may be unwilling to submit the head of euthanized livestock for testing due to the stigma attached to whoever triggers the next discovery of BSE in Canada.[29] According to the Fred Dunn, Alberta's Auditor General, "No one wants to be that number three — that third case diagnosed here," which is why some farmers may elect not to test high risk animals for BSE and just bury their dead cows.[30] But insufficient testing of high-risk animals could itself be grounds for a further downgrading in Canada's BSE status by *l'Office international des epizooties*. By July 27, 2004, it was still unclear how a sufficient number of samples would be gathered to meet Alberta's 2004 test quota.[31] No one knows if a single case of BSE remains in Canada. Cattle producers are afraid to look for it but equally afraid that no one is looking for it, betting the farm whether they like it or not. Meanwhile consumers rely on government inspection to ensure that their meat is safe.

MEAT INSPECTION

Canada's Meat and Canned Foods Act became law in 1907, one year after publication of *The Jungle*, Upton Sinclair's sensational exposé of unsanitary food handling practices in Chicago's meat-packing plants.[32] Canada's Meat Inspection Service was created as an agency of the Department of Agriculture. Any plant wishing to ship its products across provincial or international boundaries was obliged to meet federal inspection standards.

One important lesson gleaned from Britain's BSE crisis was the need to separate the government department that promotes and supports food commodity producers from the agency responsible for monitoring and enforcing food safety standards. Britain created an autonomous Food Standards Agency (FSA) in 2000, with a mandate to represent the public interest, and an independent board, which reported to Parliament through the Health Ministers. In addition to the accountability change, Britain's FSA adopted a remarkably transparent policy on the proceedings of its expert committees, giving its scientists an unusual degree of freedom to communicate dissenting views. Unorthodox and contrary scientific views and minority opinions are considered and documented so that there is a clear audit trail showing how committees reached their decisions. By exposing scientific uncertainties and clearly identifying the very real policy dilemmas of what is both a scientific and a political process, the

FSA is attempting to avoid further policy failures of the type that characterized Britain's handling of BSE.[33]

Wisely anticipating the structural problem revealed in the United Kingdom's BSE experience, Canada took pre-emptive action. The Canadian Food Inspection Agency (CFIA) was formed in 1997 to consolidate the delivery of all federal food, animal and plant health inspection programs — programs that had formerly been provided through four federal government departments: Agriculture and Agri-Food Canada, Fisheries and Oceans Canada, Health Canada, and Industry Canada. While the CFIA still reports to parliament through the Minister of Agriculture and Agri-Food, it stands at arm's length from the department that promotes agricultural output and international trade in food products.

Given the importance of its mandate and the challenging policy questions that it is likely to face, the CFIA may require even greater autonomy, with a board structure that gives science more seats at the table, as in Britain's FSA. Such a board would include private sector "stakeholders" from various agri-food sectors, but it should also have strong representation from veterinarians, and food, animal, fish, and plant scientists to bring an independent scientific perspective to bear on emerging food safety issues and the close relationships between animal and human health questions.[34] Like an auditor, the CFIA would benefit from a more independent structure. Government scientists should be given the freedom, sometimes called "whistle-blower" protection, to articulate dissenting views on the unprecedented food safety challenges emerging from industrial agriculture, innovative biotechnologies, a global food economy, and advances in health research.

Protocols for Quality Assurance

Traditional organoleptic meat inspection detects disease with the five senses, using techniques such as visual examination, incision, and palpation of various organs and lymph nodes. It is little

changed since these techniques were first developed in the 1880s.
Except for the grossest abnormalities, organoleptic inspection is
of doubtful sensitivity, and procedures such as incision have been
known to spread pathogens.[35] Considering that many recently
identified bacterial and viral pathogens are not detectable by
organoleptic methods, British veterinarians argue that the
analysis and management of risk in the slaughter and carcass

HAZARD ANALYSIS CRITICAL CONTROL POINTS

Hazard Analysis Critical Control Points (HACCP, pronounced
"hassip") is widely acknowledged as the standard quality assurance
protocol to monitor processes for safety in the food and beverage
industries. HAACP was first developed by the Pillsbury Company
in 1960 to attain the 100 percent quality assurance level required
to feed astronauts in NASA's space program.

To implement the procedure and become eligible to claim
HACCP compliance, it is necessary to work through a seven-
point process, beginning with hazard analysis and identification of
the critical control points, the stages in any process where hazards
exist. Procedures to measure, monitor, correct, and document the
hazards and preventative actions are developed. HACCP is an
unapologetically bureaucratic system that relies on measurement
and documentation to integrate quality assurance into every phase
of production.

While HACCP can reduce risk, it is no guarantee. For
example, Excel Beef (the beef producing arm of Cargill Foods in
the United States) is HACCP accredited, but in December 2003
it had to recall 13 tons of ground beef labelled as "irradiated for
food safety." For nearly three months the ground beef had not, in
fact, been irradiated at all. Even in HACCP certified plants,
errors may persist for prolonged periods.

dressing process should become the key functions of meat inspection.[36] The most common technique for risk analysis in meat production is Hazard Analysis Critical Control Points (HACCP). Many of the largest meat packing firms have already developed sophisticated new quality assurance systems based on HACCP on their own initiative. HACCP certification will eventually be mandatory in all federally inspected meat plants, as is already the case in federally registered fish and seafood plants.

The emphasis in traditional meat inspection was on ante-mortem physical condition of livestock, and post-mortem carcass dressing and meat processing — but there are possibilities that food safety may be compromised elsewhere in the commodity chain, both ante-mortem and post-packaging. Ante-mortem inspection in the pen is usually brief and arguably less important in determining suitability for slaughter than an assessment of the disease and treatment history of the animal when it was on the farm.[37] The farm is the source of many animal diseases, injuries, and other food safety hazards such as excessive tag,[38] broken hypodermic needles, and failure to observe specified withdrawal times after pharmaceutical treatment. Numerous critical control points in livestock production may create hazards. Feeds derived from rendered ruminants are now recognized as a serious hazard. This demands a new awareness of critical control points, both at the commercial feed mill, where rendered ingredients must be conscientiously segregated, and in the barn, where different types of feed may be stored. Post-production quality assurance is no less essential, from loading boxed beef on the reefer truck through retail and on to the restaurant or household kitchen. The *E. coli* O157:H7 bacterium originates on the farm, becomes a contaminant in the packing plant, multiplies if meat is improperly stored, but can be neutralized in the kitchen if beef is properly cooked.

The "farm-to-fork" concept refers to quality assurance programs that flow through the length of the commodity chain. To address food safety concerns, HACCP-style quality assurance systems need to be applied at every step in the commodity chain, beginning with calving, extending through ante-mortem inspection at the slaughterhouse-door, all the way to the consumer. Farm-to-fork quality assurance will be facilitated by the Canadian Cattle Identification Program, which was inaugurated in 2001. All cattle that move beyond their herds of origin must now have uniquely coded ear tags that remain in place up to the point of carcass inspection at the packing plant.[39] The ability to trace animals backward to their herd of origin, or forward when a herd becomes dispersed, provides an unprecedented level of information for tracing the spread of animal disease and meat safety hazards from farm to fork.

Many producers have accepted voluntary programs such as the Canadian Cattlemen's appropriately named "Quality Starts Here," which promotes best practice, but does not monitor it.[40] In Britain, the major supermarket chains sell only "Farm Assured British Beef and Lamb," a quality assurance certification program that requires producers to be inspected and subject to audits.[41] Mandatory compliance with on-farm quality assurance programs is the next logical step in Canada, but will be opposed by producers who guard their independence and object to HACCP as a bureaucratic burden.[42] Farmers will only accept quality assurance protocols when retailers send a clear market signal up the commodity chain, making certified and verified quality assurance a condition of market access.

Provincial Meat Inspection and the Regulatory Paradox

Provincially licensed slaughter plants may only sell meat within their home province. Cattle slaughter in provincially licensed plants amounted to 185,000 head in 2002 or about 6 percent of Canada's total reported cattle slaughter.[43] Large-scale federally inspected meat suppliers regard the provincially inspected meat plants as marginal and irrelevant to Canada's large export-oriented meat-packing sector. This is a fallacy with serious consequences. What happens in provincially inspected plants does have an impact on large-scale producers and their export markets. The "single stinking cow" that triggered the BSE crisis, according to Premier Klein, was sent to a provincially inspected plant and the animal's head languished on the laboratory shelf for over three months before it was finally examined and BSE was detected.

> "It was just one stinking cow, . . ."
>
> Ralph Klein, Premier of Alberta,
> Pacific Northwest Economic Region annual summit,
> Calgary, Alberta, July 14, 2003

Since its inception in 1907, federal meat inspection legislation has excluded farm slaughter and the intraprovincial meat trade from its provisions. This had the effect of reserving the higher-quality cattle and hogs for export markets while the lowest-quality cattle went to domestic consumers. Hundreds of small slaughterhouses served local butcher shops, seldom subject to any inspection. As early as 1918, the Livestock Commission of Saskatchewan noted the problem with selective federal standards.

> At present inspection operates only in those plants which do an interprovincial business, though it covers all products of such establishments, whether sold locally or outside. The consequence is that the worst stuff is reserved for local killing and consumption. Some districts notorious for bad stock are avoided by inspected plants, only to find an outlet locally.[44]

The regulatory paradox is that when two sets of regulations are applied, the highest-quality goods, which are likely to meet the criteria, are directed to the most demanding regulator, while the lower-quality goods are dispatched to the less onerous regulatory regime. As standards in Canada's federally inspected plants rise, and plants become more comprehensively equipped to meet demands for food safety, the smaller provincially inspected plants may be left to handle the higher-risk livestock.

Dr. Temple Grandin, the leading animal scientist in the field of humane livestock handling and slaughter, audited Canadian slaughter practices in 1995, 1999, and 2003. Noting the distinction between federal and provincial plants, Grandin did not observe any sick, debilitated or emaciated animals in federally inspected plants in 1995. She went on to argue that "downers" (livestock which cannot stand) and "cripples" have not been miraculously healed; they are simply being diverted to smaller plants, which are not federally inspected.[45] Canada's Health of Animals Regulations prohibit loading or transport of downers. But every province has its own animal health legislation, which does not always provide for the humane transportation of animals. Most provinces have only broad guidelines, so the handling of downers and sick livestock varies from province to province.[46] On January 13, 2004, the CFIA banned the slaughter of downer cattle in federally inspected plants licensed for export. This interim measure was designed to harmonize Canada's BSE risk management measures with those in the U.S.A. in an effort to maintain market access.[47] The effect of the CFIA ban is to divert downer cattle to provincially inspected plants for the domestic food chain. Thus provincial inspectors in small and sometimes remote plants may have to make a proportionally larger number of critical animal health decisions, but with less direct, onsite access to veterinary support than is the case in federally inspected plants.

In 1995, Dr. Temple Grandin expressed reservations about Canada's provincially licensed plants.

> There is a need to review practices in provincial plants that are not federally inspected or members of the Canadian

Meat Council. It is likely that bad things are going on in some small provincial plants. I have learned from experience that very small plants come in two basic types. They are either excellent or disgusting.[48]

Many of the provincially inspected slaughter plants that I have observed are cheerful family-owned businesses with conscientious owners and skilled workers. But few are equipped with the state-of-the-art equipment for carcass pasteurization and sanitation of cutting tools found in large plants. And I have also witnessed ineptitude and inhumane practices in provincially inspected facilities. In one case, I noted that six bullets had to be fired from a single-shot .22 calibre rifle before a steer was finally stunned into

IN ONE CASE, I NOTED THAT SIX BULLETS HAD TO BE FIRED FROM A SINGLE-SHOT .22 CALIBRE RIFLE BEFORE A STEER WAS FINALLY STUNNED INTO INSENSIBILITY.

insensibility. While stunning effectiveness is not a direct measure of meat safety, it is a determinant of meat quality.

The 2001 Report of the Provincial Auditor of Ontario observed critical deficiencies in its provincially inspected meat plants. Hazards to human health included ineffective sanitizing equipment, carcasses transported in unrefrigerated trucks, and unsanitary food contact surfaces. Ontario's Ministry of Agriculture, Food and Rural Affairs was slow to verify that corrective action was taken when abattoirs were not in compliance with food safety regulations, meat inspectors' documentation was insufficient to demonstrate that operational tasks were actually being completed, and there was no procedure for random laboratory testing to detect evidence of contaminants in the meat produced in provincial plants.[49] In August 2003, a provincially inspected plant in Aylmer, Ontario was investigated for the alleged sale of uninspected meat, slaughtering without a provincial inspector present, and processing of dead stock. No charges were actually laid, but the allegations were widely reported. Between 1991 and 2003 the firm's licence was provisionally suspended five times and on two other occasions the firm was warned about illegal slaughter and obstructing a meat inspector.[50]

These events prompted a judicial inquiry into meat regulation and inspection in Ontario. Among other problems in the provincial inspection system, Justice Roland Haines found evidence of nepotism in the appointment of meat inspectors, and pointed to deficiencies in their qualifications and training after provincial government cutbacks had replaced permanent inspectors with part-time contractual appointees.[51] He also identified conflict of interest as an issue. Unlike the Canadian Food Inspection Agency, which operates at some remove from Agriculture and Agri-Food Canada, provincial meat inspection is typically a function within provincial ministries of agriculture.[52] Thus provincial inspection authorities may feel torn between their responsibilities to consumers and their active support of livestock producers. In Ontario, Justice Haines found evidence of, "a reluctance to act decisively when the issues of public safety and client welfare collide. This only fuels the perception that public safety is sometimes taking a backseat to the agricultural business."[53]

Provinces such as Ontario claim that provincial inspection standards are equivalent to federal food standards, and that the difference between federal and provincial inspection is primarily one of scale and scope, not food safety outcomes.[54] Notwithstanding their equivalent inspection standards, provincially inspected plants are typically not as well equipped with state-of-the-art sanitation equipment, and are not as well designed and constructed to prevent contamination. The qualifications, training, and experience of provincial inspectors varies from one province to another, as does the frequency and intensity of support by professional veterinarians. At the retail meat case and in commercial or institutional dining rooms, it is often unclear whether meat was provincially or federally inspected, and it is difficult to discover where it was slaughtered and processed.

Many Canadians prefer to buy meat from locally produced livestock, and there is growing interest in organic and natural meat products, community-supported agriculture, and alternative farming practices. This trend should reinforce the role of small-scale, locally oriented slaughter plants in the commodity chain. The friendly, small-town butcher, operating a small provincially inspected plant, provides a valued alternative to national chain stores and large scale meat-packing plants. But the friendly butcher may also be processing older livestock that are more likely to be disabled or to have some zoonotic infection. Experience with locally oriented kill plants suggests that small is not always beautiful, and provincially licensed slaughter plants may need more intensive quality assurance than is presently the case.

The smaller abattoir environment poses unique challenges to meat inspection, given the prevalence of part-time kill floors that operate only one day per week, staff who are only intermittently employed in slaughter and carcass dressing tasks, and part-time meat inspectors. Some provincially inspected abattoirs are in peripheral regions, making it difficult to provide immediate support from professional veterinarians. Given the growing importance attached to food safety, the rapid developments in the biotechnology of meat inspection, and the important role played by smaller meat plants, would Canadians be better served by one rationalized system of meat inspection instead of eleven? Can we still justify two classes of inspection, one of which is *not* eligible for export and *not* acceptable for most fast-food and supermarket chains, yet satisfactory for domestic consumers?

Can more effective methods of meat hygiene and risk management be developed specifically for the needs of small plants?

BETTING THE FARM IN RISK SOCIETY

Sociologist Anthony Giddens, Director of the London School of
Economics, has identified the politics of risk as one of the most
distinctive aspects of modern society. Risk is an evaluation of a
hazard — often quantified as a probability — that may materialize
in the future. A concern with uncertain future events, justifying
institutions such as fire departments, is among the hallmarks of
modernity. Why has risk become so important? Modern society

MODERN SOCIETY HAS A CAPACITY TO CREATE "MANUFACTURED RISKS" ON AN UNPRECEDENTED SCALE.

has a capacity to create "manufactured risks" on an unprecedented
scale. Unlike the chances of being hit by lightning (a natural
hazard with an improbable but quantifiable risk), we have no
idea of the likelihood of our manufactured hazards. Cassandras
warn of sea level rise or bacterial resistance to antibiotics as catastrophic outcomes of anthropogenic global change. What is the
risk that one of these post-modern plagues may be visited upon
future generations? Civil society does not know, and scientists do
not agree. Thus Giddens says that there is a new "riskiness to
risk" creating "a new moral climate of politics" in our "risk
society."[55] Politicians are charged with a cover-up if they elect
not to take action and the worst-case scenario materializes. And
if they take action against a non-existent menace, they are
charged with scare-mongering. Science-based policy-making

can't always win — that is the fundamental problem posed by risk society.

One way to resolve this problem is to apply the "precautionary principle," a risk management tool which states that a lack of full scientific certainty should not be used as a reason for postponing decisions.[56] The precautionary principle is written into the Treaty of Maastricht, and adopted by all member countries of the European Union. To avoid the risks posed by growth hormones, the EU applied the precautionary principle in its continuing ban on Canadian and American beef imports.[57] Among most Canadian cattle producers, this use of the precautionary principle is perceived as a hypocritical pretext for a protectionist trade policy that discriminates against Canadian beef. These trans-Atlantic differences illustrate polar opposites in the moral climate of politics described by Giddens.

The precautionary principle has also been adopted by the Canadian Food Inspection Agency and by the Canadian government at large.[58] Yet applying the principle to decision-making is challenging because there is no consensus in the public's perception and tolerance of risk. Instead there is a broad plurality of risk preferences. Risk preference plurality poses a conundrum for policy-makers trying to discern whether "risk of serious harm" is truly credible. William Leiss argues that the risk of BSE was clear:

> Trouble has been brewing for Canada's beef industry for many years, during which both political and industry leaders followed the well-known three monkeys' routine ("hear no evil . . ."). The bottom line is, Canada — with a $30 billion annual beef industry to protect — has been appallingly lax in its policies designed to minimize BSE risk. In more technical language, we have been insufficiently precautionary, by a wide margin, in response to the *economic risk* represented by BSE.[59]

In the area of BSE policy, Canadians behaved as daring risk-takers. Canadians bet the farm, counting on denial and long odds to escape calamity. Canada came up short, and all Canadians are paying the price. If Canadians are fundamentally risk-averse, given that the stakes are so high, then we need to recognize that we are living in risk society and start applying the precautionary principle more consistently from farm to fork.

Glib assertions that policy decisions should be "science-based" ignore the essentially political character of risk assessment. Science and politics must interact, so that the ambiguities of scientific findings and the subtleties of scientific judgment may be communicated and shared with consumers in the climate of uncertainty that characterizes our risk society.

In coping with challenges at every stage in the commodity chain, cattle producers, beef packers, and government regulators have already demonstrated enormous ingenuity, showing evidence of innovation at every step. This chapter points to some areas where further innovation seems warranted and likely in the near term. None of these proposals is truly novel, and initiatives are already underway to address each of them; however, progress has been glacial.

- Give the CFIA and provincial meat inspection agencies greater autonomy both in their relationship to agricultural interests and internally, perhaps with a board structure that brings scientific perspectives to bear on "science-based" regulatory questions.
- Examine provincial meat inspection from a nation-wide perspective and consider some nation-wide benchmarks. Consider creative ways to implement higher national standards yet retain the essential character of small-scale meat plants.
- Extend quality assurance programs from "farm to fork."
- Use the precautionary principle, and assess risk as the product of probability and consequences to avoid future zoonotic catastrophes.

While food safety issues are changing rapidly, the challenges and ambiguities of decision-making under uncertainty will always be with us. To manage food safety risks wisely, in a dynamic policy environment, we must involve scientists more directly in decision-making processes. And we must avoid simplistic calls for science-based policy when there is disagreement, using appeals to science to validate the status quo. As Canada learned to its cost, we could be betting the farm: the odds may seem good but the consequences could be catastrophic.

A HISTORY OF FOOD (CONTINUED)

1798 Thomas Malthus first publishes his explosive work "An Essay on the Principle of Population," in which he predicts that the world's population will inevitably grow faster than food production. Malthus's theories, which paint a bleak picture for the future of humanity, will become instrumental in the development of Charles Darwin's theories of evolution and natural selection.

1802 As American ambassador to France, Thomas Jefferson is introduced to the idea of cooking potato slices in oil. Soon after, the dish is served in the White House as "potatoes served in the French manner."

1811 In Dundela, Ontario, John McIntosh plants some local apple seeds on his land. One produces a resilient and tasty apple that he names a McIntosh. Allan McIntosh, John's son, will make the apple a profitable business and the most important fruit in Canada.

1834 The first practical use of refrigeration is demonstrated by Dr. John Goorie of Apalachicola, Florida, whose device cools the air for yellow fever patients. It is not until the late 1800s that refrigeration will be used for keeping food cool.

1845–1850 A blight in the potato crop in Ireland, later known as the Irish Potato Famine, causes food prices to rise precipitously and leads to the death of a million people from famine and disease. Irish peasants are thrown off their land in the hundreds of thousands. Many people leave Ireland for the shores of North America. As a result of death and immigration, the population of Ireland decreases from 8 million before the famine to 5 million shortly after.

1851 Irish-born scientist William Thomson (later Lord Kelvin) publishes his account of the second law of thermodynamics, which will lead to a design for the heat pump, a device used to transfer heat from a low-temperature medium to a high-temperature medium. The heat pump will, in turn, lead to the development of the modern refrigerator.

▼ CONTINUED ON PAGE 96

03.

FISH OR CUT BAIT: SOLUTIONS FOR OUR SEAS

CARL SAFINA, CARRIE BROWNSTEIN

EDITORS' INTRODUCTION

In 1497, explorer John Cabot set sail from Bristol, England, looking for China. Born in Portugal — his name was originally Giovanni Caboto — Cabot had searched throughout Europe for a sponsor for his extravagant voyage until he had found backing from Henry VII of England. Cabot imagined riches of perfumes, silks, and exotic spices such as ginger, cinnamon, and pepper, which at the time were rare and very expensive commodities.

Cabot, of course, never found his way to the spices of China, but he discovered an equally valuable resource on his journey: the North Atlantic cod fisheries. He reported that the waters off Newfoundland were so "swarming with fish, which can be taken not only with the net, but in baskets let down with a stone."

After Cabot's discovery, fishermen came from Europe in droves to fish in these plentiful waters. It is estimated that over 10 million European fishermen followed Cabot's journey to fish the Grand Banks. For centuries the bountiful fish stocks were able to replenish themselves and to provide ever-growing quantities of fish for Europe and North America. And as the fishing vessels increased in size, and the catches continued to climb, the cod fishery claimed an unparalleled role in the economy of the Northeastern region of North America.

By the mid-twentieth century, a new kind of fishing vessel began to show up on the Grand Banks. The first of its kind was a

Scottish ship called The *Fairty,* a 85-metre-long behemoth weighing over 2,600 tonnes. The *Fairty* was a floating, 24/7 fishing factory. It used technology such as sonar to find the fish stocks, had enormous winch-operated nets capable of pulling in hundreds of tonnes of cod at once, and carried a full processing plant on board. As a result of these new, highly efficient fishing boats, the catch continued to climb exponentially. It reached a peak in 1968, with a catch of 810,000 tonnes of Atlantic cod that year.

Most of us already know the rest of this unfortunate story: the Atlantic cod fisheries collapsed from overfishing in the early 1990s, and despite a decade of drastically reduced fishing — resulting in unparalleled hardships visited upon the communities that had relied on the industry — the fish numbers have yet to rebound. A vital resource worth billions of dollars that fed generations has been largely destroyed within our lifetime.

The story of the North Atlantic cod fishery is not unique. Across the globe, fish populations have dropped precipitously as the mechanized efficiency of our fishing fleets — encouraged by billions of dollars in governmental assistance — has pushed our oceans to their carrying capacity and beyond. It is an awareness of this crisis that has motivated most of the work of Carl Safina. He is president and co-founder of the Blue Ocean Institute, a not-for-profit organization that is "dedicated to building a wider, more inspired cultural atmosphere for ocean conservation through science, art, and literature." He has teamed up with Blue Ocean writer and researcher Carrie Brownstein to write the following article, which tracks the history of fishing in our century and tries to show some ways that we may be able to renew our relationship with our damaged oceans.

ONE MAN'S STORY

At ninety years old, Fritz Goldstein still remembers with sharp precision the details of his lifetime in the seafood business. Stationed at his kitchen table in the outskirts of Philadelphia, his ancient eyes light up as he recounts tales of a career journey he can still scarcely fathom. Who would have known, his expression conveys, that in the early 1900s the son of a Russian immigrant fishmonger could grow up to participate in the growth and globalization of the modern seafood industry?

In his early years, Fritz awoke at three o'clock each morning to haggle with local dealers at his father's wholesale fish market on Philadelphia's bustling Dock Street. He was a fifteen-year-old with a tight schedule; after work he still had to make it across town before the first school bell rang. Fritz sold freshwater carp and whitefish hauled from the Great Lakes and the relatively more pristine waters of Wisconsin and Nebraska. The saltwater fish — croakers and porgies — travelled a shorter distance; all were caught off nearby Cape May and Wildwood, New Jersey. It was the Depression in the United States and fish was cheap — five dollars for a hundred-pound box.

The gruelling and unglamorous life of a fishmonger was never Fritz's dream. So when he graduated high school in 1932, he made other plans. Packed and ready with a scholarship to launch a football career at the University of Alabama, Fritz was intercepted by his father who pleaded for him to stay and help with the business. With a commitment to family stronger than a desire for football and academics, Fritz's decision was made. He returned to the fish market. Less than a decade later, he founded Liberty Fish Company. In partnership with his four brothers, Fritz built Liberty Fish into a major player in the international seafood industry.[1]

FISHING GOES HIGH TECH

When Fritz Goldstein first started working at the fish market in the late 1920s, human capacity to catch fish was limited by communications, transportation, and technology. Fritz recalls one harrowing journey to buy Lake Whitefish from Lac La Biche, one of Alberta, Canada's largest lakes. One way, the trip required eight airplane flights plus a twelve-mile (nineteen-kilometre) trek on a dogsled.[2]

Even when diesel engines largely replaced steam power on fishing boats after the First World War, and fishing efficiency increased markedly, some places were simply too far or too deep to fish. Most fisheries occurred relatively close to shore and consequently, there were natural refuges for fish to hide and reproduce. Deep-dwelling species were impractical targets back then, so by default some naturally vulnerable species such as orange roughy were protected from exploitation. The Second World War and its aftermath, however, not only changed the social and political landscape of the world, but dramatically transformed how and where fishing occurred.

Savvy fishers discovered that by applying naval battle technology to fishing boats, they could radically improve their capacity to catch fish. SONAR, designed to detect enemy submarines, became an effective fish finding device. RADAR allowed safe operation in dense fog. LORAN permitted pinpoint navigation to fish hide-outs with push-button ease. And with the availability of new synthetic materials like nylon, which did not rot as easily as

SAVVY FISHERS DISCOVERED THAT BY APPLYING NAVAL BATTLE TECHNOLOGY TO FISHING BOATS, THEY COULD RADICALLY IMPROVE THEIR CAPACITY TO CATCH FISH.

natural fibre nets, fishers could fish longer than before. These technological improvements made it possible for seafood buyers like Fritz Goldstein to introduce new fish to the market. On his first trip to New Zealand, for example, Fritz's customers presented him with the once-elusive orange roughy.[3] Before long, few species remained undiscovered.

THE SEAFOOD MARKET GOES GLOBAL

While seafood markets in coastal communities still feature some locally caught species, most fish markets in the developed countries now thrive on imported seafood. At major trade centres such as New York City's Fulton Fish Market, shouting fishmongers entice chefs and other buyers with a vast assortment of fish, fresh and frozen, live and dead. The world's largest fish market, Tsukiji in Tokyo, Japan, has the most diverse selection. Tautog and summer flounder from the U.S. East Coast, and lobsters from Maine are featured among fish, shellfish, and invertebrates extracted from virtually every fishable body of water on the planet.[4]

As the world's first- and second-largest importers of seafood, Japan and the U.S.A., respectively, are highly influential in determining the global fish catch. Having overexploited many of their domestic fisheries, the United States and other major importing nations now depend on developing countries to meet their demand. China and Peru report the largest catches of wild fishes, followed by Japan, the U.S.A., Chile, Indonesia, the Russian Federation, and India. The fish trade is big business today. According to the United Nations' Food and Agriculture Organization (FAO), trade in seafood products in 2000 reached US$55.2 billion.[5] Consequently, when we discuss fisheries and aquaculture in the world today, we must retain a global perspective.

The value of seafood stretches far beyond that of a commodity bought and sold in the world market. Globally, people depend on fish for food and for work. Over one billion people in the world today depend on fish for at least 30 percent of their animal protein intake. And over half of the world's population relies on fish for at least 20 percent of their animal protein. Coastal communities tend to eat more fish than inland communities. And in some small island states, fish is the sole source of animal protein. Furthermore, the FAO estimates that 35 million people worldwide are employed full or part-time in fisheries and aquaculture (seafood farming). The distribution of these workers (Asia, 85 percent; Africa, 7 percent; Europe, South America, and North and Central America, 2 percent each; and Oceania, 0.2 percent) reflects the general population distribution and predominance of labour-intensive economies.[6]

THE OCEANS FEEL THE PRESSURE

The global seafood market, as we recognize it today, grew relatively quickly after the Second World War. Global catches of wild species increased rapidly in the 1950s and 1960s as a result of the factors described previously — increased efficiency from improvements in technology, transportation, and communications. According to the FAO, the increases continued, albeit at a slower rate and with some exceptions, until peaking at 83 million tonnes in 1989. The exceptions were quite significant: in 1972 the world's largest fishery, Peruvian anchoveta, collapsed, partially due to oceanographic conditions related to El Niño. (In the mid-1990s El Niño period, the anchoveta fishery again declined substantially.) In its latest report on the status of world fisheries, the FAO suggested that catches have since recovered to levels seen in the early 1990s, prior to the latest major decline in Peruvian anchoveta: 77–78 million tonnes.

In the 1990s the FAO attributed global total fish-catch increases to production from China. China's reported catches are so high — almost 20 percent of total world production in 1998 — that they significantly affect the global total.[7] Ever since the collapse of the Peruvian anchoveta fishery in the early 1970s, scientists have warned of the upper limits to our oceans' capacity to supply fish. While the FAO has acknowledged that these claims are substantiated,[8] its portrayal of the status of the world's fisheries has been overly optimistic. Collecting statistics on the world's fisheries is clearly challenging. Relying on member countries to provide their own catch reports, the FAO has few safeguards to ensure that its statistics are accurate.

Specifically, there were some indications that China's catch reports were too high. For example, some of China's major fish populations were declared overexploited decades ago. In 2001, Watson and Pauly published an eye-opening study in the journal *Nature* about the true status of our world's fisheries. These researchers used a statistical model to compare China's officially reported catches to those that would be expected, given oceanographic conditions and other factors. They determined that China's actual catches were likely closer to one half their reported levels. The implications of China's over-reporting are dramatic: instead of global catches increasing by 0.33 million tonnes per year since 1988, as reported by the FAO, catches have actually declined by 0.36 million tonnes per year. And when catches of Peruvian anchoveta, a species whose abundance fluctuates naturally with changing environmental conditions are excluded, the declines for all other species are even more pronounced at 0.66 million tonnes per year.[9] Watson and Pauly's findings showed that fisheries are not, in fact, keeping pace with people's demand for fish. Instead, real catches had been declining since about the early 1990s.

Furthermore, even with high-tech fish-finders, fishing is not as simple as reaching down and catching a tuna by its tail. Many of the pervasive methods for fishing today are indiscriminate: fishers not only catch targeted species, they incidentally catch other species as well. When last estimated, this non-targeted catch, known as "bycatch," added up to 18–40 million tonnes (at least one-quarter of total catches).[10] These days, instead of being discarded dead, more of the non-targeted catch is being ground up and used as fish-meal for aquaculture.[11] But the impact on the ecosystem of killing such an enormous quantity of wildlife is still the same.

Today's high bycatch stems from the transition to fishing with non-selective fishing gear that occurred a half century ago. Traditionally, most tuna, for example, were caught with pole-and-line gear, which usually hooked the big tunas that fishers wanted. Today, however, far fewer fishers employ this method. Instead, fishers use purse seine nets to target yellowfin and skipjack tuna for the canned tuna market. In addition to the high volume of tunas caught, purse seines also catch substantial numbers of bill-fish, sharks, sea turtles, and marine mammals.[12] And the pelagic longline fishery, targeting the higher-value tunas and swordfish, has among the highest bycatch worldwide. Monofilament or steel longlines can stretch for miles parallel to the sea surface, with as many as 12,000 baited hooks hanging vertically per line.[13] With 100,000 miles (160,000 kilometres) of line and 5 million baited hooks set each day throughout the world's oceans, many other

species are caught in the process of fishing for tunas and swordfish. Sharks are the most substantial bycatch in longline fisheries,
causing population declines for many shark species. In the
Northwest Atlantic, most shark species caught in pelagic longlines

IN ADDITION TO THE HIGH VOLUME OF TUNAS CAUGHT, PURSE SEINES ALSO CATCH SUBSTANTIAL NUMBERS OF BILLFISH, SHARKS, SEA TURTLES, AND MARINE MAMMALS.

are declining.[14] Longline bycatch also includes many juvenile individuals of targeted species as well as billfishes, mammals, seabirds,
and endangered sea turtles.[15]

Although longlining is inherently an unselective method of
catching tunas and swordfish, with technological ingenuity fisheries can reduce bycatch of some species. Experiments in the U.S.
Atlantic, for example, showed that using circle-shaped hooks
instead of the typical J-hooks, and mackerel bait instead of squid,
reduced bycatch of leatherback and loggerhead sea turtles by
67 percent and 92 percent, respectively. Fishery managers in
Hawaii now require that Hawaii-based swordfish boats use this
more turtle-friendly gear.[16] Adoption of these methods in longline
fisheries in other regions of the world, coupled with protecting
sea turtle habitat, reducing illegal hunting of sea turtles for meat,
and adhering to fishery regulations that protect turtles in other
fisheries, could make a tremendous difference to the world's sea
turtle populations.

Shrimp fisheries, using mobile trawls to catch America's
favourite seafood, have some of the highest bycatch of all,
accounting for over one-third of discards globally when last
assessed.[17] Bycatch in shrimp fisheries includes finfish, invertebrates, and sea turtles.[18] In some shrimp fisheries, including the

U.S. South Atlantic and Gulf of Mexico, fishers are reducing overall bycatch using Bycatch Reduction Devices (BRDs) and incidental catches of sea turtles using Turtle Excluder Devices (TEDs). However, despite regulatory efforts to ensure that shrimp imported to the U.S.A. come from turtle-safe fisheries, outside the U.S.A. many shrimp fishers fail to comply with TED regulations. In Central America, for example, weak enforcement allows the majority of fishers to claim they are TED-certified without properly using the turtle escape devices.[19]

THE BROADER EFFECTS OF FISHING

Concerned about the broader implications of fishing, scientists increasingly monitor the impacts of fishing on marine communities and ecosystems. In a widely publicized study, Myers and Worm showed that longline catch rates of large predatory fishes today are a mere 10 percent of catch rates at the start of industrial fishing. They infer a 90-percent loss of large predatory fishes from the ocean. Their study marked the first demonstration of declines in whole communities among diverse ecosystems; other analyses have shown declines in single species. Declines occurred rapidly: fishing reduced community biomass by 80 percent in fifteen years.[20]

We do not yet know what the long-term ecosystem effects of removing 90 percent of predators might be. And under the modern fishery management paradigm, regulatory agencies are doing little to stop overexploitation of species before we can find out. Fishery management agencies and commissions usually implement regulatory measures after industrialized fishing has become widespread. Consequently, they're working to stabilize populations at low levels of abundance. This approach may continue to have grave consequences for fishers as they suffer from low economic yields, and also for marine ecosystems in both coastal and oceanic ecosystems.[21]

Scientist Daniel Pauly coined the phrase "Fishing down marine food webs" to describe fishers' shift from catching large predator fishes to smaller fishes and invertebrates.[22] Later, Pauly et al. analyzed species and their trophic levels (the level in the food web that a species occupies, with algae at a trophic level of one).[23] The research showed that as large fish have been depleted, fishing operations have been shifting their targets down

CONTRARY TO SOME PEOPLE'S HOPES, FISHING OUT THE LARGEST FISH DOESN'T NECESSARILY RELEASE THE SMALLER FISH FROM PREDATION.

the food chain at a rate of 0.5 to 1.0 trophic levels per decade. This demonstrates a worldwide trend in coastal and oceanic fisheries since the early 1950s. Where fisheries are most developed, mostly in northern temperate areas, trophic levels have steadily declined in the last few decades.

The consequences, Pauly et al. state, are significant shifts in the structure of marine food webs.[24] Contrary to some people's hopes, fishing out the largest fish doesn't necessarily release the smaller fish from predation. Nor does it offer more fish for humans to catch. Rather, removing the large fish increases the populations of previously suppressed species, such as invertebrates. While markets exist for some invertebrates like squid and jellyfish, other species are toxic. The Groundlings comedy group have produced a short film in which a couple dining in an upscale restaurant of the future orders the catch-of-the-day, only to find that the catch-of-the-day, today and everyday, is a bowl of jellyfish soup because that's all that's left.[25]

CAN AQUACULTURE KEEP FISH ON OUR PLATES?

Globally, aquaculture, or seafood farming, is already a significant contributor to seafood supply. According to the FAO, aquaculture is the fastest growing of all animal food-producing sectors (9.2 percent per year since 1970 compared to 1.4 percent for capture fisheries and 2.8 percent for terrestrial meat production). And it continues to contribute increasing amounts of fish, crustaceans and molluscs to total global seafood production: from 3.9 percent in 1970 to 27.3 percent in 2000. China has reported the fastest growth. However, the FAO states that China may have over-estimated production in this sector as well.[26]

Proponents of aquaculture suggest that it can lessen our overfishing burden on wild fish populations, and can enhance food supplies. (When asked in 2004 whether he ever imagined that we could catch too many fish, even ninety-year-old Fritz Goldstein replied, "Oh no, because we're farming fish now."[27]) Many people still do not know, however, that production of some species is inefficient and unsustainable. Many species farmed today are carnivores dependent on wild-caught fish for feed. Farming carnivores entails a net loss of protein and fails to conserve wild fish populations.[28] In 2001, salmon and shrimp — two of the top four groups under aquaculture worldwide — relied on fishmeal and fish oil for their feed. Presently around 29 percent of world fish production goes to non-food products, most of which is for fish meal and oil.[29]

Even if non-fish-based feeds become more commercially available and viable, aquaculture's sustainability of depends on production methods and the types of inputs and outputs. The general system-design is a good overall proxy for the operation's effect on the surrounding environment. For example, net pen systems used to raise farmed salmon allow excess feeds and fish faeces to be released directly into open bodies of water. In contrast, closed tank systems confine wastes, making it easier to control internal and external water quality. Other important factors in determining aquaculture's potentially harmful impacts include: 1) use of pollutants such as pesticides, paraciticides, and antibiotics; 2) the frequency with which species escape from fish farms, and whether escaped species are native or non-native to the farmed areas; 3) the environment's relative ecological sensitivity and whether it is occupied, converted or adversely affected by aquaculture; and 4) the presence and effectiveness of regulations on water quality, pollution, and other effects of aquaculture. Still, some aquaculture operations today are already sustainably producing seafood. Native species of filter-feeding shellfish, when suspended in bags, nets or cages — as opposed to being dredged — are a good example.[30]

IMPORTANT STEPS FOR RESTORING THE OCEANS TO BALANCE

Creating a Sustainable Seafood Market

Increasingly, the public is beginning to connect the fish on their plate with an ocean or fish farm where it once swam. Media coverage of overfishing has grown, leading more people to wonder how their favourite fish are faring. We know firsthand that consumers want to know which fish are ocean friendly and which aren't. In response to the public's question, "What's okay to eat?" we published our first guide to seafood in 1998.[31] Today, millions of guides to ocean-friendly seafood are in circulation by us at the Blue Ocean Institute and other organizations such as Environmental Defense and the Monterey Bay Aquarium.

Despite the popularity of consumer-education tools like the seafood guides, many species remain hidden from the general public eye. Most consumers are still not yet aware of what's entailed in bringing their favourite fish to the table, or if the species is healthy or in poor shape. Some of these considerations include: Does a wild-caught species have natural vulnerabilities to fishing pressure such as late maturation? Is the species abundant or depleted? Is there strong management in place? Is the species caught in ways that don't harm the environment or other creatures?[32]

The sustainable seafood movement has thus far shown that when people learn a species is in poor shape, or that catching or farming it has serious ecological consequences, they want a better option. Once they're aware of what their choices entail, it's unacceptable to eat something on the brink of endangerment. At the same time, consumers who know a fish enjoys healthy levels of abundance, and is sustainably caught or farmed, feel motivated to chose the more ocean- or environmentally friendly option.

In the food world, chefs set the trends. With the help of industry's creative marketing — like renaming Patagonian toothfish "Chilean seabass" to increase its appeal — skilful chefs can lift a fish from relative obscurity to "must-have" status on menus nationwide. A poorly managed species can suffer tremendously from a trend. The Chilean seabass craze increased illegal fishing, and caused a decline of toothfish populations to low levels. Furthermore, large numbers of endangered albatrosses and petrels are hooked and drowned as they try to steal bait from longline vessels targeting toothfish.[33]

Informed chefs, concerned about sustainability, can set new standards for how seafood is selected and promoted. Their culinary prowess can subtly if explicitly guide consumer choices. Chefs can also help provide economic incentives for improved fishery management. In 1998, around the time we published the first consumer guide to ocean-friendly seafood, over 700 top chefs on the U.S. East Coast teamed up with conservation organizations Seaweb, and the National Resources Defense Council, to launch the "Give Swordfish a Break Campaign." Nationally renowned chefs, including Nora Pouillon from Restaurant Nora (Washington, DC) and Rick Moonen, now of RM Restaurant

(New York), took swordfish off their menus. This prompted the international fishery commission, responsible for managing Atlantic swordfish, to cut catch-quotas, and the U.S.A. to close important juvenile nursery grounds. When the boycott affected

INFORMED CHEFS, CONCERNED ABOUT SUSTAINABILITY, CAN SET NEW STANDARDS FOR HOW SEAFOOD IS SELECTED AND PROMOTED.

the price of swordfish, and the management agencies felt enough pressure to implement stronger conservation measures, the boycott was called off.[34]

The campaign was effective — the number of juvenile swordfish has increased.[35] Time, and continued conservation measures, will determine whether swordfish can truly rebound. But the campaign clearly demonstrated that consumers and chefs can powerfully affect fishery decisions and help shift public consciousness. Campaigns for species protection, improved fishery management, and aquaculture reform are currently in effect for toothfish ("Take a Pass on Chilean Seabass"), Caspian Sea Sturgeon ("Caviar Emptor"), and farmed salmon ("Farmed and Dangerous"). These campaigns are undeniably increasing awareness among seafood consumers.

Changing consumer behaviour may require publicly visible events such as boycotts to draw initial attention to an issue. Boycotts can work if they have a tangible goal. Once that goal is met, the boycott ends. Making changes that last, however, requires moving beyond trend-setting, because trends are, by their very nature, ephemeral. The backlash against the anti-fur movement is good example. In 1989, People for the Ethical Treatment of Animals launched its campaign to dissuade consumers from wearing fur. Disturbing images of wild minks, foxes, rabbits, and other animals killed for fur, and the inhumane conditions at fur farms, persuaded many consumers to respond by boycotting fur coats and other fur garments.[36] Some top fashion models endorsed the campaign and it became unfashionable to wear fur. Industry felt the effects. Throughout the nineties, consumer rejection substantially decreased purchases of pelts and fur garments, so that many trappers and ranchers went out of business. The campaign also affected public policy. Several American states and eighty-five countries banned steel-jaw leghold traps. The United Kingdom, Holland, and Austria have banned farming some selected animals for fur altogether.[37] The fashion industry, however, retaliated with a marketing campaign of its own. In the current fur revival, fashion magazine covers feature some of the models who only a decade ago swore they'd rather be naked than wear fur.[38] Thus, the creation of lasting shifts in consciousness, and subsequently in behaviour, entails something deeper. Lasting change comes from developing personal relationships with the world and the living things around us.

Creating Lasting Change, Inspiring a Sea Ethic

In his 1949 book, *A Sand County Almanac*, Aldo Leopold articulated a framework for how we might consider our relationship with our environment. His idea: that our sense of community can extend beyond humanity to encompass people as well as the living landscape. His sensibility had a moral component, which he called the Land Ethic. "A thing is right," he wrote, "when it tends to preserve the integrity, stability, and beauty of the biotic community, and wrong when it tends otherwise."[39] Right actions safeguard present and future options — not just for people but for the whole living world.

Leopold's Land Ethic includes all forms of life — human and non-human — in our concept of community. It's possible that Leopold's Land Ethic (really a Nature Ethic) excluded the oceans because his own life experience was focused on the Mid-western part of the United States. A more likely reason, however, is that when he formulated his Land Ethic, he — and most of the world — was unaware that the oceans were in trouble. At that time there was little or no documentation of fishery collapses, ocean dumping, coral bleaching, or any of the other crises that have since grown acute. Now, few individuals are truly removed from impacting the oceans. One-third to one-half of the world's population now lives within fifty miles (eighty kilometres) of a coast. Even inlanders consume seafood caught or farmed in the oceans, products shipped across the oceans, or rely on energy sources, like fossil fuels, that indirectly affect the oceans through climate change. Understanding the state of the oceans today tells us that it's time we extend our sense of community below high tide — we need now a Sea Ethic.

How do we begin to see ourselves, the oceans, and the oceans' creatures as part of the same community? Mirroring the way a sense of belonging to a human community is rooted in the personal relationships that individuals have with one another, we can develop a Sea Ethic by cultivating personal connections to the ocean and ocean wildlife. Millions of people now aspire to meet the oceans' creatures on their own turf. They attach tanks to their backs, defying what once were physiological limitations to merge with the sea world. For those who find this interaction too extreme, we bring ocean life to land. We simulate the wild places. Anyone who doubts the impression that visiting an aquarium can make, hasn't seen a child pressing her face to the glass as she witnesses for her first time ever, a shark passing only inches by her nose.

Beginning a relationship with the sea doesn't require that we immediately run off to get sand between our toes. Living in the modern world, we are already interacting with the ocean in our daily lives. But one way we can honour our relationship with the sea, and become more conscious of how our choices affect ocean life, is by changing our personal approach to selecting seafood. When we peruse a menu or stand before the fish counter at a grocery store, our criteria for selecting seafood can extend

IT'S TIME WE EXTEND OUR SENSE OF COMMUNITY BELOW HIGH TIDE — WE NEED NOW A SEA ETHIC.

beyond taste and cost. We can begin thinking about and discussing which seafoods are ocean friendly and which aren't. And with reflection, we create ideas and ideals about our community in the largest sense. In essence, we formulate a Sea Ethic.

Ecosystem Management: Thinking Bigger

In ecological parlance, a "community" is defined by all the organisms — including entire populations of different species — that inhabit a particular area and that have a potential to interact. When we consider both a community and the abiotic (that is, non-living) factors that the community interacts with, we call the combination an "ecosystem."[40] Today we're interacting with our marine ecosystems on multiple levels — from manipulating abundance of individual species populations to altering climate, which ultimately affects the oceanographic conditions that drive production at the base of marine food webs. Thus, more than ever before, the time is right for an ecosystem-based approach to marine conservation.

Many marine conservationists in North America and the rest of the world hail Ecosystem Management as a framework for policy making. Ecosystem Management means looking beyond the pervasive single-species approach to the broader implications of fishing. Under the single-species approach, management policies usually address only the total catch of the target species and when, where, and how fishing for that species can occur. Unfortunately, the single-species approach has a poor record. In U.S. waters alone, where there is a formal management structure for fisheries, but most fisheries are managed on a species-by-species basis, the status of 75 percent of species populations is still unknown. Of those that we know enough about, managers have officially declared 36 percent overfished.[41] An ecosystem approach goes beyond single-species management by expanding: 1) the list of stresses on a fish population beyond fishing to include habitat degradation and general environmental quality; 2) our understanding of an ecosystem's response to fishing beyond the effect of fishing mortality on a targeted species to include other components of the ecosystem; and 3) the scope of benefits beyond the economic value of fish to include the non-monetary benefits of ecosystem services and the benefits of other human activities.[42]

Considering fisheries from an ecosystem perspective can help address the challenges of managing species and populations that are inherently unpredictable. Unlike the plants in a productive garden, where you can count exactly how many seeds you've planted and estimate with reasonable confidence how many plants your seeds will yield and where they will grow, fish are intrinsically elusive. They move and they are hidden underwater. You can't count them like seeds from a packet. Fish are subject to a wide range of variables that affect their productivity, including trophic interactions, oceanographic fluctuations, and community interactions. Although fishery scientists have a range of sophisticated tools for assessing and predicting population sizes and productivity, there will always be unknowns, especially as we still don't *know* how many fish we're actually catching. In addition to the problem of over-reporting discussed earlier, illegal, unregulated, and unreported (IUU) catches are increasing.[43] In the face of all this uncertainty, "managing the ecosystem" is extremely difficult. What we have to do is manage human activity, with an ecosystem perspective.

Conservationists commonly refer to a concept, the "Precautionary Principle," whereby we use resources conservatively today to secure their availability for the future. In the

ALTHOUGH FISHERY SCIENTISTS HAVE A RANGE OF SOPHISTICATED TOOLS FOR ASSESSING AND PREDICTING POPULATION SIZES AND PRODUCTIVITY, THERE WILL ALWAYS BE UNKNOWNS, ESPECIALLY AS WE STILL DON'T *KNOW* HOW MANY FISH WE'RE ACTUALLY CATCHING.

developed world, people plan their financial future either by investments or through government programs like social security. In developing countries, people still plan for the future — as we used to do — by having children, as a way to help them when they can no longer work. We can apply the same philosophical principle to our future food sources. By building safety measures into our management methods, we can help ensure that we have fish to eat in the future.

Ocean Zoning: A New Tool in the Ocean Conservation Toolbox

Ecosystem Management provides resource managers and conservationists with a framework for addressing the wide range of goals people have for using ocean resources. In an increasingly crowded and hungry world, we look to the oceans for many different reasons: aesthetics, conserving biodiversity, extracting food, relaxation and recreation, or even intensely competitive sports, like the single-handed boat-races around the world. These activities often conflict, creating territorial battles that sometimes erupt in the courtroom and within communities. One ongoing conflict involves recreational and commercial fishers competing over prime fishing grounds. And as society's desires change, new conflicts arise. In Cape Cod, Massachusetts, for example, residents wanting to maintain a particular aesthetic along the coastline are at odds with others who want to place energy-generating windmills in coastal waters. Resolving user-conflicts like these requires managing people and their resource use from an ecosystem perspective.

Tangibly, we can approach Ecosystem Management using tools and techniques we already know and understand. On land, for example, planning starts with assessing a need, surveying the land's capacity to meet the need, and creating blueprints that represent the plan. Many communities manage competing demands on space and resources by creating land-use plans that zone areas as residential, commercial, agricultural, industrial, and recreational. Moving away from our current open-access, free-for-all approach to ocean management, toward a method that utilizes zoning, is a way to handle the competition for ocean resources among the world's growing population. As architects for sustainable seas, we can create blueprints that *plan* for biological, economic, aesthetic, and spiritual needs.

Designing and implementing a zoning strategy requires that the public, marine-resource managers, and policy-makers understand that the ocean is not a blank space between continents, but instead is a diverse environment where some places are biological hotspots, and others vary in their ecological sensitivity. Accounting for this diversity, we can allocate appropriate areas for commercial fishing, aquaculture, shipping, scientific research, and pleasure activities like SCUBA diving, recreational fishing, and boating. Some areas will be multiple use, some restricted use, and others places will preclude resource extraction of any kind ("no-take" zones). These protected areas can help to increase marine fish production and protect marine ecosystems, and, in turn, help generate food for the future.

Worldwide, we already have several examples of successful government-supported marine zoning initiatives. Australia's Great Barrier Reef Marine Park is the most famous. Established under the Great Barrier Reef Act of 1975, and further implemented under the Great Barrier Reef Marine Zoning Plan 2003, the Marine Park works to protect biodiversity in all habitat types and maintain and enhance cultural, tourism, and recreational values. Areas are zoned for particular types of fishing (for example, some sections restrict trawling), shipping, and recreational uses.[44]

Following Australia's lead, other countries have implemented zoning programs. They include Belize's Marine Reserves at Hol Chan and Glover's Reef, and the U.S.A.'s Florida Keys National Sanctuary. While the geographic extent of these programs is small relative to our need for a comprehensive ocean management strategy, they provide an important launching point for planning future initiatives. Additionally, the U.S.A. already has various fishing-gear restrictions (no trawling and no longlining in some areas), extraction limits (oil leases), and limits on activities such as jet skiing in certain National Marine Sanctuaries. Still, there is no comprehensive approach to regional planning and management. New technologies such as wind-generators and widespread aquaculture will only further complicate future conflicts unless a zoning discussion gets underway.

We suggest that the time is right to begin formal discussions about ocean zoning. To date, premature conflicts between the conservation and fishing communities over what specific areas would be protected — and how large these areas would be — has stymied public support for Marine Protected Areas (or "no-take" zones) in the United States. People have failed to understand that no-take zones are only one type of "zone," albeit an important one in a comprehensive zoning strategy.

Fritz Goldstein smiles softly as he concludes his stories of memorable travels around the world in search of new seafood sources

THE TIME IS RIGHT TO BEGIN FORMAL DISCUSSIONS ABOUT OCEAN ZONING.

and lifelong business partners and friendships. In his palm he holds a tiny, delicately carved figurine of a Vietnamese fisherman pulling his catch from a net. Fish-inspired artwork displayed throughout his apartment is the last remaining relic to his half-century in the seafood business. And so for Fritz, telling his story rekindles feelings of happiness and pride.

Imagination and ambition, enabled by developments in communication, transportation, and technology, led Fritz Goldstein and other well-meaning architects of the modern seafood industry to re-define the perception of the oceans held by the generations before them. The capacity to fish where no-one had gone before transformed their image of the oceans from a blank yet dangerous void between continents to a seemingly inexhaustible source of food and business opportunity. In their eyes, their relationship with the oceans undoubtedly was an improvement from years past.

In the last few decades, our natural curiosity prompted us to further explore our ocean world. In the process, we learned that the ocean is far more alive and intricate than we had ever imagined. From below the surface, we extracted images of multi-coloured fish staking their territory among vibrant coral reefs, sharks dwelling in deep ocean caves, and migrating giant bluefin tuna chasing their bait at breakneck pace. With this imagery, we triggered human fascination. And people began to care.

We cannot heal the oceans overnight. Pollution, invasive species, habitat destruction, overfishing, aquaculture, coastal development, and climate change are all threatening our oceans today.[45] With inspired imagination, intelligence, motivation, and skill, however, we can reconfigure our current relationship with the seas. Acting from a place of hope, we can restore abundance to the seas.

A HISTORY OF FOOD (CONTINUED)

1853   Responding to a picky customer in a Saratoga Restaurant, Native American chef George Crum thinly slices his fries before frying them. They are such an immediate hit that they appear on the Moon Lake Lodge Menu as Saratoga Chips. Crum soon opens his own restaurant. Saratoga chips will largely remain a local specialty until Herman Lay mass produces and sells them throughout the United States in the 1920s.

1864   Master scientist and inventor Louis Pasteur develops the "germ theory," which claims that micro-organisms are active in the process of fermentation. Sponsored by Emperor Napoleon III, who is concerned about the economic costs resulting from the loss of wine to diseases, Pasteur applies this theory and discovers that micro-organisms can be significantly reduced and their growth slowed by heating wine to 55°C for only a few minutes. This discovery will lead to a range of new developments including large-scale wine making, beer brewing, and pasteurizing. Pasteur's germ theory will also be instrumental in understanding the development of diseases such as rabies, cholera, and anthrax, and will lead directly to the development of the first vaccines.

LATE 1860s   Using beef fat instead of dairy, Hippolyte Mège-Mouriez in France creates a spreadable substitute for butter, in response to a challenge by Emperor Napoleon III. Butter has become a staple of most diets, and Napoleon wants a substitute for his troops that is less exposed to price volatility. Because of its pearly texture and colour, Mège-Mouriez names his creation after the Greek word for pearl, *margarites*.

1882   Thomas Ahearn, an engineer in Ottawa, Ontario, makes the first electrically cooked meal when he installs his "electric range oven" in the Windsor Hotel.

1884   John Harvey Kellogg and his brother, Will, patent the formula for corn flakes after discovering that once wheat is floured it can be steamed and rolled into a flake. The patent is a culmination of John's years of study as the head of the Western Health Reform Institute of Battle Creek, a research institute founded by members of the Seventh Day Adventists to promote healthy eating. The elder Kellogg is a pioneer in food research. A fight between the brothers will leave Will with the sole rights to sell corn flakes through his company, The Kellogg Toasted Corn Flake Company.

▼ CONTINUED ON PAGE 124

04.

THE HIGH-TECH
MENU
WILLIAM I.
ATKINSON

EDITORS' INTRODUCTION

To really understand the world's obsession with genetically modified/engineered organisms and food technologies, it's helpful to remember the story of the Moravian friar. No one thought the young man would amount to much, let alone start a scientific revolution that would rage for more than a hundred years. Born into a peasant family in Heizendorf, Austria, Johann Mendel had very few options in life. Too poor to pay for an education, he joined an Augustinian monastery at Brunn, one known for its devotion to learning and science. But his early years at the monastery showed a startling lack of promise.

The abbot gave Johann a new name, Gregor, and sent him off to study at the University of Vienna. It was a dismal failure. Gregor disliked the city and the pressures of the university and he flunked out, returning to the monastery humiliated. But one experience in Vienna did lodge in his mind, and that was the work of a biologist named Frank Unger. Unger's research into inheritance traits struck Mendel as practical and sound, reminding him of the real-life experiences he had had growing up on a farm. Mendel decided very quietly to embark on some experiments on his own.

Mendel decided to study the common garden pea, known to biologists as the *Pisum.* In 1856 he began to grow and crossbreed various strains of the garden pea, keeping track of the seeds and the colour and size of the stems and leaves and the plant. To artificially cross-pollinate the plants, Mendel would snip the pollen-bearing part of the plant off — a process known as castration — and then dust on the pollen from a different plant. Then he would painstakingly wrap the individual plants to protect them from pollinating naturally and ruining his experiments. Imagine this amateur gardener spending years in his black monastic robe, tweezers and brush in hand, growing more than 28,000 pea plants. Some thought he was going insane.

But Mendel got startling results. When he bred a short plant with a tall plant, the hybrid product came out tall, not, as Mendel imagined it would be, of average size. Mendel postulated that each plant carried what he called "hereditary units," some of which are "dominant" and some "recessive." With these first experiments, Gregor Mendel became the father of the genetic age. He was the first to begin to understand the roles that genes play in evolution.

And so, the obscure monk, publishing in an obscure journal about the obscure subject of breeding peas, turned away from science and retreated into the monastery. Eventually Mendel rose to the position of Abbot, but he would never see the profound impact his work would eventually have.

Today, genetic modification of plants is a multi-billion-dollar business, with champions and detractors. Mendel never imagined such creations as the 1994 Flavr Savr tomato, the genetically altered tomato that has its winter shelf life increased, or gene-altered tobacco plants or Golden rice, a rice bred to contain vitamin A, or strawberries with frost-inhibitor genes or pigs with human genes. The modern world of science and food have become intermingled today. But for all the controversy about genetics, technical ingenuity remains a huge part of the story of our food supply, and so, in the following article, acclaimed author Bill Atkinson looks at the history of high-tech food, with an eye to both the past and the future.

"**FOOD**," the columnist Richard J. Needham wrote, "is always worth whatever it costs." This is because food is on a short list of things — water, sunlight, love — that are vital to our conception and development. Food goes beyond the material to the mythic. It isn't just on shelves, stoves, and tables: literally and figuratively, it constitutes our hearts and minds. Even business, so cold and precise when it deals with microchips and auto parts, takes on a warmer glow where food is concerned.

Still, sheer scale intervenes. How to comprehend so vast a subject as nourishment? Happily, like other enterprises of equal greatness — war, politics, science — food can be understood through the interaction of technology with history. Even better, tracing food's technical history also lets us make shrewd forecasts about its future. This chapter presents some examples.

FROM UNCERTAINTY TO SCIENCE

Growing, storing, and transporting food poses problems that technological ingenuity can effectively address. While knowledge-based solutions have varied over the centuries, the problems have stayed the same. One such problem is food's tendency to spoil. Let's look at the history of this key technology.

All animals eat, and compete with us for food. Wolves cull

our herds, mice ravage grain stores, seals can strip full gillnets clean. But the fiercest of all predators are invisible: the bacteria. There's nothing in existence that some bacterium won't try to eat. Most food preservation is nothing more than safeguarding food from micro-organisms, either by forcing the wee beasties into hibernation or else by killing them outright.

Traditional ways of preserving food took the first option: shutting bacteria down. Bacteria need water; take it away and they close up shop. So people learned to dry food, exposing it to sun or hanging it in smoke-filled rooms. Or they mixed food with salt. The atoms in sodium chloride have an insatiable appetite for water, and alternating strips of fresh meat between 1-cm layers of salt desiccates the meat to the point where any germs it contains no longer function. A variant of dry-salting is pickling, which soaks food in a saline solution. Its concentration of sodium ion exceeds bacterial tolerances, killing the bacteria or knocking them out.

Cold-weather cultures also learned that lower temperatures slow food decay. Meat cooled to just above freezing stays edible for weeks; if frozen, it can be thawed and eaten months later with no ill effects.

Like all early preservation methods, drying, salting and cooling could not be explained from first principles. They worked, was all. Not until van Leeuwenhoek invented the microscope in the seventeenth century did we see microfauna, and not till Pasteur's insights two centuries later did we realize how voraciously van Leeuwenhoek's animalculae attacked our foodstuffs. Bacteria probably caused the mysterious deaths of Sir John Franklin and his fellow explorers in 1845–46. Franklin was well funded; his equipment and provisions were the era's state of the art; his food was preserved with the latest and most scientific method, canning. But Franklin's tins didn't just seal out the ambient spoilage principle, bacteria. They also sealed in some of the deadliest germs in existence. Franklin's biographers speculate that the Arctic expedition's canned food was packed on tables teeming with blowflies by workers who knew nothing of hygiene. This turned Franklin's food into a deadly cocktail. Botulinum-A, the nerve toxin produced by *Clostridium botulinum*, is so lethal that a few milligrams heaped on a pinhead could kill everyone in central Toronto. It's possible that the deaths of Franklin and his men were hastened by food poisoning, compounded (as insult to injury) by lead poisoning from the cans.

Had Franklin left a few years later, new knowledge would have seen him home. Two decades after the English expedition Pasteur, Koch, and their fellow microbe hunters had revealed the microbial cause of a host of diseases, from tuberculosis to anthrax. Previous ages had attributed these scourges to swamp mist, excess blood, or the phase of the moon; Pasteur and his fellow-researchers found the real villains were bacteria.

As inevitably occurs, new scientific data quickly led to improved practical remedies. Pasteur's most famous discovery bears his name: pasteurization.

Well-boiled food contains no live bacteria. If immediately sealed into sterile cans, the food remains without bacterial degradation until the container is breached. But the heat that kills germs also breaks down complex nutrients (making food lose taste) and fibre (turning it into a gooey, unappetizing mush). Pasteurization is a compromise: it heats food gently until *most* bacteria are dead. The process, which works best with milk, juice, and other liquids, retains flavour and nutritional value. When pasteurized foods are then refrigerated, their shelf life increases a hundred times. A litre of milk that would spoil in two hours if left at room temperature lasts up to two weeks in the fridge.

Commercial pasteurizing methods vary. You can heat raw milk to 62.8°C for half an hour, or to 72.8°C for 15 seconds. Ultra-high temperature pasteurization (UHTP) is hotter and briefer:

1–2 seconds at 141°C, above the boiling point of water. UHTP kills all germs, thus sterilizing food completely. While UHTP is too rough to use on cow's milk, its effects on the taste, texture and nutritive value of rice milk are not noticeable. That's why rice-milk packets in grocery stores need no refrigeration.

Refrigeration to above the freezing point, or else below it (freezing) came to prominence from about 1830 to 1930. The first refrigeration used water ice. Initially the ice was hand-sawn from winter lakes, packed in insulating sawdust, stored in large

AS OFTEN HAPPENS, THE OLD TECHNOLOGY SPAWNED WORDS THAT LONG OUTLASTED THE TECHNOLOGY: MY GRANDMOTHER WENT TO HER GRAVE CALLING HER REFRIGERATOR THE "ICEBOX."

urban ice houses, and distributed by horse-drawn wagons to city households. A thirty-centimetre cube of ice might last a household a week. From 1910 to 1930 the same distribution system remained in place, but mechanical refrigeration replaced natural winter ice.

As often happens, the old technology spawned words that long outlasted the technology: my grandmother went to her grave calling her refrigerator the "icebox." We take artificial ice for granted, but it was the wonder of its day. It created entities as diverse as geographically dispersed as cruise ships and the National Hockey League. The RMS *Titanic*, for example, boasted the most advanced refrigeration system in the world.

To make ice, a cooling medium circulates through a closed loop. The medium begins as a gas, which is mechanically compressed until it liquefies. This generates heat, which is radiated away — hence those black coils on the back of your fridge. The liquefied coolant enters the cold area as a liquid, cools further as it reverts to a gas and absorbs ambient heat, and returns to the compressor for another go-round. The cycle repeats until the cooled area is as chilly as desired.

The elegant technology of artificial ice followed the same dispersal route as electrification. It began in Paris and London *circa* 1880 and had reached most large Western cities by 1910. Then, beginning slowly in the 1930s and more rapidly in the great consumer explosion after the Second World War, refrigeration became one of the first consumer technologies — decentralizing from large urban ice houses into individual homes. City households were the first to get refrigerators; then rural electrification sent the farmhouse icebox to the antique shop along with the wood-fired stove.

Practical refrigeration had vast social and economic effects. It's no exaggeration to say that the technology permanently changed the face of North America. The chops and vegetables in a 1925 icebox were probably as local as the ice: few had travelled more than twenty kilometres from farm to kitchen. When Calvin Coolidge was president, only non-perishables — robust foods such as root crops and live cattle — were shipped long distances. The widespread adoption of refrigeration sparked a fifty-fold increase in the distance over which food could safely move. Small gasoline engines powered stand-alone cooling units for boxcars and trucks. Refrigeration gave farmers the same worldwide markets for their vegetables, fruit, and dressed meat that manufacturers had long enjoyed for their mass-produced knives, nails, and other imperishable dry goods.

At the same time as the home refrigerator decentralized food storage, refrigeration and transportation centralized production. Now, regions such as California's Salinas Valley could grow fruit for the entire U.S.A. Put to wheat, 200 million hectares of Canada's prairie heartland could function a global breadbox.

Some saw this trend early and others grew rich on it, but nobody did both. In his novel *East of Eden*, the American writer

John Steinbeck tells how his father foresaw the transformation of rural America by the transport of refrigerated foods. But an early attempt by Steinbeck *père* to ship vegetables to Los Angeles failed when his expensive cold-cars were mistakenly sidelined for days, spoiling their contents and costing Mr. Steinbeck his life's savings. As in other technical sectors — Bell in telephony, Edison in lighting, Gates in microcomputer operating systems — it was the Johnnies-come-lately who took the profits, leaving the concept-proving pioneers neither glory nor gold.

I have dealt at length with food preservation not because it is more important than growing or preparing food, but because it is more technology-intensive than anything except genetic improvement and nanotechnology. Food preservation nicely illustrates the whole process of technical change. First comes pure knowledge: new insights into food. This knowledge is then put to use, to buttress traditional techniques and to replace old empirical methods with better ones. The word *progress* has lost some of its lustre, but the historical progress of food preservation is beyond dispute. The next time someone laments the wastefulness of modern packaging or the woeful lack of nutrients in store-bought foods, mention this:

- Twice as much food was spoiled by microbes seventy years ago as it is today.
- "Organic" foods are not detectably richer in nutrients than other produce.
- "Organic" foods are not perceptibly lower in toxins than standard foods.
- Like the botulinum that afflicted Franklin, most food toxins are 100-percent organic.
- Preservatives such as sulfites and butylated hydroxytoluene (while you wouldn't want to eat them by the spoonful) are far less harmful in trace amounts than the natural toxins they inhibit, which is why we use them.

- Even common wheat fungi produce a metabolite called atropine, which triggers hallucinations. Medieval folk ate 110-percent organic. It didn't keep their life expectancy from being a third of ours, but it did create a lot of witch trials.

Like all change, technical improvement is the art of the possible. Will people accept it? Will old methods and devices prove so entrenched that a new idea goes nowhere? Can capital be found to nourish the idea, or will cash-deficiency smother it in the cradle? Assuming the idea survives infancy, will potential users be distracted at a crucial point by political turmoil or hard times? Will the idea be a flash in the pan or prompt the growth of an enormous new sector like microchips or lasers? The only answer to such rhetorical questions may be, "Wait and see."

While technology may tackle any problem at any time, the biggest single factor in an invention's widespread acceptance is whether or not it solves a pressing problem. At first glance, further advances in food technology hardly seem urgent. The First World knows more than enough to safeguard its produce against unacceptable spoilage; the Third World has yet to adopt even the older technical solutions. This is too simplistic a view. New ideas are in universal demand, both in the First World, where cutthroat competition repays even the smallest advance, and in the Third World, where ingenuity minimizes life-cycle consumption. I'll provide some examples towards the end of the chapter; in the meantime, four technical trends in food seem poised for especially vigorous growth. They are: ZDQC, GM/GI, functional foods, and nanoscience.

ZDQC: ZERO-DEFECT QUALITY CONTROL

Actuaries are applied mathematicians who work for insurers, governments, and health authorities. Their duties include calculating risk assessments, quantitative statements that attempt to clothe the misty future with hard fact. Some risk assessments match limited medical resources to limitless health-care demand. It's bad economics to spend $250,000 replacing Aunt Minnie's hip when she's 105, but good economics to give four-year-old Jimmie a heart-lung transplant. A common approach in such assessment is "equivalence of risk." In mathematical terms, a 1-in-10 risk of losing ten dollars is equivalent to the certainty of losing one dollar. But this strict scientific equivalence breaks down in the face of factors that are more subjective and non-technical — in a word, human.

Here's an example. Those who live near a nuclear reactor find it perfectly acceptable that their risk, expressed as maximum anticipated decrease in life expectancy, is one in 2 million. Rephrase this as equivalent risk, however, and you get a different response. Tell the reactor's neighbours that all 2 million of them will die in agony after a core breach, and the remote likelihood of the event no longer matters. Statistically, a 1:2,000,000 chance of 2,000,000 deaths is equivalent to 2 million people each shortening their life by twenty minutes. In human terms, the two risk-assessment statements are as different as chalk and cheese.

Similar effects apply in agri-food.

Britain is one of the few places in the world where the misfolded proteins called prions have demonstrably moved from animals (bovine spongiform encephalopathy — BSE — or mad cow disease) to humans (Creutzfeldt-Jakob disease or *kuru*). This has led to fifty deaths in the last thirty years. In a country whose population is 60 million, a simple risk assessment yields one death per 36,000,000 person-years of exposure. Yet while these odds make being struck by lightning seem a safe bet, they have spooked beef consumers in Britain and throughout the world. The cause of this reaction is a simple risk equivalent: *British beef may turn your brain to porridge.* The event is idiotically remote, but it's also so horrifying that it's unacceptable at any odds. *Kuru* is like accelerated Alzheimer's: you lose your short-term memory, then your long-term memory, then your fine motor control. Next to go is your gross motor control; then your bladder and bowels log off. It's so ugly a death that it's put droves of consumers off U.K. beef despite the low probability.

Canada has an even lower chance of BSE–human transmission. Strictly speaking the odds are zero for, and infinity against, since Canada has never recorded a case. Yet here as well, two diseased cows among tens of millions have sparked unease among consumers. This is true not just domestically, which would be bad enough, but in export markets. At press-time several nations still had their borders closed to Canada's live cattle, processed beef products, or both.

The only way to effectively address mad-cow is zero-defect quality control, a philosophy so stringent that it tolerates no BSE whatsoever. In ZDQC, *every cow in Canada* would be tested three times: at birth, maturity, and slaughter. Each animal's DNA would be logged so that every shred of resultant food product

THE ONLY WAY TO EFFECTIVELY ADDRESS MAD-COW IS ZERO-DEFECT QUALITY CONTROL, A PHILOSOPHY SO STRINGENT THAT IT TOLERATES NO BSE WHATSOEVER.

could instantly be pedigree-traced back to clean stock. Furthermore, everyone — foreign and domestic consumers, governments, media, whomever — would continually be briefed on ZDQC results. All this will be less expensive than today's billion-dollar handouts and multi-billion-dollar losses, because ZDQC works. In thirty months, France's ZDQC program restored both consumer confidence and market evaluation of French beef to pre-BSE levels — in some cases beyond that benchmark. Buoyant beef sales prove it.

Another example of ZDQC, well-established but generally unknown, comes from the pork industry. Trichinosis is a parasitic disease of pigs that is transmissible to humans through infected meat. If left untreated, it can cause death within weeks of ingestion. But the 100-micron-long nematodes that cause trichinosis are kept from swine by monitoring the animals' diet. Pig carcasses are tested at slaughter, and consumers know to cook pork thoroughly. Result: a ZDQC program that's empirical but effective.

It wasn't always that way. A century ago hundreds of Canadians contracted trichinosis yearly and dozens died — a record infinitely worse than BSE's. But since then, the pork industry has arrested trichinosis so rigorously that new infections are a non-issue. After reading the mad-cow headlines, many consumers have replaced beef (which they consider non-ZDQC and suspect) with pork (seen as ZDQC and non-suspect). This trend will increase with each scare headline. Lessons for the beef industry are clear.

FROM GM TO GI

For many people, today's biggest worry is the GMO or genetically modified organism. Yet here too, technology offers reassurance. GMO is too broad a term: *everything alive* is a GMO. Nature constantly muddies the genome of every species. Every baby is a jumble of its ancestors' genes. And for millennia, traditional plant breeders have used inbreeding, crossbreeding, grafting, and other rule-of-thumb techniques of genetic modification to isolate and fix desirable traits. Every dog breed on Earth stems from this type of GM intervention; so does nearly every plant and animal species that gives us food. Holstein cows look nothing like the aurochs, the ancient bovine hunted by our Cro-Magnon ancestors. Good thing, too: a bull aurochs weighed two tonnes and could squash a human hunter like a roach. In its natural state, maize produced a seed packet no bigger than your thumb — traditional GM yielded today's fat ears of corn. Wheat, one of the world's most important food species, does not even *exist* in nature. It was created over centuries by Middle Eastern farmers who interbred a variety of grasses. Without GM in any form, *H. sapiens* would be stuck in the Stone Age.

Those opposed to genetic food engineering insist that by GM we mean *transgenic* modification — taking genes from one species and stitching them into another. Yet even that is old hat to nature: bacteria, our pint-sized competitors for foodstuffs, do it all the time. Photomicrography has imaged disease germs such as cholera in the act of extruding tiny hollow tubes called F-factors. Through these, the bacilli inject genes that encode powerful enterotoxins into wildly different bacterial species. With its genome so modified a normally innocuous gut symbiont, the bacterium *Escherichia coli*, evolved a strain called O157:H7 that causes human illness and death. Last year's 73,000 cases of *E. coli* poisoning in the U.S.A., and the 61 fatalities recorded in that country, all result from a perfectly natural form of GM — organic, as it were.

The activists' complaint about GM involves the scientific characterization of such natural transgenic techniques, their modification, and their application to complement traditional methods of plant breeding. Yet this approach poses few or no dangers and is too useful to let die. Moreover, it harnesses the power of genetic diversity.

Diversity is the key to life: with plants as with people, it takes all kinds to make a world. And plants are infinitely various. Some have evolved genes for drought resistance, thickening bark to reduce evaporation or holding water in internal cisterns. Other plant genes break down poisons, repel predators, or shrug off herbicides.

The genes of still other plants recruit certain animals that distribute their seeds, while teaching less useful animals to avoid them. A family of chemicals called capsaicins (cap-*say*-shunz) form the heart of one such system. Capsaicins make peppers hot: they hit mammals, including us, like a punch in the mouth. But birds are immune — their tongues and digestive systems lack the capsaicinoid receptors that relay capsaicins' false cry of *fire*. The pepper plant invites birds to dine on its seed pods; the birds happily comply, and afterwards excrete intact seeds — increasing the plant's geographical range and thus its survivability. But a big mammal that might graze the pepper plant to the ground is sent packing with its head on fire. Sorry, mister, you're not useful. Bouncer!

Plants evolved such striking abilities because they had to. As immobile or "sessile" species, they can't run away in response to fire, flood, insect attack, or other stresses. They must stay put and handle the threat with genetic creativity. This has given Earth's flora genes that, singly and in clusters, produce amazing effects. It makes perfect sense for plant geneticists to seek these effects, isolate and sequence the genes that encode them, and import this DNA into the genome of a food plant that lacks it.

Applications are limitless. Has a traditional plant-breeding program given you barley so top-heavy with seeds that its stalks break in a windstorm? Add a stem-strengthening gene from sunflowers. Is your cold-resistant Durham Hard wheat susceptible to rust? Import a gene from a weed on which *Puccinia graminis* cannot grow. And so on. Activists find this transgenic work unnatural; one wonders what horrible results they imagine. Giant triffids stuffing humans in their leafy mouths? The central fact for all GM debate is that *not one adverse human reaction to a GM food has ever been documented,* anywhere. But while the anti-GM activists have yet to adduce a scrap of evidence that GM foods are unsafe, that doesn't damp their rhetoric. As the adage has it:

When the facts are with you, pound the facts. When the facts aren't with you, pound the table.

It might be argued that GMO technology reduces genomic diversity in food flora. Yet that is also the case for every other plant-breeding technique ever used. Developing a new grain, for example, nudges out any number of marginal forms that evolutionary forces automatically insert into the natural genome. Certainly, engineering a tomato resistant to caterpillar attack, and then spreading clones of this one genome around the world, suppresses a myriad of other tomato types — just as immunization

IT MIGHT BE ARGUED THAT GMO TECHNOLOGY REDUCES GENOMIC DIVERSITY IN FOOD FLORA. YET THAT IS ALSO THE CASE FOR EVERY OTHER PLANT-BREEDING TECHNIQUE EVER USED.

reduces diversity by eliminating the habitat of the smallpox virus. It's been remarked that education and gardening are so successful because most natural forms are stunted. If this be diversity reduction, give me excess of't.

In fairness, the activists have one point. Even when GM foods modify plant diversity in useful ways, their heavy-handed application sometimes puts pressure on the human diversity in farming. Yet strictly speaking these are issues not of technology but of monopoly marketing, expressed through technology. It's like seeing *The Grapes of Wrath* and concluding the Dust Bowl Okies were disenfranchised by the bulldozer technology that smashed their shacks. The problem with big, heartless firms ham-handedly introducing GM technology rests not with the technology but with big, heartless, ham-handed firms. The issue is political.

Although transgenic plant engineering is a simple idea, the technology that makes it work is complex. Even after a useful gene has been found, decoded, and synthesized, it's hit-and-miss whether it can be successfully stitched into another plant's genome. Even if it can be placed, the gene may never work as planned, for scientists still cannot control exactly where an imported gene will stick in the genome of a transgenic host. Yet location affects how strongly a gene is expressed, or even if it's expressed at all. A hundred attempts may be needed before a transgenic experiment is complete — and that's just the beginning of mass production. Plant geneticists are patient.

GMOS: AN AFRICAN PERSPECTIVE
by Florence Wambugu

It's needless to re-emphasize that food security is by far the most urgent priority of the African continent. If current trends continue, the absolute number of hungry people will rise in Sub-Saharan Africa from 344 million in the year 2000 to 435 million in 2010. In addition, nutritional deficiency and inequity of food distribution is expected to increase in a similar trend.

Among the multitude of problems that make agriculture difficult in Africa are poor soil fertility, uncertain rainfall, the lack of roads in rural areas to transport yields to market, uncertain local and global markets, and ever-fluctuating prices. It is therefore impossible for any one technology — or solution — to overcome all these problems. But in my view, GM technologies can help.

Recent biotech techniques have enabled both private and public sector research to make advances in two exciting areas that promise to be of great benefit in Africa: bio-fortification, and drought-resistant technology.

In Kenya and many other Sub-Saharan countries successive droughts, pests, and diseases have reduced maize yields. GM technologies can protect against these conditions. For example,

Africa is likely to benefit from the first drought-resistant maize plants that also resist the Africa-specific virus, maize streak virus. These are being developed at the University of Cape Town under the leadership of award-winning molecular biologist, Professor Jennifer Thomson.

Also in the pipeline for Africa's GM future is the Ugandan genetically modified banana cultivars that will curb banana bacterial wilt disease. These will be released from Kawanda Agricultural Research Institute, which is supported by the Rockefeller Foundation. The disease was the main cause of production constraints that reduced banana production countrywide.

Spurred on by the success of the GM "Golden Rice" — which has provided a miracle solution for vitamin A deficiency, a condition that causes severe effects in children and pregnant women across the developing world — African scientists have developed the New Rice for Africa (NERICA), a high-yielding rice that is not restricted to growth in marshy paddies and is perfect for Africa's dry conditions. Professor Monty Jones, Africa's first World Food Prize winner, hopes to see NERICA accepted across the continent. This rice has a phenomenal potential to reduce the continent's poverty, hunger, and malnutrition.

GM technology could also revolutionize how Africans are vaccinated against various diseases. During the smallpox era, it was less difficult to defeat the sickness because needles could be re-used; this not possible, now, given the HIV/AIDS pandemic. Today the three most costly components of any vaccine campaign are transportation, the needles, and the necessity for cold storage. This is why bio-pharming is important. South Africa's Council for Scientific and Industrial Research has joined a research consortium that is working on the development of various methods to add pharmaceutical proteins to plants.

As a continent Africa has much more to benefit from GM technology than our preoccupation fear, doubt, and uncertainty.

The benefits far outweigh the risks. GM technology came on stream globally in 1996. Between then and 2003, its rate of global adoption has grown at double-digit figures — higher than any other form of technology in history. According to the ISAAA "Global Status of GM Crops" report of 2003, GM crops are currently being grown by at least 7 million farmers in eighteen countries worldwide. It's time for Africa to put aside all hindrances to redirect their finances, time and energy toward building the laboratories and capacity required to develop our own Africa-specific GM crops.

The longer it takes us, the further we fall behind.

What might the future hold for GMO work? Science constantly extends and refines our control of things, and will probably solve the genomic-locale problem within five years. This will greatly accelerate plant-transgenics applications. But the biggest boost to transgenic work will come from marketing, not science. It will be the replacement of pejorative terms like "Frankenfood," and even of neutral terms like "genetically modified," by the optimistic (and exact) phrase, "genetically improved." This is precisely what transgenics does: it enhances our foodstocks. It makes life better for farmers, producers, and consumers. It cuts pesticide use, doubles solar energy capture in food species, and puts more nourishing food on more tables at less cost. Plant transgenics is an advance as pivotal as the first food-species domestications in the Late Paleolithic. We can salute its achievements by writing, saying and thinking *GI* in place of *GM*.

FUNCTIONAL FOODS

Language reveals the spiritual overtones of food — *bread of heaven, water of life*. A similar mysticism emerges in a health movement called "neutraceuticals" or "functional foods."

As Agri-Food Canada defines them in its Summerland Research Program, "functional foods . . . do more than provide energy and essential nutrients to sustain life and growth. . . . [They] deliver physiological benefits in management and prevention of diseases." AFC makes a strong qualitative case for neutraceuticals. Flaxseed for example, of which Canada produces nearly half the world's total, contains dietary substances such as gamma-linolenic acid, an antioxidant that seems to combat cancer. Alpha-linolenic acid, a slightly different fraction of flaxseed oil, lowers blood pressure and reduces serum concentrations of low-density lipoproteins or "bad cholesterol." Other functional foods cited by AFC include evening primrose oil, which suppresses inflammation and improves ectopic eczema; hempseed oil, whose gamma-linolenic acid appears to boost the immune system; and even that ancient winter-morning standby oatmeal. The beta-glucan in oats, says AFC, "lowers serum cholesterol." Beta-glucan is also "being produced and marketed to the pharmaceutical and cosmetics industries as a new product that moisturizes, revitalizes and smoothens [sic] the skin." (At this point I am reminded of Samuel Johnson's definition of oats — "A grain fed in England to horses, and in Scotland to men" — and the Highlander's rejoinder: "An' *that*, sir, is why Scotland is famous for her men, and England for her horses." It's the beta-glucan, you see.)

But even scholarly papers on neutraceuticals, such as those from Agri-Food Canada, raise questions. Isn't *all* food functional? Individually and in aggregate, what we ingest must satisfy basic needs. Grain starch is converted by salival enzymes and gastric acids into our universal energy currency, glucose. Meat gives us amino acids that we reassemble into vital proteins like keratin for hair and nails, insulin for glucose conversion, and — in a wonderful circularity — the very enzymes that break down meat. Dozens of different foodstuffs, such as broccoli, buffer the effect of those damaging electron thieves called oxidants, implicated by science in a range of ailments from aging to cancer. The calcium in milk and cheese is essential to bones; via a cellular on-off switch called calmodulin, the same metal that also controls key life processes; and water is the solvent that keeps our body's chemicals meeting and combining in a million necessary ways. And so on. Functionality seems merely a complex synonym for good nutrition.

Over the millennia, we humans have added new foods to our must-have list. Several million years ago our prehuman ancestors lost the genetic ability to synthesize vitamin C, also called citric acid or ascorbic acid. We now get this essential nutrient from external sources. Those who neglect to do this get a deficiency disease called scurvy: their teeth fall out, old wounds reopen, their kidneys fail. Vitamin C prevents this, and reverses active scurvy in all but terminal cases. Should we define lemons, limes, and other vitamin-C sources as functional foods? The jury is out. Neutraceuticals, while socially hot, remain scientifically unproven; functional foods may be less a genuine trend than something that's trendy.

Certainly, the functional food concept is subject to abuse. In 2000 the U.S. Federal Trade Commission (FTC) successfully sued the marketers of several neutraceutical supplements because their claims to cure ADD, ADHD, and hyperactivity were unsubstantiated. While the FTC avoided using the word *fraud*, it posts these warnings on its Internet sites:

- Most neutraceuticals have never been effectiveness-tested on children.
- The U.S.A. has no federal standards for neutraceutical quality or purity.
- Neutraceuticals advertised as "natural" are not necessarily safe.
- Mainstream medicine does not conspire to suppress neutraceuticals.
- Claims of fast cures for several ailments at once are unfounded.

The U.S. National Council Against Health Fraud explicitly cautions consumers against self-dosing with neutraceuticals. The council cites a cardiac patient who ate so much broccoli that she neutralized the effect of her blood-anticoagulant medications.

"If food companies want to do constructive nutrition education," concludes Dr. William Jarvis of the NCAHF, "they should debunk the widely held misconceptions that our soil is depleted, our food supply is poisoned by additives and pesticides, our foods are devoid of nutrients, nutritional approaches can remedy most ailments, [and] sugar causes hyperactivity."

NANOSCIENCE

Certain technologies shine from history. Fire permanently changed our species from prey to predator. Farming dulled our diet but sustained large cities. The scientific method, whose blend of skepticism and starry-eyed enquiry shows us how the world works. Weapons, steam, anaesthetics, electricity, computers, flight. To this list must now be added something called nanoscience.

Nanos is Greek for "dwarf"; in science, the prefix *nano-* means "one billionth." So 0.000000001 m = 1 nm; a billionth of a metre is one nanometre. How small is that? If a nanometre were magnified to the size of your little fingernail, that fingernail would be bigger than Montreal and your thumb would be the size of Florida. This is the strange, hidden world that nanoscientists explore. They don't need to go far to find it, either: the realm of the nanometre constitutes all matter, from dust to stars to humans.

Nano*science*, like all science, begins with curiosity: finding out what atoms and molecules get up to in their tightly constricted quarters. Those facts are put to work by nano*technology*, the nanocosm's engineering arm. Both nanoscience and nanotechnology are currently at work. We're not only exploring the nanocosm, we're shaping it.

Nanoscience is revolutionary because for the first time it lets us directly view the foundations of matter and energy, rather than imagining a set of cobbled-up constructs. We don't need to *assume* molecules any more: with new instruments such as the scanning tunnelling microscope we can see them directly. Nanotechnology promises to be a transforming technology as much as farming or fire. It will leave no technology unaltered or unimproved — least of all the technologies of our foodstuffs.

Consider metals. Alloys like bronze, steel, and duralumin literally support our civilization. Metals frame our offices and schools. We drive in metals, communicate through them, skate on them. But before nanoscience appeared, we didn't fully know

NANOTECHNOLOGY PROMISES TO BE A TRANSFORMING TECHNOLOGY AS MUCH AS FARMING OR FIRE. IT WILL LEAVE NO TECHNOLOGY UNALTERED OR UNIMPROVED — LEAST OF ALL THE TECHNOLOGIES OF OUR FOODSTUFFS.

how metals did what they did. Metallurgy gave us rules of thumb: what colours a forging should show before you temper-quench it (straw-purple-blue), or the pulling force required to snap a rod of bridge-grade steel one square centimetre in cross section (3.5 tonnes). But what happened at the nanoscale, while theories abounded, was not known.

Metals' biggest mystery was the disparity between theoretical calculations and observed properties. The math was clear: metals should be a lot tougher, stronger, and harder than they were. Observations on the scale of one micron — the microcosm — suggested a reason for this performance gap. At room temperature, all metals except mercury freeze solid; but under microscopic examination, what seems solid metal is a mess. It is a wilderness of voids, cracks, lumps, discontinuities, and inclusions.

Even if metal is forged and machined under conditions so precise that its microstructure appears perfect, at the nanoscale (a thousand times finer than the microscale) it is as helter-skelter as a garbage heap. Theory assumes that metal atoms are perfectly aligned and bonded, and they're not.

At least they haven't been till now. Integran Technologies, a nanotech firm in Toronto, has found ways to assemble metal atoms to theoretical perfection. Integran creates full-size metal parts whose nanostructure is theoretically ideal. Strength is triple, hardness is quadruple, resilience and wear resistance are multiplied by a factor of ten. Integran alloys resist fatigue, the silent killer that suddenly snaps metal parts in half even when they flex within their theoretical limits. Integran's alloys resist creep, the glacially slow and ultimately fatal flow of hot metals under load. Integran technology makes metals easier to weld, form, and machine, and decreases their tendency to crack. In this particular nanotechnology, theory and reality converge.

This is about to revolutionize our use of metals. Imagine military armour thinner than tinfoil. Skate blades that never need sharpening. Full-sized cars stronger and stiffer than a tank, yet with twice today's fuel efficiency. Food-processing factories the size of breadboxes that automatically churn out powdered milk or freeze-dried broccoli. In the next ten years, metals nanotechnology will transform the food industry. It will change everything from farm implements to energy production.

Nor will nanotech restrict its revolution to metal items. Research underway in Dutch laboratories is homing in on the Greens' holy grail: a reliable, low-cost panel that silently and continuously converts sunlight to electric power. Imagine a farm that does not have to buy external energy of any kind. That is more self-sufficient than the best farm today, but with many times the wealth creation per capita. This isn't science fiction: nanotechnology is already taking nanoscience into the marketplace. You may have used nanotechnology without knowing it. The DoubleCore, Wilson's top-of-the-line tennis ball, gets its name from an extra layer of nanomaterial inside its standard shell. The new layer is invisibly thin and weighs less than the ball's production tolerances, yet as an air barrier it is more efficient than iron. It imbeds nanoscale particles of a fluorine compound in a layer of butyl rubber 800 microns thick, and these nanoparticles put an impenetrable maze in the path of air molecules.

When a tennis pro smacks a DoubleCore ball, it flattens from a sphere to a pancake; its interior volume shrinks by 90 percent; the air inside undergoes a short, sharp, 1,000-percent pressure spike. Yet the enclosed air does not escape. When the ball rebounds to a sphere, its internal pressure and its bounce-characteristics remain unchanged. Air exfiltration in a hard set of tennis finishes off a normal ball within an hour. Wilson had to toughen up the DoubleCore's outer fuzz because players were wearing it bald without affecting its play behaviour.

What nanotech is doing for sports it will soon do for every aspect of food — not just seed production and produce transport, but production and consumption as well. The same "passive" nanotechnology inside a tennis ball will soon appear in vehicle tires, making them last longer and reducing their rolling friction so they use less fuel.

And consider food preservation, our model for technical innovation. Laboratories in Japan's Tsukuba research complex use nanoscience to isolate and synthesize a natural protein that lowers water's freezing point. At $-30°C$, when even normal saltwater is frozen solid, water treated with this protein is still a pumpable slush. Replacing standard heat-transfer media such as ethylene glycol or chlorofluorocarbons, the Japanese compound loafs rather than races through coolant coils. Its longer dwell-time, combined with its Antarctic chill, permits refrigerators and air conditioners that are twice as energy-efficient. In concert with this slo-mo compound, Tsukuba nanoscientists have also developed a method of scoring invisibly small trenches inside cooling coils, at right angles to fluid flow. The cold slush rides across the incised grooves on cushions of air, cutting pump friction in half and further reducing energy demands.

I'll give two more examples, out of thousands:

- Sciperio, a technology-incubator firm in Oklahoma, uses nanoscale engineering to change surface properties at the flick of a switch. The Sciperio compound starts off as hydrophilic, or water-bonding. When left it in the air for a few hours, it attracts water molecules by the trillion, bonding them as tightly as flies to flypaper. At this point the surface is made hydrophobic or water-repellent, allowing the accumulated water to slide into a collector. The result is unlimited pure water from thin air, even dry desert air. Think about the applications. Hydroponics and drip irrigation that do not touch natural aquifers. Cooling, including food refrigeration and air conditioning, that uses water evaporation but that doesn't steal a single drop from any lake, river, or well. Mobile refrigeration technology that doesn't need fossil fuels any more than it requires block ice.

- The promise of nanoscience will be particularly fruitful when allied with genetic improvement. In a sense, today's GI techniques work on faith. They introduce certain chemicals to other chemicals in certain sequences and verify results indirectly. They work with 1,000,000,000,000,000,000,000,000 molecules at a time. While this by-guess-and-by-God approach has had its successes, nanoscience will rise as far above standard GI as this GI has above empirical plant breeding. With nanoscience, GI practitioners won't have to guess what they're doing. They'll see it directly in real time, controlling molecular assembly as it happens. GI technologists will snap together genes to predetermined patterns as a carpenter follows plans to build a house.

The twentieth century decoded life; the twenty-first century will master it. At the 2000 Human Genome Conference in Vancouver, I heard a research team from Brandeis University discuss how every current antimycological agent attacks a single point in the metabolic pathway of fungi. But the Brandeis group had found other points of vulnerability in the armour of every fungal pest from wheat rust to bread mould, and were developing new techniques to stop fungus in its tracks.

More of this technical elegance is on the way. From gene to seed, from soil to store, everything about food technology is about to undergo revolutionary improvement. The world will be richer, safer, and healthier as a result.

A HISTORY OF FOOD (CONTINUED)

1886   Atlanta-based pharmacist Dr. John Smith Pemberton invents a drink described as a "brain and nerve tonic" that contains small amounts of cocaine. The name — Coca Cola — is coined by Pemberton's accountant, who also designs the original logo (the same one used today). Pemberton's sales for the first year are a meagre $50, and he will sell the company in 1891 for $2,000, before dying that same year. In 2004, Coca Cola will serve over 800 million drinks a day.

1892   The "crown cap" is invented, which revolutionizes the American soft-drink industry by allowing beverage companies to manufacture drinks that retain their carbonation until they are opened.

1907   Canadian chemist John McLaughlin patents Canada Dry Ginger Ale in a soda water bottling plant in Toronto.

1909   Charles Saunders combines two different strains of wheat, Red Fife and Hard Red Calcutta, creating the revolutionary Marquis Wheat. The hearty new strain has been developed to give high yields and mature early in order to prevent destruction by frost. By 1920, almost all the wheat grown in the Canadian Prairies will be Saunders's Marquis, and Canada will become the breadbasket of the world.

1910   In order to create a snack for hungry fishermen, Arthur Ganong of St. Stephen, New Brunswick, combines nuts and chocolate and invents the first chocolate bar. It costs five cents. Ganong will go on to become a candy giant.

1916   Processed cheese is patented by Ontario-born businessman J. L. Kraft. His technique allows cheese to keep longer and will eventually become the basis for the Kraft cheese empire. * Clarence Saunders opens the first modern grocery store or "super market" — called the Piggly Wiggly — in Memphis, Tennessee. When asked why he chose such a goofy name, Saunders replies, "So you would ask." Saunders will be recognized as the pioneer of bulk price buying and selling, and even the automated checkout. Piggly Wiggly will still be in business in 2004.

1920   It is believed that Henry Ford (inventor of the Model T car and the moving assembly line) invents the charcoal briquette, with help from Thomas Edison.

▼   CONTINUED ON PAGE 154

05.

DIET FOR A SMALLER PLANET: REAL SOURCES OF ABUNDANCE

FRANCES LAPPÉ, ANNA LAPPÉ

EDITORS' INTRODUCTION

When BBC reporter Michael Buerk began to cover the Ethiopian famine in 1984, he struck a nerve. Confronted with footage of an enormous humanitarian disaster, Britain and much of the rest of the world mobilized an unprecedented response. The movement was spearheaded by an unlikely leader: the lead singer of the band the Boomtown Rats, Bob Geldof. Geldof and his friends organized a huge benefit concert called Live Aid, which aired simultaneously from Wembley Stadium in London and JFK Stadium in Philadelphia. An estimated 1.2 billion people watched the concert in 170 countries, which inspired Buerk himself to call Live Aid "the biggest shared event in human history." And along with the hit single "Do They Know It's Christmas?" Live Aid raised over $180 million for relief in Africa.

As well-intentioned as Live Aid was — and it was — 1.2 million people still died in the Ethiopian famine of 1984. How many more would have died without the aid, without the attention, we will never know. But in the end, the size of the tragedy blots out the size of the charity.

And then something worse happened. The world's attention left Ethiopia and focused on the next tragic thing. There is never any shortage. In Ethiopia, however, things got worse. A potent witch's brew of war, deforestation, poor irrigation, chronic disease, and population growth continued to bubble. Twenty years after the first famine, in 2002, Ethiopia was again on its knees. Prime Minister

Meles Zenawi warned that an even worse famine would result if aid was not mobilized again. This time, however, the call fell on deaf ears. By 2002 the world was more concerned with the ongoing conflict in the Middle East. Ethiopia somehow managed to avoid a full-scale famine that year, but millions were still weak and in need of food.

Ethiopia is not alone in its constant fear of famine. In places like Afghanistan, Sudan and its western region, Darfur, China, and even in places like the United States, hunger is a serious problem. In 2003 the Food and Agricultural Organization in the United States published its State of the World Report and concluded that 842 million people were undernourished in 1999–2001. Given these bleak statistics, we have to ask ourselves, what causes famine in the first place? Why is there hunger? Does the world simply not produce enough food for everyone?

When Frances Moore Lappé wrote her groundbreaking book *Diet for a Small Planet* in the 1970s, she was in part motivated to try to answer these tormenting questions. What she discovered shocked her. The world, she realized, produces more than enough food to feed everyone. In other words, there's no good reason for anyone to starve. She concluded that, in fact, with a little ingenuity and common sense, we could feed a growing population with ease. The pessimists were simply wrong.

The book became an international bestseller, and one of the most influential books of her generation. In this chapter Frances has teamed up with her daughter Anna, the co-author of her latest book, *Hope's Edge: The Next Diet for a Small Planet,* to continue exploring the paradox of food and famine, as they look at the environmental, political, and social issues affecting global food production — problems for which the world is starving for answers.

MY DAUGHTER AND I are walking down a basement hallway at UC Berkeley's Agriculture Department. I've brought her to the spot where thirty years ago I burrowed myself in the Ag Department library to write *Diet for a Small Planet*. At the ripe young age of twenty-six, I had responded to the experts' cry, daily echoed in the media, that we faced imminent global famine. Books like Paul Ehrlich's *The Population Bomb* had just exploded, along with the even more alarming title: *Famine 1975* by the brothers William and Paul Paddock.

I wanted to dig deeper, asking, *Is hunger inevitable? Why is there hunger at all?* My research returned a startling fact: there is more than enough food to feed the world. At the time, this claim was heresy. I was saying the experts were wrong. I secretly feared I'd misplaced a decimal point. But the research held. And what I discovered then is just as true today: the world produces more than enough for all of us to thrive.

Thirty years later, the two of us decided to revisit the themes of *Diet for a Small Planet* asking why hunger in a world of plenty. Beginning the research for our book *Hope's Edge*, an exploration of holistic, community-based solutions to hunger, we returned to where *Diet* had been conceived. We searched for the library where I had pored over U.N. documents and other data to understand the world food crisis.

But the dimly lit hallway was empty; the library long-since relocated. As we turned to leave, Anna spotted a lone article tacked to an otherwise barren bulletin board. It read: "World Demand for Food Expected to Outstrip Production." We looked at each other, stunned. Headlines exactly like this leaping off the daily papers had been my motivation to explore the root causes of hunger thirty years ago. Here we were reading a headline dated November 7, 1999, proclaiming the same scarcity scare.

Articles like this were helping fuel the campaign for genetically modified foods, or GMOs — plants bred with technology that inserts DNA from another species in ways that nature and traditional breeding never could. Corporations developing and marketing GMOs were telling us we should swallow — literally — what many argue is risky technology or face scarcity in a hungry world. By this logic, blocking GMOs is tantamount to taking food from the mouths of the starving.

There are a few critical kinks in this logic. Most glaring of all is that our food crisis is not a crisis of scarcity. We already produce enough food to feed the world. In fact, we have grain alone to provide nearly 3,000 calories per person (not even counting all the beans, potatoes, nuts, fruits, root crops, and vegetables produced). That's enough not only to feed us, but to make us all chubby![1]

Yet, hunger is still widespread. Although advances have been made in certain regions of the world, almost one in six people on the planet is undernourished today, according to the United Nations Food and Agriculture Organization.

No, the root of the tragedy is not the scarcity of food; perhaps it has never been. Rather, hunger is caused by a scarcity of democracy. By democracy we don't mean merely the institutions of democracy — multiple parties, constitutional protections, a tripartite governmental structure. We mean *living democracy* in which everyone has a say in their own futures and in which, therefore, the right to life's essentials, including food, is protected. Since no one chooses to go hungry, the very existence of hunger is proof that democracy has not yet been realized.

Without such a living democracy, what happens? Here in perhaps the richest country in the world, it means that almost 35 million people live in households experiencing food insecurity.[2] And in the Global South, India — a country with all the formal trappings of democracy — has the world's greatest number of hungry people. Half the children under the age of four suffer from malnutrition, while surplus grain pours out of over-full warehouses.[3] When we travelled to India in 2000, the government minister in charge of food distribution himself acknowledged to us, "Ours is not a problem of scarcity, it's a problem of plenty."[4]

Without a living democracy, we end up creating the very scarcity we say we fear. With income and wealth so skewed within and among countries, hungry people don't have the wherewithal to buy the food they need. So the market, responding only to wealth, ends up creating a farming system that shrinks artificial oversupply — artificial because it reflects not real demand, only market demand. Worldwide, we now feed almost half of all grain to livestock that return to us in meat only a tiny fraction of the

THE WORLD FOOD CRISIS IS MORE ACCURATELY A WORLD *DEMOCRACY* CRISIS. MORE AND MORE PEOPLE ARE CUT OUT OF DECISION-MAKING ABOUT LIFE'S ESSENTIALS AS CONTROL OVER LAND FOR FARMING, SEEDS FOR PLANTING, AND THE MEANS FOR BUYING AND SELLING MOVES INTO FEWER AND FEWER HANDS.

nutrients we feed them.[5] Cattle, for example — ruminants prized for turning inedible substances into protein-rich food — consume in the U.S.A. sixteen pounds of grain and soy, plus thousands of gallons of water, to produce just one pound of steak.[6]

The world food crisis is more accurately a world *democracy* crisis. More and more people are cut out of decision-making about life's essentials as control over land for farming, seeds for planting, and the means for buying and selling moves into fewer and fewer hands. Billions are left to pick up the crumbs, forced to sit on the sidelines in the making of the most fundamental questions of our time.

THE BLINDERS OF MEASUREMENT

Understanding hunger and democracy, we see the striving to create abundance with new eyes. Typically, when we think about abundance, we turn immediately to the question of production. But once grasping the social roots of the hunger crisis, we can see that thinking of abundance simply in terms of output misses the mark.

Consider the parallel with a reliance on the ubiquitous indicator for economic well-being and wealth: the Gross Domestic Product, a measure of the total dollar value of all goods and services made and purchased within a year. We assume an increasing GDP is progress; its careening down is bad.

For decades, economists and savvy citizen organizations have been knocking at the door of government institutions, arguing that the GDP is a flawed indicator of progress. Many argue it often measures just the opposite. In 1968, Robert F. Kennedy said the GDP "measures everything . . . except that which makes life worthwhile." The San Francisco-based non-profit Redefining Progress has articulated just this problem; car crashes are a boon, just think of those repairs or new cars needed; divorce a windfall, think of costly lawyers, psychiatrist visits, separate homes. And cancer and death? Cancer treatment is a multi-billion-dollar business and the funeral industry is one of the strongest in the economy, with little competition and a guaranteed clientele. Yet despite its limitations, we still rely on the GDP. In the process, the measurement itself turns our attention away from aspects of our economy — and our lives — that determine real wealth.

The GDP does not meaningfully measure our social health — infant mortality, illness, morbidity, crime, depression — nor does it even accurately measure our economic health. The GDP can go up while unemployment, poverty, and inequality do too. The GDP also doesn't capture the depletion of natural resources that ultimately undermines long-term economic, social, and physical well-being: the loss of forests, farmland, and soil fertility. And the list goes on.

Using strategies to broaden indicators of agricultural "productivity," economists have been developing alternative indicators that do measure this more complex — and accurate — picture. Redefining Progress's Genuine Progress Indicator (GPI) is one. Developed in 1995, it uses the accounting framework of the GDP, but adds in the economic contributions of household and unpaid work, while subtracting negatives such as crime, pollution, and family breakdown. The GPI is updated every year to "document a more truthful picture of economic progress," according to its founders.[7]

Similar to the GDP's myopia, a narrow-minded focus on agricultural production can blur a critical truth — that we can have more food and yet more hunger. Focusing narrowly on production draws us away from the essential challenge: ensuring that people actually get to eat and that what we produce, and the ways we produce it, are healthy for us and for the Earth, now and in the future.

Today's food system bypasses this essential challenge; it not only leaves nearly a billion people hungry, it also means that many who *do* have access to food are getting sick from what they eat. In fact, more than a billion people around the world are *overfed*.[8] And many of these are mal-fed. In the United States, the mortality and health care costs of obesity-related diseases now rival those from smoking, according to the U.S. Centers for Disease Control and Prevention.[9]

In order to perceive and promote *true* abundance, we must look beyond mere measurements of gross production. We must remember that the heart of the hunger crisis is the faltering of democracy. When it comes to food and farming, people go hungry because they are denied democratic participation in decisions governing the most fundamental aspects of production: land, seeds, capital, and trade.

THIS LAND IS MY LAND, THIS LAND IS YOUR LAND

One needn't be a farmer, agricultural economist, or a plant scientist to grasp that what is grown and who has access to it depends in large measure on who controls the land. To make this obvious point come to life, we traveled to Brazil as part of our research for *Hope's Edge*.

We were drawn to Brazil because, in part, it suffers among the world's most extreme inequalities of income and wealth (fourth, behind Sierra Leone, Central African Republic, and Swaziland). Just three percent of landowners control more than half of Brazil's arable land, much of it left idle.[10] In fact, while Brazil's arable land totals 964 million acres (390 million hectares), one-third of it — a land area the size of Peru — goes unused.[11]

Such staggering inequality helps explain why Brazil is a striking example of the disconnection of production from the creation of abundance that would end hunger. While Brazil has become one of the world's largest agricultural exporters, tens of thousands of its children die every year from hunger and more than 5 million rural people have no land at all.

The concentration of control over Brazil's land has gone hand-in-hand with government policies favouring export-oriented agriculture and large, industrialized operations that push small farmers off the land and provide few jobs to the rural landless. This agricultural system has fuelled massive urbanization. In the past thirty years, 30 million people have fled rural areas for the cities, causing untold pressures on Brazilian cities to feed, house, and support these new residents. By the 1990s, Brazil had changed from a largely rural country to an urban one, with 75 percent of Brazilians living in cities.[12]

Brazil is the world's second leading exporter of soy products, the largest exporter of coffee and orange juice, and a major exporter of poultry and sugar. Hunger there is obviously not caused by inadequate production.[13] So, for decades, Brazilian church leaders, farmers, and human rights and hunger activists have seen clearly that narrowly focusing on increasing agricultural output could never eradicate hunger. To reduce hunger requires asking what is keeping the poor from *feeding themselves*. The answer in Brazil, as in much of the world, is that the poor are denied fair access to land. In fact, over several centuries, it's been actively taken from them.

Many of the largest Brazilian landholdings today can be traced back centuries to when the Portuguese Crown carved up the country's vast acreage. Since then, wealthy landowners have used political favours and legal loopholes to expand control at the expense of the poor.

For centuries efforts by peasants to gain fairer access to land had been defeated, snuffed out with peasant blood. But opening for real change began toward the end of Brazil's military dictatorship, which held power between 1964 and 1985. During Brazil's transition to democracy, leaders of religious communities and social movements came together to form the Landless Workers Movement or MST, an acronym from its Portuguese name, *Movimento dos Trabalhadores Rurais Sem Terra*, to push for just land reform.

As the fledging democracy drafted its constitution, the MST and others struggling for the rights of the landless ensured that a clause was included to allow the government to expropriate and redistribute idle land in order to fight hunger. The constitution now reads:

> It is within the power of the Union to expropriate on account of social interest, for purposes of agrarian reform, the rural property which is not performing its social function.[14]

Despite this clear constitutional mandate, the MST frequently has had to resort to civil disobedience to pressure the government to make good on the constitution's promise. Often fighting against the wishes of local, state, and national politicians more responsive to wealthy landowners than landless peasants, the MST has helped to settle more than a quarter of a million families on 17 million acres (7 million hectares) of formerly idle land.

This achievement has been at great cost. In the struggle for land, the Landless Workers Movement has lost more than 1,000 members to violence, more than all those "disappeared" during Brazil's military dictatorship.

As the MST grew, its leadership told us, the movement also evolved its understanding of where solutions lie. "We started out working on access to land," a former nun and now an MST organizer had told us at a member-training seminar deep in the rural heart of the southern Brazilian state of Parana, "but soon we realized that every aspect of life has to be included—health, gender, education, leadership, philosophy . . ."[15]

With members in almost every Brazilian state, the MST has not only settled hundreds of thousands of families in new communities; it has developed educational programs, schools, businesses, health clinics. In the process, the movement has multiplied five-fold the incomes of the formerly landless and drastically reduced infant mortality among its members.[16] With a growing consciousness about the need to insure sustainability, the movement also created the first organic seed line in Brazil. "It's not just that farming without pesticides means less hazard and lower costs for us," one farmer told us when we asked why they were choosing organic methods. "Why would we go to all this trouble and risk to grow food that's just going to hurt people? We are concerned about the people in the cities, too."[17]

What lessons does the Landless Workers Movement hold for other countries? For countries of the Global South, the lesson is that fair access to land, generated by a strong, vocal civil society, is possible, although far from easy.

For industrialized countries, where farmland is ever-more concentrated in large farms and farmers are increasingly mere contract workers for non-farm corporations, Brazil's example calls us to ask: What would fairness look like here?

We can see the struggle for greater fairness in citizens throughout the United States challenging corporate control of farming. In nine Midwest states, farmers and their allies have initiated and passed laws prohibiting corporations from owning farmland. These states collectively produce over 30 percent of the U.S.A.'s agricultural output, according to the Community Environmental Legal Defense Fund. In Pennsylvania, ten townships passed similar ordinances outlawing corporations from owning farmland. Two have gone even further. They've passed "corporate rights elimination ordinances" which deny corporations constitutional protections of persons, including those in the commerce and contracts clauses of the constitution. Proponents of these ordinances discovered that such restrictions offered the only protection from corporations introducing huge hog-confinement operations, causing serious environmental and health hazards in their communities.[18]

Here, land fairness would also mean a critical review of the contracting system, in which farmers lose decision-making power to corporations. By 2001, these contract farmers made up 36 percent of the total value of all crop and livestock sold in the United States — and nearly *all* poultry production.[19] In these contract arrangements, it is the farmer who shoulders all the debt and all the risk from crop loss or livestock illness.

Moreover, here, fairness might not begin with land·redistribution per se, but with a call for remaking a government subsidy system that disproportionately rewards large farms at the expense of small, family-owned ones.

When most people hear "farm subsidies," they imagine our government helping poor, struggling farmers survive, not enhancing the bottom line of our nation's largest corporations. But between 1995 and 2002, 10 percent of the biggest and often most profitable crop producers collected 71 percent of all subsidies,

IN OTHER WORDS, OUR TAX DOLLARS ARE GOING TO BIG BUSINESS, WORSENING THE INEQUALITY IN POWER OVER OUR NATION'S FARMING PRACTICES AND LAND.

averaging $34,800 in annual payments, while the bottom 80 percent received only $846 on average per year, according to a report from the Environmental Working Group.[20]

In 2002, the U.S. government spent more than $12 billion on farm subsidies, of which nearly $2 billion went to corn producers alone. In other words, our tax dollars are going to big business, worsening the inequality in power over our nation's farming practices and land. These multi-billion-dollar subsidies also help keep the prices for raw material artificially low. This means big savings (effectively subsidies) for ConAgra, Altria (formerly Philip Morris), Cargill, and other agribusiness giants who trade and process the subsidized commodities.

Government agricultural research, moreover, disproportionately goes to industrial farming, not to innovations in sustainable methods. In fact, the Sustainable Agriculture Research and Education program represents less than one half of one percent of USDA research and education funding annually.[21]

Imagine the abundance possible if we were to radically redirect research dollars to sustainable practices. Imagine the abundance that could emerge from subsidies helping small farmers stay on the land, protecting natural environments with sustainable practices and ensuring the health of communities able to consume local foods raised without chemicals, now and for future generations.

SEEDING THE FUTURE

Land and resource inequality is easy to observe; but control over other vital aspects of food and farming is more challenging to perceive. I think about this when I remember my son's insights more than three decades ago. I had just taken my children, then three and five years old, on a research trip to Guatemala. One day the three of us climbed to the top of a nearby hill and looked out over the town where we were staying. With a child's wisdom, my son Anthony asked: "Why do so few people have all the land and all the other people have to live so close together?"

Land inequality was easy for even a five-year-old to see. Inequality over the control of seed supplies is harder to perceive, but equally as critical. Along with the other most basic natural elements — soil, sun and water — seeds are essential to farming and food. Since the advent of agriculture more than 10,000 years ago, farmers have been saving and sharing seeds year-to-year. But over the past century a steady stream of laws — primarily in the

United States but now going global through world trade agreements — have transferred ownership and control over seeds from farmers to corporations.

Just one hundred years ago *all* crops in the U.S.A. were grown from farmer-bred varieties, according to Hope Shand, research director of the ETC Group, a Canadian-based organization that examines the social and economic impacts of new technologies.[22] At the turn of the last century, a government program actively encouraged the sharing and saving of farmer varieties. In 1897, at the peak of its seed sharing promotion, the U.S. government gave away 22 million seed packets, Shand reports. The prevailing wisdom was that the more you encourage sharing and experimenting with seeds, the more farmers will breed diverse, high-yielding, healthy crops. In the twentieth century, that very principle was turned on its head.

Late-nineteenth-century seed-sharing programs operated from the belief that the more you give, the more abundance you gain. Today's version of a market economy is based on the opposite premise: It assumes that what you give away you lose. During the twentieth century, the scarcity model won; the abundance principle lost.

Starting with the Plant Patent Act of 1930, which allowed the patenting of asexually reproduced crops but excluded food crops, and continuing with the landmark 1970 Plant Variety Protection Act and key amendments in the 1990s, corporations have gained increasing rights over crops and now food crops too, according to Shand.

In 1994 the U.S. Congress passed a critical amendment to the Plant Variety Protection Act, critical because "it amended the Act to restrict the amount of proprietary seed that farmers can save for re-planting and prohibited farmers from selling harvested seed to other farmers," Shand explains. "It was a first step in eroding the principle of farmers' rights in the U.S. legislation, which had previously recognized the farmers' exemption — the right to save and sell proprietary seed."[23] This amendment built on the power given to corporations by the 1985 ruling of the U.S. Patent and Trademark Office, which made utility patents available for plants, bioengineered ones as well as those bred naturally.

Concentration in the industry has also increased in the past several decades. Since 1970, multinational companies have bought or taken control of nearly a thousand, once independent, seed companies.[24] By 2002, Monsanto had spent more than $8 billion acquiring seed and biotech companies. Today, virtually all companies protect their plants with patents, with just one, Monsanto, accounting for virtually all genetically modified soybean seed technology grown in 2000 worldwide,[25] and the top ten seed firms now control nearly one-third of the $24.4 billion commercial seed market.[26]

Shand, and others who study corporate control over seeds, point to a number of dangerous consequences of this dynamic. One is decreasing diversity within the seed gene pool, which in turn makes our food system more vulnerable to disease.[27] Because measuring seed diversity is challenging, estimates vary

VIRTUALLY ALL COMPANIES PROTECT THEIR PLANTS WITH PATENTS, WITH JUST ONE, MONSANTO, ACCOUNTING FOR VIRTUALLY ALL GENETICALLY MODIFIED SOYBEAN SEED TECHNOLOGY GROWN IN 2000 WORLDWIDE, AND THE TOP TEN SEED FIRMS NOW CONTROL NEARLY ONE-THIRD OF THE $24.4 BILLION COMMERCIAL SEED MARKET.

about the percent of plant species that have disappeared. In one example, the authors of *Shattering: Food, Politics, and the Loss of Genetic Diversity* found that 97 percent of the varieties in a turn-of-the-century list of vegetables from the U.S. Department of

Agriculture are now extinct.[28] Possible cross-pollination and other contamination by GMOs further threaten plant as well as wildlife diversity and ecosystem health.

In response to concern about GMOs contaminating the seed-lines of non-GMO plants, the United Nations ratified the Cartagena Protocol on Biosafety in September 2003. It establishes rules governing the introduction and import/export of GMOs, which now make up the majority of certain U.S. crops. Today, 38 percent of corn, 80 percent of soy, 70 percent of cotton, and more than 60 percent of canola in the United States are genetically modified.[29]

Globally, these four crops — soy, cotton, canola, and corn — account for most genetically modified acreage. By 2003, one-quarter of the 672 million acres (272 million hectares) of these crops planted worldwide, or roughly 167 million acres (68 million hectares), was transgenic.[30] But while GMOs continue to spread, the rate of growth has been slowed by citizen concern worldwide, with only six countries growing 99 percent of all genetically modified foods.[31]

In a drive to protect profits derived from patented seeds, some corporations use the legal system to enforce their rights against farmers. They send investigators into communities to ensure that farmers are not illegally saving seeds, suing those farmers who are perceived to be violating the law. According to Shand, Monsanto has filed more than 475 lawsuits against farmers in the U.S.A. for patent infringement and violation of technology user agreements.

Although proponents claim GMOs will help farmers to "feed the hungry world," critics argue that lawsuits such as these, plus a research focus neglecting the crops and seed qualities most used and needed by the poor — such as drought resistance — reveal the real corporate goal: increasing market share and profits, not ending world hunger. In fact, A. F. Leu, the chairman of the Organic Federation of Australia, points out that the latest direction of GMO technology is toward "BioPharm" where plants such as corn, sugarcane, and tobacco "are modified to produce new compounds such as hormones, vaccines, plastics, polymers, and other non-food compounds. All of these developments will mean that less food is grown on some of the world's most productive farmland."[32]

The debate over GMOs reflects the underlying crisis of democracy. For example: even the Food and Agriculture Organization of the United Nations, a public body whose explicit commitment is to end hunger, now spends its precious time cajoling global seed corporations to refocus at least some GMO research on the needs of the poor.[33] It responds to an agenda that's *already* been set — set by a handful of corporate giants. By contrast, an action agenda of the majority of the world's farmers — mostly small, subsistence producers — would likely be quite different. Why not instead direct the $3 billion now going annually to seed biotechnology toward improving water and soil-saving practices? Such a reallocation using local, low-cost materials, along with spreading local seed-breeding and exchange, could free third-world farmers from dependence on the corporate giants.

The GMO path was deliberately undertaken in a manner to avoid public deliberation, giving citizens no opportunity to weigh risks and benefits.[34] Yet in 2004, less than a decade after GMOs became widely used, the Union of Concerned Scientists reports that in the U.S.A. "seeds of traditional varieties of corn, soybeans, and canola are pervasively contaminated with low levels of DNA sequences derived from transgenic [GMO] varieties."[35] While no farmers or consumers asked for this technology, we, the public, bear the as-yet unknown health consequences of such genetic contamination, let alone the ecological risk.

What does the control over seeds have to do with hunger and with real abundance? Everything. Almost one and a half billion small farmers in the developing world depend on saved seeds as their primary seed source; these are people whose average income barely creeps above two dollars a day, often not even above one. Imagine what it would mean if these farmers were suddenly required to pay distant corporations for every seed they planted. Imagine what it would mean for these farmers to relinquish centuries-old local agricultural practices for techniques and products developed and controlled by faraway corporations over which they have no say?

We don't need to imagine. We can look to another agricultural revolution and learn from history. Today's "Gene Revolution," after all, is in many ways a reprise of the 1960s

ALMOST ONE AND A HALF BILLION SMALL FARMERS IN THE DEVELOPING WORLD DEPEND ON SAVED SEEDS AS THEIR PRIMARY SEED SOURCE; THESE ARE PEOPLE WHOSE AVERAGE INCOME BARELY CREEPS ABOVE TWO DOLLARS A DAY, OFTEN NOT EVEN ABOVE ONE.

Green Revolution, which used technological innovation to increase yields across the developing world. The key to the Green Revolution was the development of high-yield hybrid seeds, or what critics of the technology call "high-responding" because they require extensive application of inputs — including water, fertilizer, and pesticides. Although hybrid seeds produce "heterosis" or hybrid vigor (crossing two genetically distant parent plants creates offspring "superior" in terms of yield), this benefit disappears after the first generation.[36]

In a recent speech, Norman Borlaug, father of the Green Revolution and the 1970 Nobel Peace Prize winner, provided statistics to prove that the Green Revolution doubled, and even trebled, cereal production in some regions of the developing world from 1961 to 2000.[37] But his accompanying PowerPoint slide also showed a *thirty-five-fold increase* in fertilizer use in those same regions and increased reliance on tractors, irrigation, and other expensive technology. Borlaug also failed to mention sinking water tables, salinization, deteriorating topsoil, and farmers displaced from the land. Nor did he mention increasing rates of suicide among farmers facing insurmountable debt and devastating crop loss.

In 2002, when we visited the Punjab, the much-heralded proving ground of this technology, we were struck by the social and ecological devastation. The Green Revolution not only depleted natural resources (soil and water), it also depleted financial ones. Farmers were encouraged to take out loans for costly inputs and to buy expensive farming equipment. Driving along the dusty Punjabi roads, we saw countless abandoned tractors, left to rust by farmers who could no longer make their payments.

In one village, we spoke with a group of more than fifty Sikh farmers. One gestured to the men around him, explaining that almost all his neighbours were deep in debt to the banks, many on the brink of losing everything. "Two years ago, the bollworm [a moth that attacks cotton] and crop failures swept through Andhra Pradesh," Afsar Jafri, a scientist promoting organic cultivation with the Indian activist farmers' network, Navdanya, told us. In one district Jafri researched, pesticide use had increased two thousand percent in the past three years, but crops still failed. The bollworm had become resistant. The year before, in a nearby village, hundreds of farmers had committed suicide, many by drinking the very pesticides partly responsible for their indebtedness.

The cautionary tale of the Punjab is just one illustration of what can happen when a myopic focus on production blinds us to the systemic effects of a technology. A similar myopia reveals itself in the push for GMOs.

But around the world, citizen organizations are seeking to protect the diversity at the heart of abundance. They want to ensure that small farmers around the globe, dependent on seed saving and sharing, can continue to do what they have done for generations.

We travelled to India to learn about just such an organization: the farmers' network Navdanya, started by internationally renowned environmental activist and physicist Vandana Shiva to protect farmers' seed rights, seed diversity, and traditional practices.

On one of our first nights in the country, we slept on a narrow cot in a bare room with only jars of seeds for company, in the foothills of the Indian Himalayas. The room was one of Navdanya's seed saving hubs.

The next morning, we traveled to Uttirchha, a village of about eighty families whose white-washed stone homes clung to the hillsides. As far as we felt from our respective American homes in New York and Boston, the presence of the industrialized world surprised us. Decisions in far-off boardrooms and distant courtrooms directly affected the villagers, who were celebrating a recent win in the European patent offices. W. R. Grace, along with the U.S. Department of Agriculture, had taken out a patent on the Indian neem tree. Navdanya, along with several other international groups, had filed suit, arguing that the patent unfairly claimed "ownership" of knowledge that had been developed over centuries by Indian farmers and healers. Navdanya helped bring a delegation to the hearings to deliver a protest petition with half a million signatures. In a rare win, the patent office overturned that patent, stating "claims were not novel in view of prior use, which had taken place in India."[38]

Navdanya is also encouraging villagers to be proactive in protecting their biological heritage. The morning that we sat with village elders in Uttircha, they showed us their community biodiversity registry, a creative strategy to create "community intellectual rights" that would have comparable legal standing to corporate intellectual property rights. Their registry was an oversized hand-bound book with sample specimens of plants. Each page included details about a specimen's uses — medicinal, edible or both. The village elder, Darshan Lal Chowary, told us: "We'll have more than one thousand plants in here before we're finished. Now, no one can come into our community and claim a patent on these plants and tell us they've discovered the plant's uses. Anyone who wants this will have to get our permission first."[39]

Navdanya and farmers' rights organizations around the world are working to ensure that community intellectual rights can stand up in international courts and be recognized by such councils as the World Trade Organization. In 1994, for instance, the Third World Network developed the Community Intellectual

NAVDANYA AND FARMERS' RIGHTS ORGANIZATIONS AROUND THE WORLD ARE WORKING TO ENSURE THAT COMMUNITY INTELLECTUAL RIGHTS CAN STAND UP IN INTERNATIONAL COURTS AND BE RECOGNIZED BY SUCH COUNCILS AS THE WORLD TRADE ORGANIZATION.

Rights Act, "to establish a *sui generis* system for the protection of the innovations and the intellectual knowledge of local communities."[40] Navdanya's work builds on this legal language.

Navdanya is also active on the ground, providing technical assistance to promote traditional seed sharing and saving. We visited the community seed bank at the Navdanya organic demonstration farm, housed on Dr. Shiva's family homestead near Dehra Dun, India. We drove out down narrowing dirt roads from the city whose population has exploded since Dr.

Shiva was a child. It wasn't harvest season so the fields were dormant, but the farmers led us into large rooms filled with jars and bushels of seeds. The floors were covered with tarps layered with thousands of seeds, waiting to be dried, labeled and preserved in their own containers. Along with their work on the farm, Navdanya members travel to nearby villages, teaching organic farming principles, and gathering more seed savers — and sharers — for the network.

Navdanya is actively involved in promoting organic farming, not only in the region near Dehra Dun but across the country. In the Punjab, we heard the painful stories of farmers who had bought the Green Revolution promise. Navdanya trainers tried to convince many to try organic practices — a hard sell for those desperate for a quick fix. Shortly after we returned from our trip, though, Afsar Jafri, wrote to tell us that more than one hundred farmers in the village we visited had begun using Navdanya's traditional wheat varieties and organic practices. Though yields were roughly half to three-quarters what they had produced with Green Revolution varieties, the farmers were fairing much better. Their cost of production without chemicals was *one-quarter* what it had been.[41]

Wider surveys of sustainable techniques show even more promise. In the world's largest study of sustainable agriculture, researchers from the University of Essex in England analyzed more than 200 projects in 52 countries, covering 70 million acres (28 million hectares) and involving nearly 9 million farmers. The research indicated that crop yields increased on average 73 percent under sustainable methods, and concluded that "sustainable practices can lead to substantial increases in per hectare food production."[42] In cases where yields per acre of cereals had not increased, substantial improvement still occurred in "domestic food consumption or increasing local food barters or sales through biointensive gardens, or better water management."[43]

The projects the researchers analyzed were not just isolated, small communities. They included 223,000 farmers in southern Brazil using "green manures and cover crop, doubling their yields of maize and wheat" — and, as well, 200,000 farmers in Kenya, 45,000 in Guatemala and Honduras, 100,000 in Mexico, and more than one million wetland rice farmers in Bangladesh, China, India, Indonesia, Malaysia, Philippines, Sri Lanka, Thailand, and Vietnam.

Navdanya's work is part of this growing international movement promoting sustainable practices, seed sharing, and community intellectual property rights. Their efforts remind us that supporting community rights over seeds is a critical way to ensure abundance now, and in the future. Many of these efforts are connected through Via Campesina, an international co-ordinating body, bringing together peasant organizations, small and middle-scale producers, and indigenous communities in Europe, Northeast and Southeast Asia, South Asia, North America, the Caribbean, Central America, and South America, and Africa.

SHOW ME THE MONEY

Another essential ingredient for creating abundance — often ignored, if obvious — is income for producers. Not income for ADM or Novartis or Monsanto, but for small family-farmers living on the land.

Economist and Nobel laureate Amartya Sen wisely notes that falling prices to farmers depress production; yet, while we've seen precisely that trend over the past several decades, little has been done on an international level to respond. Since the 1950s, real prices for grain have shrunk by two-thirds. Some commodities, like coffee, recently fetched their lowest price in history. On average, all commodities, save fuel, now bring farmers less than half as much as they did thirty years ago.[44]

Sitting with a coffee-farmer near Nairobi, Kenya, a few years ago, we learned firsthand what these abstract figures can mean. Farmer Mumo Musyoka had to work all year for her coffee harvest; yet after subtracting payments for inputs and the middlemen, coffee prices were so low that she came out with zero income. And, as she told us, if you don't make any money on your coffee yield, "you can't eat your crop."

So it would seem obvious that a critical component of increasing production — and particularly *sustainable* production — is to ensure that small farmers get a fair price for their work. Instead, unfair prices within an unfair trade system is the norm.

The coffee trade is one of the best examples. Coffee is the second most valuable commodity in the world after oil, but low

IT WOULD SEEM OBVIOUS THAT A CRITICAL COMPONENT OF INCREASING PRODUCTION — AND PARTICULARLY *SUSTAINABLE* PRODUCTION — IS TO ENSURE THAT SMALL FARMERS GET A FAIR PRICE FOR THEIR WORK.

world prices have left 25 million small farmers in fifty countries in dire poverty.[45]

Coffee prices hit their lowest levels in part due to political decisions that date back to the late 1980s when the U.S.A., under the Reagan administration, pulled out of the International Coffee Agreement. Without this system, which had helped to stabilize prices and production, prices plummeted and production skyrocketed as farmers struggled to make up in volume what they were losing in price. This of course pushed prices down even further.

The result was tens of thousands of displaced farm families. The tragedy triggered the birth of a movement to create a coffee trading system based on fair, not exploitative, prices.

Seventy percent of the world's coffee is grown by small family farmers, who often have no choice but to sell to middlemen who pay as little as 25 cents per pound (55 cents per kilogram). With fair trade, farmers are ensured $1.26 per pound ($2.78 per kilogram) and slightly more, $1.41 ($3.11 per kilogram), for organic (still much less than we pay here). When the world price rises above that floor, farmers get paid more.

Since 1999, TransFair USA, a California-based non-profit organization, has been certifying fair trade products to sell in the United States, and business is booming. TransFair USA–certified coffee almost doubled in 2003 compared to the previous year, jumping from 9.8 to 18.7 million pounds (from 4.4 to 8.5 million kilograms). The fair trade movement is now expanding beyond its coffee programs, certifying not only coffee but cocoa, tea, and bananas, and — starting this year — mangoes, pineapples, grapes, and bananas. Across the globe, these fair trade efforts are benefiting more than one million family farmers in forty-five countries in Latin America, Africa, Asia, and Europe.[46]

Fair trade also has positive ripple effects on the environment — and for future abundance. Small coffee-farmers are some of the best stewards of the land, many still growing coffee in traditional ways, under the shade of forest overhang and without chemicals. "Fair Trade supports some of the most bio-diverse farming systems in the world," according to leading expert on agroecology, UC Berkeley Professor Miguel Altieri.

Today, the fair trade movement is a rapidly growing international network with enormous potential for continuing to transform the health and well-being of communities worldwide.

RETHINKING ABUNDANCE

We were asked to contribute a chapter about solutions to hunger, about how we might best realize abundance. At first, we began trolling through studies showing that organic, biodynamic small- and medium-sized farms could compete with the production levels of large-scale industrialized North American farms. We started pulling together research that revealed the hidden costs of industrial agriculture — the polluted waterways, air, and soil — costs not accounted for in production totals. Our initial instinct was to show how, acre-by-acre, sustainable farming systems outdo industrial ones.

The evidence wasn't that hard to find. As we've noted, studies are proving that sustainable approaches can produce comparable and even higher yields than the chemical model.[47]

But while a snapshot, yields-per-acre analysis is one way to measure productivity, another is to look at the productivity of the land over time. Here, sustainable agriculture beats industrial farming hands down. One of the fundamentals of sustainable agriculture is the understanding that the soil is alive — and healthy soil is the cornerstone of productive farming — quite the opposite to industrial, extractive farming where soil fertility is something to be created with the right combination of chemical inputs.

More and more research on sustainable practices informs us that accessible, low-tech, sustainable solutions produce comparable yields to industrial agriculture. They also best meet the needs of third-world farmers. Jules Pretty, lead researcher in the University of Essex report, explains: "Above all [sustainable practices using cheap, locally available technology] most help the people who need help the most — poor farmers and their families, who make up the majority of the world's hungry people."[48]

This premise — that there is enough, that third-world farmers can feed themselves — forces us to ask the harder questions about what elements of our social, economic, and international trading systems create hunger amidst plenty? What is democracy if it is not about each person having a voice to secure lives and their share of the future?

Asking these questions, in turn, forces us to talk about power, including the power over land, seeds, income, and trade, which determines who does and does not eat on this abundant planet. It forces us to acknowledge how we ourselves create scarcity from plenty.

Turning aside from these deeper questions, GMO and extractive, industrial agriculture promoters foment the fear of famine — a fear that blinds us to the solutions at hand.

That was exactly the aim of the alarming headline from the article tacked to the bulletin board in that deserted UC Berkeley hallway. Such fear promotion, diverting us from real causes and real solutions, seems to be everywhere. Consider President George W. Bush's comments in 2003 at a biotechnology conference: "We should encourage the spread of safe effective biotechnology to win the fight against global hunger."[49]

Either risk untested technology or face famine — we must remind ourselves what we need *not* fear. There is enough food to feed the world. There is enough. Repeat it twice.

Fear is a funny thing. When we feel it, we look for quick answers, sure bets, fast fixes. Feeling fear, it's easy to get tunnel vision; it's harder to hear nuanced arguments. But we need not let the fear-mongers set up shop in our minds. Instead, we can stay open to the complexity of hunger's roots.

As important as production levels are in measuring success, other indicators might fall off our mental map if we're not careful. We can measure true abundance, for example, in whether all human beings have access to healthy food. To achieve such abundance, we can rethink and remake control over land, seeds, and trade, as the ingenious social movements we've described here — from the Landless Workers Movement to the Navdanya movement to the fair trade movement — are doing. Refusing to succumb to the scarcity scare, these movements help us to understand the relationship between democracy — in its richer, more participatory forms — and the creation of sustainable abundance.

A HISTORY OF FOOD (CONTINUED)

1928 The bread slicer is invented, followed shortly by the modern toaster.

1930 Mahatma Gandhi and hundreds of followers begin their 320-kilometre (200-mile) trek to the village of Dandi on the Arabian Sea to break the British salt tax. By illegally collecting salt from the ocean-side, Gandhi puts into practice his method of civil disobedience, which eventually helps lead to India's independence in 1947. * Pablum, the world's most famous baby food, is invented by Alan Brown, Theodore Drake, and Fred Tisdall, three doctors at Toronto's Hospital for Sick Children. The vitamin-enriched precooked cereal goes on to be credited with saving thousands of babies' lives.

1932 Soviet leader Joseph Stalin's policies result in mass famine in the Ukraine, a fertile country that has been under Russian control since the time of the Czars. Much of the grain that feeds the Soviet Union traditionally comes from Ukrainian farms, but Stalin's program of forced collectivization saps the will of the independent farmers and significantly reduces output. To make matters worse, Stalin insists that 45 percent of all grain in the Ukraine be shipped to Russia. This policy, which is at least partly a response to the aspirations of the Ukraine to become an independent country, will in effect condemn over 6 million Ukrainians to death by starvation.

1935 Following a conversation with a truck driver who has lost a shipment of chickens because the storage compartment overheated, Frederick M. Jones invents the first automatic refrigeration system for long-haul trucks. His system will be patented in 1943, and will be converted to ships and railway cars, forever changing the North American food industry.

1938 On a handshake, Irish inventor Harry Ferguson and Henry Ford cement a deal that will mass produce the Ferguson System and create millions of tractors worldwide. Ferguson's patented system — which he painstakingly developed between 1910 and 1936 — allows for a tractor to undertake numerous heavy tasks, from ploughing fields to cutting grass. His developments will eventually be manufactured and popularized by the Massey Ferguson Company.

1940s In response to food shortages during the Second World War, canning becomes a common method of preserving foods.

▼ CONTINUED ON PAGE 190

06.
OVERFEEDING THE FUTURE

KELLY BROWNELL

EDITORS' INTRODUCTION

In 1998, Sue Barr was wider than she was tall. Weighing five hundred pounds, she stood 65 inches high and 70 inches wide. Doctors classified her as morbidly obese because she — along with six million other Americans — was more than 100 pounds overweight. By her own admission, Barr was destined to a shortened, virtually immobile life, until she found a miracle cure: a radical procedure called bariatric surgery.

This year, Sue Barr will be joined by over 140,000 other people who will have bariatric surgery. As popular as it is, however, it's not risk-free. According to the American Society for Bariatric Surgery, which promotes the procedure, 10 percent of patients will suffer serious complications after surgery from infections, pulmonary problems, or other effects. All of these risks, however, are acceptable to people like Sue Barr. Her battle against fat was a life-and-death struggle and she believes she's won. Today Barr weighs 153 pounds.

What is so astonishing about stories like Barr's are how common they have become. According to the American Obesity Association, approximately 127 million adults in the U.S.A. are overweight and 60 million are classified as obese. In Canada the battle of the bulge is being lost as well. According to a 2004 Stats Canada report, about 15 percent of adult Canadians are considered obese and 33 percent are considered overweight. How did we get so fat so fast? What are the costs of it? And what can we do about it?

These are questions that Kelly Brownell has been thinking about for a long time. You might know Brownell from his appearance in the hit documentary film *Super Size Me,* where filmmaker Morgan Spurlock ate McDonald's for a month and monitored what happened to his body. As the director of the Yale Center for Eating and Weight Disorders, Brownell is an internationally known expert on eating disorders, obesity, and body weight regulation. In his bestselling book *Food Fight,* Kelly outlines various strategies to combat what he calls the current "toxic food environment," ways that vary from labelling the caloric content of all food to, more radically, imposing a tax on unhealthy food.

Brownell's ideas have struck a chord. In the last year, six U.S. states have started debating legislation to put nutrition information on all menus, while some states are talking about eliminating fast-food advertising aimed at children. All of this has made Kelly Brownell few friends in the fast-food world. "Like a weed or a virus, health nanny Kelly Brownell's idea for a 'Twinkie tax' on high-calorie and high-fat foods has spread as far as England and New Zealand," wrote the Center for Consumer Freedom on its website in July 2003. For its part, the Center for Consumer Freedom, "a nonprofit coalition of restaurants, food companies, and consumers working together to promote personal responsibility and protect consumer choices," collected negative comments about Brownell's ideas and his personal appearance and served them up to its readers. Brownell is hardly surprised by the vitriol. After all, the stakes in the war on fat are high. This year, for example, the Krispy Kreme company saw its stock fall more than 45 percent, a loss the doughnut makers attributed to the public war on fat.

So who is winning the war on fat? To find out about the action on the front lines, we turn to Kelly Brownell.

CONSIDER THE FOLLOWING:

1) In its peak year, the primary U.S. government nutrition education program (called 5 a Day) was given $3 million for promotion. The food industry spends one thousand times that much to advertise fast foods, just to children.

2) The most recognized corporate logo in China, aside from those of Chinese companies, is KFC's.

3) Ronald McDonald is the second most recognized figure in the world, next to Santa Claus.

4) Creating major news in September of 2002, McDonald's announced that by February 2003 it would change the oil used for its fried products to decrease (but not eliminate) trans fats. McDonald's President Mike Roberts spoke of a "healthier nutrition profile" in heralding the company's concern for public health, and the CEO lauded his company for being a "leader in social responsibility." In February of 2003, the company quietly announced a change in plans (there would be a "delay"). The delay is still in effect.

5) Kraft Foods announced in 2003 it would cut portion sizes of some products to "help arrest the rise in obesity." Less than a year later, Kraft announced this plan had been scrapped.

6) Promoters to the juvenile market have declared the cell phone

their next horizon, noting that tens of millions of children power up a cell phone at the same time each day (after school). Satellite technology allows marketers to know a child's precise location, and enables them to beam advertisements, coupons, and directions to nearby eating establishments.

7) The Food Guide Pyramid created by the U.S. Department of Agriculture (USDA) recommends that meat, poultry, fish, and eggs comprise 14 percent of the diet, yet 52 percent of USDA food-promotion resources are allocated to these foods. The pyramid recommends 33 percent of the diet from fruits and vegetables, but they receive 5 percent of the USDA budget. The meat and dairy industries "outlobby" the fruit and vegetable sectors by orders of magnitude.

This list could include thousands more. Stampeding technology, corporate interests, authorities caught unaware, and the market stigmatization of overweight people (which emphasizes personal over corporate responsibility) have created an environment that guarantees poor diet, physical inactivity, and obesity. The world now faces a crisis of overfeeding.

Until recently, a book on feeding the future would have focused solely on the need to feed the world's population. Without a doubt, hunger is still a major issue, but it will soon be surpassed in many countries by overconsumption as the leading public health nutrition issue. In countries not traditionally considered prone to obesity, such as Mexico, Brazil, Morocco, Thailand, and China, hunger and obesity coexist. The World Health Organization (WHO) has declared obesity a global epidemic, increasing in every country throughout the world.

Words like "crisis," "epidemic," and "global emergency" used to describe a public health problem evoke a predictable backlash of blame on those affected by obesity. Such has been the case with AIDS, tobacco, drug abuse, and other problems. Business interests are commonly pitted against public health, and there are calls for change focusing either on the individual or broad social factors. Food must now be considered in a similar light.

The world faces important questions about what and how we eat. Who is responsible for increasing rates of obesity? What are the causes? What are the relative contributions of poor diet and physical inactivity? Can the food industry be trusted? Must children be protected from a "toxic" environment? What must change?

In this chapter I focus on the causes and consequences of overfeeding the world, and, most importantly, on some solutions.

OUR BIG FOOD PROBLEM

The most visible consequence of poor diet and physical inactivity, obesity involves a cascade of other medical, social, and psychological issues. The explosion of media coverage has brought attention to this significant problem, but its downside implies that obesity is the only consequence of modern living. In fact, poor diet and sedentary lifestyle are risk factors for many major chronic diseases

FOR THE FIRST TIME IN NORTH AMERICAN HISTORY, EXPERTS HAVE ASKED WHETHER CHILDREN WILL LEAD SHORTER LIVES THAN THEIR PARENTS.

independent of a person's weight. For example, children in affluent countries frequently show detectable signs of heart disease, regardless of weight.[1] For the first time in North American history, experts have asked whether children will lead shorter lives than their parents.

Throughout the 1980s and 1990s, paper after paper in the scientific literature showed that obesity is increasing around the world. Rates are burgeoning in industrialized countries (the U.S.A., Canada, Britain, Australia, and so on), in particularly wealthy countries such as Saudi Arabia, but also in little-known island nations and developing counties. Clinics for the treatment of obese children opened in Beijing, where only decades ago malnutrition was the most serious problem.

In 1998, the WHO released a report declaring obesity a global epidemic. Since then, the organization has been at the forefront in raising global awareness, documenting rising weights in country after country and highlighting the associated disease burden.[2] The WHO has also proposed proactive solutions, as we will see later.[3]

Related to many of the leading causes of death, obesity is also involved in problems such as sleep disturbance, pain, and arthritis that can affect quality of life (see Table 1). The risk of coronary heart disease increases nearly 60 percent in men and 179 percent in women, and risk for diabetes increases fivefold for men and eightfold in women as weight increases from normal to very obese. The poor diet and inactivity causing obesity contribute independently to many of the same outcomes. Rand Corporation economist Roland Sturm has shown that obesity's health effects now surpass those of smoking, and that it carries the same risk as aging two decades.[4]

Since poor diet and inactivity can affect health, they are likely to have other powerful impacts. Lost productivity, a less alert work force, and declining school grades are some. It is well documented that poor diet affects cognitive and intellectual performance in undernourished children, and the same could well occur in the case of overnutrition.

Researchers estimate obesity-related health care costs in the U.S.A. alone to be $75 billion, with taxpayers financing about

Table 1
MEDICAL CONDITIONS ASSOCIATED WITH OBESITY[5]

Osteoarthritis	Heat Disorders
Rheumatoid Arthritis	Hypertension
Birth Defects	Impaired Immune Response
Breast Cancer	Impaired Respiratory Function
Cancer of Esophagus	Infections Following Wounds
and Gastric Cardia	Infertility
Colorectal Cancer	Liver Disease
Renal Cell Cancer	Low Back Pain
Cardiovascular Disease	Obstetric and Gynecologic
Carpal Tunnel Syndrome	Complications
Chronic Venous Insufficiency	Pain
Daytime Sleepiness	Pancreatitis
Deep Vein Thrombosis	Sleep Apnea
Diabetes (Type 2)	Stroke
End Stage Renal Disease	Surgical Complications
Gallbladder Disease	Urinary Stress Incontinence
Gout	

half these costs through Medicare and Medicaid.[6] In a study of 200,000 employees of General Motors, researchers estimated that obese individuals incur up to $1,500 more in health care costs per year compared to normal-weight peers.[7]

Not So Obvious Consequences

Obese individuals incur severe social stigmas. They include a phalanx of negative characteristics such as laziness and lack of motivation, and also charges of core personality and integrity defects (being stupid, dishonest, dirty, and more). An imperfect body reflects an imperfect personality, so the thinking goes, hence bias and discrimination can be justified by the old adage that people get what they deserve and deserve what they get. These attributions result from cultural norms in which obesity is repulsive, that link social status with physical attractiveness, and construct weight as a matter of personal control. Research clearly shows that overweight people are targets of discrimination in areas central to health and happiness (employment, housing, income, and health care).[8]

Given the prevalence of obesity, it is natural to ask whether a more overweight population would lead to less bias. In a 1961 study, a group of researchers showed children line-drawings of children who were obese or had a variety of physical disfigurements.[9] The majority ranked the obese child as the one they would least like to have as a friend. Latner and Stunkard repeated the study recently and found even stronger bias against the overweight child.[10] Weight stigma is very difficult to shake.

If bias and discrimination affect the happiness and well-being of stigmatized groups, they affect health. The experience of bias may affect health directly, say by influencing risk factors such as blood pressure, lipids, or immune function. Bias can also exert influence through psychological factors (such as vulnerability to depression), which in turn influence health or it can alter a person's experience with the health care system. There are studies showing that overweight individuals are less likely to obtain preventive care, perhaps due to shame from interacting with providers and fear of negative comments.

Combining the more and less obvious consequences of unhealthy eating with sedentary lifestyle and obesity, we see problems that cannot be ignored. Tremendous human suffering is occurring. Young adults in their twenties and thirties now suffer from complications of Type 2 diabetes (formerly called adult onset diabetes), which begins before the age of ten. Some are blind, some have limbs amputated, and some have died.

In other words, overfeeding the world is a crisis by any standard — one that demands aggressive, innovative action. How to take action depends in great part on how nations construe the causes.

HOW THE WORLD GAINED SO MUCH SO FAST

The world is increasingly exposed to what I have labelled a "toxic environment," in which food and agriculture companies produce too many calories, particularly in meat and highly processed foods. Food has become artificially inexpensive and is engineered to maximize taste. Reasonable at first glance, this exacts a tragic price on both health and the environment. The U.S.A., Canada, Britain, and Australia exemplify these negative conditions, but nearly every country is following suit.

Eating is influenced by a number of factors, the most powerful being accessibility, convenience, promotion, taste, and cost (see Table 2). Each has been distorted in ways that encourage unhealthy eating.

Table 2
PRIMARY FACTORS THAT AFFECT HUMAN EATING[11]

Unhealthy Foods	Healthy Foods
Highly accessible	Less accessible
Convenient	Less convenient
Promoted heavily	Barely promoted
Good tasting	Less tasty
Cheap	More expensive

The Multiple-Causes Distraction
It is standard to say that obesity has multiple causes — to cite

biology, psychology, and the environment as contributors. This explains everything and nothing at the same time. Of course obesity has multiple causes — everything does, but not all causes are equal. Much depends on whether we look for causes in individuals or in larger groups like a country or even the world.

Conceptualizing the cause of obesity for an individual necessitates understanding a variety of factors, including biology, a person's upbringing, psychology, and socio-economic status. But when one looks to population increases in obesity, we ask, for example, why Japan has more obesity this year than last, why some nations are heavier than others, why an entire population is vulnerable to changing diets, and what might be done to reduce the problem. From this point of view, there is a clear explanation for rampant obesity — the environment has become fattening or "obesigenic."

Because so many people are overweight, we can infer that most individuals have a "willing" biological profile that fosters high energy intake and the efficient storage of energy as body fat. The environment, however, causes energy intake to rise and calorific expenditure to decline. High levels of obesity in developed countries, and low levels in poor countries, cannot be explained by population genetics, particularly considering studies documenting weight gain as a predictable consequence of moving from a country with little obesity to another with more.

In the absence of a fattening environment, few people will become overweight. Obesity occurs as the environment promotes unhealthy eating and inactivity. The cause is the environment, and the environment in a growing number of countries is an ideal recipe for fattening the population.

Global Changes and the Nutrition Transition
Barry Popkin and his colleagues have done the most careful and extensive work on the "nutrition transition" that occurs as nations

modernize.[12] He and colleagues define five patterns that characterize this transition:

Pattern 1: Collecting Food. Food comes from hunting and gathering. The diet is high in carbohydrates and fibre and low in fat. Activity levels are high and there is little obesity.

Pattern 2: Famine. Diet is less varied, scarcity occurs, and malnutrition is common. Obesity is rare.

Pattern 3: Receding Famine. Consumption of fruit, vegetables, and animal protein increases, as do inactivity and leisure time.

Pattern 4: Nutrition-related Non-Communicable Disease. The diet is high in fat, cholesterol, sugar and other refined carbohydrates, and low in polyunsaturated fat and fibre. Sedentary behaviour increases. Obesity increases as does chronic disease.

Pattern 5: Behavioural Change. The desire to prevent disease leads to changes in diet and physical activity, sometimes self-driven by consumers and other times stimulated by government action.

Popkin notes that many countries are in Patterns 3 and 4. Developing nations in particular are transitioning from receding famine to energy-dense diets and declining physical activity. A good example is China, where in the 1970s 10 percent of calories came from fat. Now one-third of families eat a diet with more than 30 percent of calories from fat, the number of televisions has risen dramatically, and the number of jobs requiring physical labour is decreasing. Popkin notes that in countries like China, with rapid advances from food shortages to a healthier diet, the line is quickly crossed where eating too much, and corresponding weight gain, become key concerns.[13]

Willingness to Damage the Environment

As you might expect, supporting the growing calorie-needs of a world gaining weight requires more food. This issue is particularly acute when one considers that highly processed foods and certain meats are particularly resource intensive. To get the staggering amounts of cheap food the world consumes, the food system must be structured for mass production. To fully understand the obesity crisis, one must look at how food is produced. This is what Michael Pollan did in an important article published in 2002.[14]

Pollan, a well-known food and agriculture writer, bought a cow that was raised for beef. He followed the cow from farm to fork, in order to document exactly this part of the food chain. Pollan considered the amount of energy used to raise the cow, compared to the energy the cow would later introduce into the food supply. One analysis is that fully 283 gallons (1,071 litres) of oil are used to bring a 1,250-pound (570-kilogram) steer to your table.

Most of us are not aware of the considerable energy from fossil fuels required to create hamburger or steak. Energy is needed to produce the fertilizers and pesticides applied to feed-grain and corn; for the hormones injected into the cow to optimize its growth; to truck the meat to distant markets, and to keep it refrigerated. Also relevant is the environmental damage (such as the 12,000-square-mile (31,000-square-kilometre) "dead zone" in the Gulf of Mexico from nitrogen and pesticide runoff into the Mississippi River), pollution created from shipping, and depletion of the world's energy supplies. In Pollan's words, "We have succeeded in industrializing the beef calf, transforming what was once a solar-powered ruminant into the very last thing we need: another fossil-fuel machine."

The energy quotient of Pollan's cow can be supported by many different examples. An estimated 2,200 kcal of energy are needed to produce a 1-kcal can of Diet Coke. In parts of India, public outcry has denied water licences to Coca Cola and Pepsi, where they have significantly affected groundwater resources to the point of producing shortages for local residents.[15] Table 3

Table 3
PERCENTAGE OF U.S. ENVIRONMENTAL IMPACT ATTRIBUTABLE
TO FOOD PRODUCTION[16]

Climate Change: Greenhouse Gases	12%
Air Pollution: Common	17%
Air Pollution: Toxic	9%
Water Pollution: Common	38%
Water Pollution: Toxic	22%
Habitat Alteration: Water	73%
Habitat Alteration: Land	45%

shows estimates of the environmental impact of food production.

One could argue that overconsumption occurs where food and agriculture industries exploit the environment to maximize production, and governments fail to intervene.

Food subsidies are another little-known factor allowing high consumption at low consumer-cost. Raising the 1,250-pound steer requires a great deal of feed, and most cattle in North America are raised on grain and then on corn. Corn can be an expensive crop, but the U.S. government subsidizes the farmers, making certain the price of corn remains artificially low, which in turn allows the fast food restaurant to sell you a "super-sized" beef patty for a startlingly low price. And then what happens? Consumption of beef and similar products escalates.

The same dynamic helps sell soft drinks. Many soft drinks are sweetened with high fructose corn syrup, which again comes from subsidized corn crops. It costs companies like Coca Cola and Pepsi little to sweeten a litre of water and sell it for a few dollars. This allows companies to increase portions at virtually no cost, again making overconsumption more likely.

The Key Determinants of Eating

Table 2 shows so much the reverse of what is needed that one could say the food system is totally backward.

Unhealthy food is ubiquitous. The proliferation of vending machines, fast-food restaurants, convenience stores, and eating opportunities in gas stations, shopping malls, and drug stores, makes food everywhere available around the clock. Long gone are school days when children ate only during lunch periods, when highway rest stops were not oriented around fast food, and when snacks were not designed for automobile cup-holders. High-calorie foods are available from drive-through windows, in microwaveable containers, and carry-out packages. Hurried lifestyles increase the value of convenience, particularly for second-income families. Unhealthy foods far outnumber healthy foods.

Most troubling is the massive promotion of unhealthy foods directed at children. The typical American child sees 10,000 TV advertisements per year, mostly for soft drinks, fast foods, candy, sugared cereals, and snack foods. Children at all ages (even very young children) are affected in ways that health experts deplore — hence the repeated, and repeatedly ignored, calls for regulation.[17] Leading sports stars, cartoon characters, and music celebrities continue to promote unhealthy foods.

Product placements in movies and video games, virtual product placements in reruns of television shows, television food promotions in schools (for example, Channel One, the education channel, now runs in 12,000 U.S. schools), vending machines in schools (which lend themselves to advertising), all these — and more — add to the commercial bombardment. Children receive a great deal of nutritional "instruction," most of it delivered by a food industry that has strong incentives to maximize children's consumption of unhealthy foods.

Taste is a key determinant of human eating. In general, foods high in sugar, fat, or both, taste good. Such foods tend to thwart any regulatory system the body may have, so that weight gain occurs. Our ancestors ate as much energy-dense foods as they could. Their dietary pattern enabled them both to survive periods of scarcity and thus contribute to the gene pool. This once-adaptive tendency is now mismatched to modern conditions of abundance.

Cost is another important cause of obesity, especially for poorer individuals. Studies show that a market basket of healthy foods costs more than a basket of unhealthy foods. People in some neighborhoods do not have access to supermarkets, and therefore pay a premium in small markets, even in the rare cases when the markets carry items like fresh fruits and vegetables.

Consider pricing incentives. Fast-food restaurants have package ("value-added") meals that offer the customer more when foods are grouped together. Larger or "supersized" drinks

STUDIES SHOW THAT A MARKET BASKET OF HEALTHY FOODS COSTS MORE THAN A BASKET OF UNHEALTHY FOODS.

and fries are retailed at an apparently slighter additional cost. The concept of more product for less money isn't inherently bad, but it is applied almost exclusively to unhealthy foods. If one buys six oranges rather than three, the price per orange does not decline.

Pricing incentives for larger portion sizes create a real problem. Value can be added to the consumer by offering the same amount of food for a lower price, or by increasing the amount for smaller price increases. The latter approach maximizes producer profits. Big portions, highly desirable for the industry, redefine a reasonable serving. The current small serving of fries at fast-food restaurants was once the large size; soft drinks, once in 8-oz. (237-ml) bottles, are now in 12-oz. (355-ml) and 20-oz. (591-ml) servings; and a muffin, once the size of a baseball, is now softball size.

Paul Rozin and others have made a cultural comparison of serving sizes in the United States and France.[18] The French serve smaller portions of attractively presented and nicely prepared foods than Americans. French meals (even at fast-food restaurants) are eaten slowly, and their amount is not enough for leftovers. (The "doggie bag" is unknown in much of the world.)

Research by Barbara Rolls and others shows that people served more food eat more.[19] Consumers are drawn to large portions, and the food industry exploits this by attaching words like "super," "mega," and "extreme" to their foods. Thus the same hype plays out over and over: the consumer who buys more food, consumes more. And the companies maximize profits from selling larger portions. A fast-food patron may happily pay 39 cents to "upsize" to the largest size of fries and drink, and the bargain is struck. The incremental cost to the company is small, and it also seems minimal to the consumer. But excessive calorific intake can be the consequence.

These powerful and unrelenting factors encourage unhealthy eating. It occurs partly because of the food industry's marketing practices, which are woven into economics, technology, and the fabric of modern life. To identify the threads, to reverse the troubling situation we now face, which has already had a profound global impact, environmentally and individually, will require nothing short of aggressive action.

CAN THE FOOD INDUSTRY BE TRUSTED?

In *Food Politics*, Marion Nestle documents how profoundly the food industry has influenced legislation, regulation, and public policy related to nutrition.[20] Her examples include the industry's undue influence in establishing the U.S. Food Guide Pyramid, and in blocking attempts to regulate food advertising directed at children. Food and agriculture companies demand that governments act in their interest, and that politicians grant their wishes.[21] Nonetheless, agribusiness claims it can be trusted, and that the obesity problem will not be solved without industry involvement. The language of cooperation and "involvement of stakeholders" is used to justify this stance.

The food industry is no monolith. Generalizations cannot apply to all players. Organic tomato growers, supermarkets now specializing in organic, natural, "whole" foods, Girl Scouts selling cookies — these are part of its diversity. But the industry does include massive companies like Kraft (large enough to own Nabisco), McDonald's, PepsiCo (large enough to own Frito-Lay), and Coca Cola. To complicate matters, companies that sell unhealthy products nearly always sell healthier ones as well, so it can be difficult to separate the good from the bad. McDonald's, for example, has yogurt and salads on its menu. Yet, as we have seen, it has indefinitely delayed in coming through on its promise to change cooking oils. And it has a massive budget to promote energy-dense foods to children.

Some food companies devote considerable resources to publicizing healthier new products, hoping perhaps to escape the tidal wave of unhealthy food marketing. Creating the appearance of corporate social responsibility is now a priority, but whether appearance is matched by substance is yet to be determined. As the food industry faces new challenges, we can revisit important lessons learned from the deadly history of another industry, tobacco.

Tobacco companies asked for the same privileges food companies now demand, namely that their promotions be taken at face value. Tobacco companies, like the food industry, claimed concern for public health, pledged cooperation with the government and health authorities, introduced filtered cigarettes they claimed were better for consumers, and assured the public they had the best interests of children at heart. These tactics were accepted by government authorities for years, with tragic consequences. The food industry, which also asks to be trusted, makes many of the same arguments as did tobacco companies almost to the word.

In *A Question of Intent*, David Kessler, former Commissioner of the U.S. Food and Drug Administration, wrote "Devised in the 1950s and '60s, the tobacco industry's strategy was embodied in a script written by the lawyers. Every tobacco company executive in the public eye was told to learn the script backwards and forwards, no deviation was allowed. The basic premise was simple — smoking had not been proved to cause cancer. Not proven, not proven, not proven — this would be stated insistently and repeatedly. Inject a thin wedge of doubt, create controversy, never deviate from the prepared line. It was a simple plan and it worked."[22] The script was written and performed by lobbyists, public relations firms hired by the industry, scientists paid by the industry, members of congress financed by the industry, the main industry trade association (Tobacco Institute), and of course company executives themselves.

The Food Industry Playbook

How does the food business resemble tobacco? In a paper I wrote with Kenneth Warner, examining tobacco and food industry responses to health crises, we noted striking similarities in the scripts (playbook) used by the food and tobacco industries to still public concern and stall or prevent policies that would hurt business.[23] The fact the food industry has a script is indisputable. Trade associations, some of the same public relations and advertising agencies formerly used by tobacco, scientists funded by the industry, and of course company spokespersons — all have their parts in the playbook. The key features are as follows:

- Introduce products perceived to be healthier.
- Publicize corporate social responsibility.
- Fund programs focusing on physical activity.
- Claim that lack of personal responsibility is at the heart of the population's unhealthy diet.
- Plead that personal freedom is at stake, hence government should not contemplate regulation or legislation.
- Vilify critics with totalitarian language, characterizing them as the food police, leaders of a nanny state, even "food fascists," and accuse them of desires to strip people of civil liberties.
- Emphasize physical activity over diet.
- State there are no good or bad foods, hence no food or food type (soft drinks, fast foods, and so on) should be targeted for change.
- Dispute the science to plant doubt.

The first three items in the playbook may have positive consequences, but vigilance is in order. The industry often introduces products that are made to sound healthy. Examples are snack and drinks with "fruit" in the name. Cynicism about corporate social responsibility is also natural, given the tobacco experience. In 2000, Philip Morris spent $115 million on social causes such as the arts, helping flood victims, and supporting shelters for abuse victims. The company spent $150 million publicizing these acts. The remaining six parts of the script are likely to have negative consequences.

The food industry notes that food is different from tobacco, in that people have to eat. Hence, the argument goes, big food can profit as much if people eat healthier foods. In their attempts to alleviate controversy, industry insiders argue that we are all on the same side. This argument can be challenged on several grounds. A move by the public toward healthier foods means lower sales of foods with high profit margins (highly processed convenience foods). But the stark reality is more important: the only way the population can lose weight is if food intake goes down (and activity increases), hence less food must be sold overall. This places the industry squarely at odds with public health priorities.

Given these factors, the world must assess whether food companies can be trusted. It must also decide whether the industry should be included or excluded from policy decisions. But there are other ways of establishing an industry's trustworthiness. One is to examine the use or misuse of science.

Industry (and Government) Disputing Science

A robust literature currently exists on the impact of food advertising directed at children. In the U.S.A. alone, children under twelve spend $35 billion a year on their own, and influence another $200 billion of household spending.[24] A number of scientists and authoritative organizations have examined the available science, reaching a remarkable consensus.

For example, the World Health Organization concludes that, ". . . marketing affects food choice and influences dietary habits, with subsequent implications for weight gain and obesity."[25] The American Psychological Association concurs: "Such advertising efforts, in our view, are fundamentally unfair because of young children's limited comprehension of the nature and purpose of television advertising, and therefore warrant government action to protect young children from commercial exploitation."[26]

The American Academy of Pediatrics has issued this position statement: "Advertising and promotion of energy-dense, nutrient-poor food products to children may need to be regulated or curtailed."[27] In a comprehensive report, the Kaiser Family Foundation reached a similar conclusion: ". . . it appears likely that the main mechanism by which media use contributes to childhood obesity may well be through children's exposure to billions of dollars of food advertising and cross-promotional marketing year after year, starting at the youngest ages, with children's favorite media characters often enlisted in the sales pitch."[28]

In an excellent review article, Mary Story and Simone French conclude, "The research evidence is strong showing that preschoolers and grade school children's food preferences and food purchase requests for high sugar and high fat foods are influenced by television exposure to food advertising. . . . The heavy marketing of high fat, high sugar foods to this age group [< age 8] can be viewed as exploitative because young children do not understand that commercials are designed to sell products."[29]

These statements, based on considerable science, paint a clear picture. Contrast the industry's position, exemplified by William McLeod, representative of the Grocery Manufacturers of America (the world's largest food industry lobbying group), in response to questions about the damaging effects of advertising to children raised by Kaiser Family Foundation report: "There is very little evidence that we have seen. As a matter of fact, I think the conclusions in the report we've heard today indicate that the jury is still out." McLeod added, "The evidence that is not in these studies and the evidence that I don't think we are ever going to see is that advertising is telling kids or encouraging kids to eat too much or exercise too little."[30]

Here is another food industry spokesperson on the issue. When asked, "What, if any, is the relationship between marketing and obesity?" Shelley Rosen, speaking for McDonald's, said, "There is no connection." And, "When you ask if obesity is a marketing and communications issue, the answer is no."[31]

The science on soft drink consumption, calorie intake, and body weight reveals a similar pattern. Here, the considerable literature ranges from laboratory studies with animals to large-scale human epidemiology studies. First, let's look at the conclusions from scientists. A research paper by David Ludwig and colleagues on soft drinks and childhood obesity concluded, "Consumption of sugar-sweetened drinks is associated with obesity in children."[32] George Bray, Samara Nielson, and Barry Popkin, who conducted research on obesity and high fructose corn syrup (HFCS) in beverages, concluded, "It is becoming increasingly clear that soft drink consumption may be an important contributor to the epidemic of obesity, in part through the larger portion sizes of those beverages and from the increased intake of fructose from HFCS and sucrose."[33]

In yet another research paper, Samara Nielsen and Barry Popkin looked at changes in beverage consumptions: ". . . soft drink consumption is rising and is a significant contributor to total caloric intake for many individuals, especially children and adolescents." Further to the point, "This would seem to be one of the simpler ways to reduce obesity in the United States."[34]

Now for the soft drink industry position, as stated by the industry's trade association. According to the National Soft Drink Association, "Soft drink consumption by children is not linked to pediatric obesity, poor diet quality, or a lack of exercise."[35] Sean McBride, the spokesperson of the National Soft Drink Association, was asked to respond to schools' eliminating soft drinks. Employing the familiar diversion tactic of physical activity, he stated that obesity "is about the couch and not the can."[36]

The industry's disingenuous response on children's food advertising and soft drinks illustrates larger problems. There are many other cases where industry competes with public health and where its actions are the opposite of what health experts recommend (for example, snack foods in schools, fast food consumption and obesity, and agriculture subsidies). The education system is one place where this conflict is acted out.

In some countries, the sale and promotion of unhealthy food in schools has occurred for so many years that it has become part of the funding equation for education. The problem is especially acute in the United States. It is common for schools to have "pouring rights" contracts with soft drink companies, multiple snack food machines with high-calorie products, food company logos on scoreboards, abundant food advertising on "free" news channels (such as Channel One), and homework programs rewarding children with free food from companies like Dunkin Donuts and Pizza Hut.

Schools often perceive these arrangements as consistent with their educational mission: food sales fund important programs, appear to be a "free" source of money, and allow communities to provide less funding for education. The soft drink industry exploits these relationships for both money and public relations (they boast of their caring about children and their role in education).

In fact, these connections drain money from communities. Children put money into the machines and the companies take away the profit. The band uniforms or school trips the money supports are purchased by children and their parents, but with the industry first taking its share. And beyond the direct profits from sales, the industry benefits from the massive advertising exposure on vending machines, sports spectators seeing logos on scoreboards, and more.

Business self-interest may be expected, but governmental failure to correct the situation, or worse yet, collusion in ways that damage public health, especially troubling. On the issue of children's food advertising, does the U.S. government side with science/public health or with the industry?

The U.S. government found itself isolated from the world community in 2003–04 by its stiff opposition to a report of the World Health Organization that proposed a global strategy for confronting problems with diet, inactivity, and obesity.[37] In particular, the sugar industry exerted heavy pressure on both the

U.S. government and the WHO to change recommendations that sugar intake should decrease. Part of the U.S. response to the report was a pointed letter to the WHO from an assistant to Secretary of Health and Human Services, Tommy Thompson, saying, "The assertion that heavy marketing of energy-dense foods increases the risk of obesity is supported by almost no data."[38] The Federal Trade Commission chairman, Timothy Muris, took the same stance on food advertising directed at children: "A ban would be ineffective because there is no reason to think that the ads kids see make them obese."[39]

Example after example could be interpreted as collusion between government and the food industry. National nutrition policy in the U.S.A. is established by the USDA, whose primary task is to help the food industry sell more products. For years there has been an open "revolving door" of industry executives running the USDA and then returning to industry. A few examples occurred in 2004 when the head of the USDA appointed a deputy chief of staff who was vice president of legislative affairs with the International Dairy Foods Association, along with a director of communications who had worked with the National Cattleman's Beef Association.

There is abundant evidence that the food industry has not always acted in the interests of the public eating less food or better food. Which prevails when public health and profits are in conflict? Kraft's and McDonald's highly visible pronouncements suggest that the answer is clear. McDonald's promised to use healthier oil for its fried foods, and Kraft said it would offer its food in smaller portions. To date, both companies have failed to follow through on their announcements. Public opinion may ultimately force the industry to act differently, or courageous government officials might one day overlook business interests and be creative with legislation and regulation. Until that day, a skeptical eye must be turned to industry's pleas that it be trusted.

NECESSARY SHIFTS IN THINKING

Fundamental shifts in public opinion are necessary before unhealthy eating habits can change. Public opinion did turn against the tobacco companies, permitting unprecedented policy

THERE IS ABUNDANT EVIDENCE THAT THE FOOD INDUSTRY HAS NOT ALWAYS ACTED IN THE INTERESTS OF THE PUBLIC EATING LESS FOOD OR BETTER FOOD.

changes: the smoking ban in public places, very high taxes, forbidding the use of an icon — Joe Camel — that allegedly encouraged children to smoke, and so on. The realization that there were victims (children being seduced to smoke, nonsmokers hurt by secondhand smoke), awareness of the human toll produced by smoking, and the release of internal documents from the industry showing callous, calculating behavior designed to maximize sales of products that can kill users — all this facilitated an enormous attitude shift. When the history of the obesity issue is finally written, key shifts in public opinion will probably be seen as preceding key advances.

Some of those changes may be occurring already. We see children as a protected group. Nations safeguard children by requiring immunizations, mandating the use of safety restraints in automobiles, and more. There is increasing recognition that great harm has occurred by not protecting children from conditions that lead to unhealthy eating and a sedentary lifestyle. Moves to ban soft drinks and snack foods from schools and to regulate children's food advertising are examples of actions based on a needed shift in thinking. There are more.

Individual Responsibility Versus National Failures

The time-worn argument against legislation is that eating is matter of personal responsibility, and that the "nanny state" should not tell people what is good for them because it infringes on free ·choice. It is a powerful argument, and one that bears refuting.

As an aside, there *are* food police who tell people what to eat. That police force is the food industry with billions of dollars at its disposal to convince people, particularly children, what to eat. Even if the government were willing to fight the industry, as it finally did tobacco, the resources it could bring to the effort would be trivial in comparison.

In an article I wrote with Marion Nestle, we noted four fundamental points in response to the argument that personal responsibility is the cause and solution to the obesity problem:[40] Fundamentally wrong, the argument cannot be supported by either science or common sense. The rate of obesity increases year after year, in country after country. It is difficult to argue that the world's people were less responsible in 2002 than in 2001 or that irresponsibility is sweeping the globe.

Secondly, the argument ignores biology. Humans like foods high in sugar, fat, and calories as a survival strategy. Lab animals, responding strictly to their biology, can triple their body weights when given access to high-fat, high-sugar foods found at any convenience store. Imagine the folly of attributing the animals' normal weights to the exercise of responsibility, and the heavier weights to failures in animal character.

Thirdly, the argument fails to lead to constructive action. For years, food companies have urged that people should eat better and exercise more — in other words, should be more responsible. How much higher can obesity rates climb before such blandishments are seen for what they are?

Finally, the personal responsibility approach is a trap. It insists that the environment should remain unchanged, that the food industry will do business as usual, and that pious government officials will continue to defend the status quo while claiming credit for taking action. The picture startlingly resembles the history of the tobacco industry, which argued that damage caused by dangerous products were the fault of the people who used them.

Bottom-Up Versus Top-Down Priorities
(Creating Social Contagion)

Will change occur from the top down, with central governments taking the lead? Or will it come from the bottom up, with grassroots, local, and state changes forcing central change? It appears that the victories are occurring in a bottom-up fashion in the United States, but Europe and Scandinavia there is more hope for constructive action from the top.

In the U.S.A. the federal government talks much about obesity. Looking beyond this rhetoric, one sees minimal allocation of resources — and the classic escape tactic, imploring people to be more responsible. Outside North America, central governments are more likely to take constructive action. The British government is considering action to limit food advertising directed at children, and politicians are debating food taxes. Sweden prohibits advertising aimed at children. Finland has undertaken impressive health promotion efforts. Such efforts must be tracked and evaluated so other countries can consider taking action.

At the local level, many impressive changes are occurring.[41] School districts are banning soft drinks and snack foods, school lunch programs are improving in some areas, communities are building bike/walking trails, there is increasing pressure on schools to add back physical education, organic gardens are being built on school grounds and are integrated with the core education, calls are being made for regulation of children's advertising, and more. Even though the support for such programs is insignificant compared to food industry promotion, these programs can become models for other communities and may ultimately have a major impact.

These programs have national or even global potential, but only if evaluated and spread around the world. Rapid evaluation of these efforts would be very helpful, as would better understanding about how positive contagion can occur (when other communities adopt successful programs).

SPECIFIC ACTIONS

A number of actions have been suggested for reducing obesity. The key is to develop cost-effective preventative approaches that improve diet and enhance physical activity.

It is important to hold the food industry accountable. We should insist it earns the trust it seeks. Constructive actions, say when a company introduces a healthier product, cannot excuse countless damaging practices. It would be helpful to establish specific criteria that industry must meet to be considered trustworthy. A beginning would be for the industry to develop a new playbook. That playbook would include the following criteria:[42]

- Promote only healthy foods to children, and ultimately, minimize promotion of unhealthy foods to adults.
- Cease sales and promotion of unhealthy foods in schools.
- Change marketing, pricing, and promotion strategies that encourage overeating and the consumption of unhealthy foods.
- Alter the industry focus from personal responsibility to environmental changes that encourage and enable people to make healthy decisions.
- Place approximately equal emphasis on diet and physical activity.
- Permit objective parties to interpret science and avoid manipulating science as a marketing and public relations tool.

- Acknowledge that personal freedom is enhanced as the environment becomes healthier.

One suggestion my colleagues and I have repeatedly made is to introduce a food tax. A lightning rod for controversy, the proposal has been attacked with great vehemence by the food industry, food trade associations, and conservative political groups. Once thought completely radical but now part of legitimate debate, a food tax is being considered by several national governments.

A tax could be conceptualized in several ways. The most dramatic would be to impose a tax on unhealthy foods. The tax would be large enough to decrease consumption, and to raise sufficient revenue to subsidize the sale of healthy foods. Research would be needed to determine the necessary level of tax.

Less radical would be a small tax on soft drinks, snack foods, and fast foods to generate revenue for needed programs.[43] For instance, a U.S. national tax of one penny per soft-drink can

ONE SUGGESTION MY COLLEAGUES AND I HAVE REPEATEDLY MADE IS TO INTRODUCE A FOOD TAX.

or bottle would raise $1.5 billion per year. The revenue would be much larger if the tax were just two pennies, and was applied to other classes of foods. I have recommended that the revenue be earmarked for a "nutrition superfund" that could be used to promote healthy eating to children.

Such small taxes are now in effect in a number of American states and municipalities, but in all cases have been implemented to raise general revenues rather than to improve nutrition. Such taxes are acceptable to the public. The challenge is to earmark the revenue to healthy eating.

Based on what is known, my colleagues and I have suggested a number of actions that might be considered to improve the nutrition landscape.[44] The hope is to develop approaches that offer promise in preventing obesity, change conditions in ways that improve diet and physical activity, and are cost effective.

Social Attitude Change

- Focus on environmental change and recognize that personal resources (responsibility) can be overwhelmed when the environment is toxic.
- Replace the "no good foods or bad foods" stance with a public health focus on what foods must be generally consumed.
- Recognize that treating obesity is very difficult and can be costly, thus making prevention and children the priorities. See obesity as a matter of social justice: As obesity is highest in low-income groups, social justice and race issues are linked with diet, inactivity, and obesity. Correcting social disparities is one means of fighting obesity. Civil rights, anti-poverty, anti-hunger, and community organizations might be allies for public health experts working on obesity.

Global Priorities

- Learn from successes in countries such as Finland and Mauritius about large-scale efforts to change diet and activity.
- Support research to understand transitions in nutrition and activity.
- Emphasize disparity issues and the impact of obesity on developing countries.
- Work with the WHO as the prime organizing unit.
- Establish a world culture where promoting unhealthy food is unacceptable.

Physical Activity
- Develop national strategic plans to increase physical activity.
- Earmark transportation funding for non-motorized transport.
- Design activity-friendly communities and offer incentives for activity.
- Build and promote exercise opportunities in communities, schools, worksites, and physician practices. Promote walking and biking to school.

Commercialization of Childhood
- Prevent exploitation of children as market objects.
- Protest the use of cartoon characters and celebrity endorsements to promote unhealthy foods.
- Discourage product placements in movies, TV shows, videogames, and food company web sites with games for children.
- Encourage legislators to prohibit marketing of products to children, or at least to create equal time for pro-nutrition messages.
- Create a nutrition "superfund" to promote healthy eating, perhaps from fees placed on food advertisements or small taxes on the sale of unhealthy foods.
- Promote media literacy (advertising inoculation) among children.

Food and Soft Drinks in Schools
- Identify how eating and activity affect academic performance. Education and public health officials should be allies in this effort. Soft drinks and snack foods will be banished from schools, the instant schools officials learn that poor diet is affecting standardized test scores.
- Prohibit TV programming with food promotion, rid schools of food company logos and references to unhealthy foods in educational materials, have only non-food fundraisers, and use only healthy foods as academic incentives.

- Improve school lunch programs and use the cafeteria as a learning laboratory.
- Find alternatives to snack foods, soft drinks, and fast foods.
- Improve nutrition and activity instruction.
- Use zoning laws to prohibit food establishments from operating near schools.
- Have only healthy foods/beverages in vending machines.

Portion Sizing
- Raise awareness that larger portions lead to more eating, encourage companies to sell and advertise reasonable portions, and educate people on serving sizes.
- Require food labelling at restaurants, and food companies to list the number of USDA servings on the front of containers.

Economic Issues
- Increase awareness of the fundamental imbalance of incentives to eat well versus poorly, and highlight the connections of poverty with obesity.
- Engage programs such as the U.S.A.'s National School Lunch Program, Food Stamp Program, Head Start, and WIC (the special supplemental nutrition program for women, infants, and children) to fight poor diet.
- Change the food price structure, first by lowering costs of healthy foods and perhaps by increasing the costs of unhealthy foods.
- Think of food taxes not as punitive measures but as a means to support nutrition programs.

Interacting with the Food Industry and Government
- Support positive industry changes, but also increase public awareness of industry tactics that influence policy and promote unhealthy eating.

- Challenge the industry for hidden funding of political and nutrition front groups.
- Encourage bold action free of industry influence among political leaders.
- Curb food commercialism in public institutions (such as ads in museums, in hospitals, on police cars).
- Promote activities known to help with body weight (for example, breast feeding, decreased television watching).
- Mobilize parents to demand a healthy environment for their children.

Explore Innovative Coalitions
- Making coalitions of concerned groups increases the power of social movements. Because improved diet should boost academic performance, explore coalitions with education groups, and also with traditional medicine. Other creative avenues could include connections with groups focused on environmental sustainability.[45] Improving dietary habits would benefit these groups as well as public health.

SUMMARY

Poor diet, inactivity, and obesity are severe global problems. Modern conditions, which have bred the obesity pandemic, simply must change. This will require considerable attention to the food and physical activity environments, bold action on the part of national leaders (who must be separated from their food company interests), support of creativity at the grass roots, considerable funding, and the will to persist in the face of vexing systemic problems.

Blaming individuals for obesity, table-pounding exhortations for increased personal responsibility, and protecting the food industry's status quo do not work. They have been tried for years and have failed, yet they are precisely what many in government propose as a means of moving ahead. Helping the population make responsible decisions by creating an environment that promotes rather than prevents healthy eating and activity is a worthy goal, but it will require fundamental changes in the economics of food, the activity environment, and the way the food industry does business.

Positive signs exist. Awareness of the problem is increasing, the media are publicizing obesity as a public health issue (not just how to diet), and government leaders are beginning to resist industry pressures. Grassroots victories have occurred, and are having a contagious effect. Support of these movements offers the greatest hope of progress. But it has yet to be combined with the work that legislators must do.

A HISTORY OF FOOD (CONTINUED)

1953   Gerry Thomas, a marketing employee for Swanson foods, invents the TV dinner as a way to utilize 240,000 kilograms (520,000 pounds) of excess turkey. The turkey is packaged in a three-compartment tray, with peas and sweet potatoes, and sold for 98 cents. Interest in the television, still a relatively new concept for North American consumers, helps propel interest in the TV dinner, which will pioneer a huge business for Swanson.

1954   Food inventor and entrepreneur Ray Croc drives all the way to San Bernardino, California, to see the excitement generated by a hamburger restaurant owned by brothers Dick and Maurice (Mac) McDonald. The restaurant — called McDonald's — serves hamburgers and milkshakes at reasonable prices, with very short turnaround times. The concept draws long lineups. Seeing the potential in franchising this "fast food" concept, Croc obtains the rights from the brothers to be a franchise agent, and soon opens a new McDonald's restaurant in Des Plains, Illinois. In 1961, Croc will buy out the brothers for $2.7 million. The company's shares will be worth over US$35 billion in 2004.

1959   Chinese revolutionary leader Mao Zedong's Great Leap Forward leads to the largest famine in history. The crisis results in part from the effort to mobilize Chinese labour away from traditional agricultural development and toward large-scale industrial development, considered to be more valuable to the nation's economy. This results in a decline in agricultural output, which will be made worse by natural disasters in 1960. The leaders of the country will not realize or respond to the problem, and will allow the country to continue exporting grain even after the famine has begun. It is estimated that somewhere between 15 million and 40 million Chinese perish in this famine.

1962   Canadian scientist Edward Asselbergs invents instant mashed potatoes. Through work at the Department of Agriculture in Ottawa, Ontario, his technique for dehydrating potato flakes is used to create other foods and provide nutrition to developing countries and the military.

1968   The total catch for cod in the Grand Banks off the coast of Newfoundland reaches its peak of 810,000 tonnes. Despite the introduction of larger vessels, larger nets, and more sophisticated equipment, the cod catch will continually decline from this date onwards.

▼   CONTINUED ON PAGE 236

BRAND BARONS AND THE BUSINESS OF FOOD

DAVID WHEELER, JANE THOMSON

EDITORS' INTRODUCTION

In 1929, a modest Canadian scientist with thin lips and thick eyebrows changed the history of food forever. He was an unlikely culinary revolutionary, and even today this giant of science rarely gets the credit he deserves. After all, who goes to the grocery store, sees the long aisles of frozen food, and thinks of the name Archibald Gowanlock Huntsman?

Born in Toronto in 1883, A.G. — as he was affectionately known — was educated as a doctor before turning to his great love, marine biology. He moved to New Brunswick to become the curator of the St. Andrews Biological Station, where he began a lifelong study of salmon.

By 1926 the Biological Board of Canada — which later became the Fisheries Research Board — wanted to investigate the possibilities of freezing and selling Canadian fish. They hired Archibald Huntsman to do the job. It took two years of experimentation until Huntsman perfected the quick-freeze process. In 1929, the first packaged, quick-frozen food was brought to market in Halifax and Toronto. The product had the rather uninviting, tasteless name of Frozen Ice Fillets. The Ice Fillets were a hit, however, and Huntsman was keen to develop and market the project. But the fishing industry lost interest. After all, where would the average family keep a Frozen Ice Fillet anyway? General Electric had only just released the first refrigerator in 1927, and few households owned one. So by 1931 the Ice Fillet project was dropped.

Huntsman went on to have an extraordinary career, rising to become the president of the Royal Society of Scientists in Canada, but he never pursued the potential of frozen food. And so, as is so often the case in science, another man seized on the idea and made a fortune. That man's name is Clarence Birdseye.

If Huntsman was a serious academic, Birdseye was a jack-of-all-trades entrepreneur. Born in Brooklyn, New York, Birdseye studied biology at Amherst College for a few years. But university life didn't suite Birdseye, so he quit school and went to work as a trapper and naturalist for the U.S. government. When he was posted to Labrador, Canada, he noticed how the natives preserved their food in the freezing weather. When the food thawed, Birdseye was amazed to discover that it still tasted fresh. Right then he knew he had the next food revolution in his hands. He just had to find a way to duplicate the process mechanically.

Returning to New York, he formed Birdseye Seafood Inc. and, with buckets of brine, ice, and a seven-dollar electric fan, he set about trying to create what would become flash-freezing. After years of experimentation, he perfected the process, packaging fish as well as vegetables and meats in waxed cardboard. In 1930, a year after Huntsman first introduced the process, Birdseye went into business. Birdseye eventually sold his flash-freezing process and his patents to General Foods, a company that he helped found, for $22 million, and he went on to become a legend.

David Wheeler and Jane Thomson might consider Clarence Birdseye one of the early brand barons. We asked Wheeler and Thomson to examine how new ideas from moderns versions of A. G. Huntsman might make it to the rapidly changing marketplace. Here is their examination of ingenuity in the business of food.

IN JULY 2004, we received another extraordinary e-mail from a former student at York University, Farouk Jiwa, updating us on his latest triumph. Farouk is Director of a Kenyan food company, Honey Care Africa. Established in the late-1990s as a for-profit business, Honey Care is now Kenya's largest producer of high-quality honey. Farouk had just returned to Kenya from Washington, where he signed an agreement with Jim Wolfensohn, President of the World Bank, to extend the Honey Care model in East Africa through a combination of grant funding and commercial investment.

The World Bank deal, made under the "Strengthening Grassroots Business Initiative," a department of the International Finance Corporation, was just the latest in a string of international awards and commercial investments won by Farouk and his colleagues. Farouk is now a celebrity in the world of sustainable food and entrepreneurship.

What is fascinating about the Honey Care model is that Farouk has built a highly innovative business model that supports thousands of rural village-based bee-keepers with loans, simple technology, collection services, and training, while paying them the highest possible prices for their honey — direct, immediate, and in cash. Honey Care also maintains effective relationships with a wide range of financial and development agencies keen to support the growth of a business with such clear social, ecological, and economic pay-offs. From a business perspective, Farouk has established a network of win-win relationships, and a set of virtuous cycles between partners, suppliers, and customers, undreamt of by even the most sophisticated entrepreneurs. Honey Care is a powerful beacon for technological and social ingenuity in the food business.

This chapter explores the "business case" for responding to what many contributors to *Feeding the Future* believe is a gathering global crisis in food quality and distribution. Our exploration is guided by two fundamental questions:

- How can we ensure that technological and social ingenuity in food production and distribution promotes the common good: that is, the interests of ordinary people and the natural environment?
- How can we strike the optimum balance between the common good and the need for private sector organizations to create economic value from food production and distribution?

Let's begin with the first question by examining one highly successful historical example of social innovation and ingenuity in the food industry: the nineteenth-century emergence of co-operative businesses in food production and retailing.

BUSINESS INGENUITY AND THE COMMON GOOD

Our story begins in 1844, in Rochdale in the Northwest of England. In that year a group of working-class social activists formed a mutual, self-help organization called the Rochdale Society of Equitable Pioneers. Inspired by the experiments of early social entrepreneurs such as Robert Owen and William King, the Rochdale Pioneers envisioned a co-operative approach: a "self-supporting home-colony of united interests" that would include agricultural production and food retailing. The experiment was founded on a number of core principles that the co-operative movement has maintained, more or less intact, to this day (Birchall, 1994).

Agricultural production co-operatives grew rapidly in Europe in the years following the establishment of the Rochdale Society. Commencing around 1860, particular success was achieved in Germany, and thereafter in Italy, France, Belgium, Switzerland, and Denmark (Wheeler & Sillanpää, 1997). In Britain, the Co-operative Wholesale Society's Farmcare business remains the country's largest agricultural producer, with more than a hundred farms under management and a strong environmental ethic. Farmcare claims to be at the "forefront of organic and integrated crop management research and its effect on wildlife" (Farmcare, 2004).

In 1895, the International Co-operative Alliance (ICA) was founded to represent the interests of national co-operative organizations.[1] Constituent parts of the ICA, representing hundreds of millions of agricultural and fisheries workers around the globe, include the International Co-operative Agricultural Organization (ICAO),[2] and the International Co-operative Fisheries Organization (ICFO).[3] According to the International Co-operative Information Centre, 150 years after the founding of the co-operative movement, co-operatives control 99 percent of Sweden's dairy production, 95 percent of Japan's rice harvest, 75 percent of western Canada's grain and oil seed output, 65 percent of India's sugar production, and 60 percent of Italy's wine production (International Co-operative Information Centre, 1994). Scotsburn (Nova Scotia) and Gay Lea Foods (Ontario) are two examples of successful Canadian dairy industry co-operatives, both of which are answerable to their producer members and both of which employ several hundred workers.

This story of the growth and establishment of a global movement in co-operative food production and distribution is instructive for three reasons:

- First, it demonstrates that a great deal of food production and distribution around the world today is directed by *producer or consumer-controlled enterprises* rather than shareholder-driven, for-profit multinational corporations, agribusinesses, and food conglomerates: i.e., the organizations usually targeted by food and health activists and anti-globalization campaigners. This is not to imply that co-operative organizations are socially or environmentally perfect, merely that they are an alternative business model to large corporations.

- Second, it demonstrates that *social innovation* in business — in this case the invention of stakeholder-controlled food production, distribution, and retail enterprises — has had a profound effect on the way food has been, and continues to be, produced, distributed, and consumed globally.

- Finally, as with the Honey Care Africa case, this story demonstrates that when principles of social as well as technological ingenuity are applied simultaneously, *enormous value can be created* for ordinary people, both as producers and consumers.

Let's return to these points later in the chapter. Meanwhile, we will address our second fundamental question: how to strike the optimum balance between the public interest and the needs of private sector businesses to create economic value.

STRIKING A BALANCE BETWEEN CORPORATE INTERESTS AND THE COMMON GOOD

Recent controversies over food production, distribution, and quality described elsewhere in this book have led to a generally pessimistic view of the private sector in co-managing the world's food systems. From concerns about the range of chemical toxins and biochemically active contaminants of meat and produce (for example, dioxins, furans, PCBs, antibiotics, and hormones), to trans fats and problems of obesity in children raised on a diet of high-fat, fast foods — a wide range of issues have served to focus consumer disquiet over the private sector's role in providing safe and wholesome food supplies in the industrialized world. Two of the most potent recent controversies were the outbreak of Bovine Spongiform Encephalopathy (BSE) or mad cow disease that cost the lives of millions of cattle and hundreds of people in Europe, and the raging debates over genetic modification (GM) of basic seeds and foodstuffs such as corn and soy.

Professor Maxime Schwartz of the Institut Pasteur in Paris has described how the emergence of the BSE epidemic among cows, and its deadly human equivalent Creutzfeldt-Jakob disease (CJD), could be linked directly to intensive farming. Although meat and bone meal has been added to cattle feed since the latter part of the nineteenth century, "the use of these meals, especially for dairy cows, greatly increased after the 1960s and 1970s, with the development of intensive agriculture to maximize productivity" (Schwartz, 2003). While acknowledging the absence of definitive proof linking BSE with hundreds of deaths from CJD mediated by fast food, Professor Schwartz cites a study of diets and geography in Britain that "made it possible to correlate the incidence of CJD and the consumption of foods such as hamburgers, sausages and meat pies."

If BSE shook public trust in meat products and their corporate purveyors, then genetic engineering has certainly raised the stakes for public acceptance of innovation in the food business. Many commentators have traced the growing public disquiet over GM foods and the motives of the food biotechnology companies. In his book *Travels in the Genetically Modified Zone*, Mark Winston, a professor of biological sciences at Simon Fraser

University, described the corporate public relations disasters and consequent societal responses to GM foods: "My forays into industry left me ambivalent about the complex scientific-corporate conglomerate that has evolved in the biotechnology

IF BSE SHOOK PUBLIC TRUST OF MEAT PRODUCTS AND THEIR CORPORATE PURVEYORS, THEN GENETIC ENGINEERING HAS CERTAINLY RAISED THE STAKES FOR PUBLIC ACCEPTANCE OF INNOVATION IN THE FOOD BUSINESS.

business" (Winston, 2002). Although convinced of the potential benefits of GM foods, he concluded, "We have made considerably greater progress in achieving scientific breakthroughs than we have in managing the chaotic controversies that swirl around them. The biotechnology experience has revealed a deep chasm between science and public awareness."

Peter Pringle makes much the same point in *Food Inc.* Criticizing the polarization created both by clumsy biotech food corporations and by their opponents, Pringle believes, "GM groceries are not Frankenfoods any more than a transplanted heart is today's Frankenstein. They are scientific creations full of both promise and potential hazard. These experimental foods deserve respect from those who discover them, call for more caution from those who regulate them and grow them, and finally, at the end of this real food chain, demand close study by those of us who eat them." (Pringle, 2003).

Clearly the public is skeptical. As a result, business organizations such as the Foods and Consumer Products Manufacturers of Canada believe that mandatory labelling of GM foods should be avoided because opinion polls suggest that 57 percent of consumers read "contains genetically modified ingredients" as a warning, and that 27 percent would actively seek out non-GM alternatives (FCPMC, 2002).

In the cases of BSE and GM, technology and efficiency juxtaposed with issues of public health and nutrition exposed the very real difficulty policy-makers face in drawing the right line between benefits and risks. Risk-benefit equations were not fully understood by regulators or the protagonists. As a result, consumers — particularly in Europe — were left reeling. The general public felt unprotected by governments and assaulted by corporate interests. More recently, this has driven stricter regulatory controls in various countries, causing companies like Monsanto and Bayer to back off GM wheat and maize projects in North America and Europe.

Already there is a widening gap between Europe and North America on what constitutes acceptable risk. In Europe, the adoption of the "precautionary principle" may severely curtail sales of agricultural and other chemicals that cannot be proven absolutely harmless. Who derives the benefits and who bears the risks will be a central feature of future debates about innovation and ingenuity in the food business in both the industrialized and developing worlds (Rifkin, 1998, 2004).

When we turn to problems of food quality and availability in the developing world, the issue of genetic modification becomes even more complex. According to Lester Brown of the Earth Policy Institute, the worldwide grain shortfall of 105 million tonnes in 2003 was "easily the largest on record." Rather chillingly, Brown suggests that with population growth,[4] climate change, water shortages, and other factors, further grain shortfalls in coming years could take the world into "uncharted territory" where world grain stocks would be down to less than fifty days rather than the seventy days required for global food security: i.e., stable prices and supply (Brown, 2004).

It was for precisely these reasons that the United Nations Food and Agriculture Organization published a major report in

May 2004 entitled *Agricultural Biotechnology: Meeting the Needs of the Poor*. It backed the use of biotechnology, provided that benefits flowed more quickly to poor farmers in the developing world. Releasing the report, Dr. Harwig de Haen of FAO warned that biotechnology, including genetic engineering, is not a panacea against world hunger, but it can raise farmers' incomes, increase food supplies, reduce prices, and improve nutritional quality.

Organizations like the International Service for National Agriculture Research and the Pew Initiative on Food and Biotechnology have drawn similar conclusions (ISNAR, 2002; Pew, 2004). But, like FAO, many independent foundations and research organizations identify the main barriers to feeding a world approaching 9 billion people as more than just the transfer of technology, citing a range of political, economic, and social factors. Thus, questions of unfair subsidies to industrialized nations' agricultural producers (both in the co-operative and private sectors), lack of capacity in the developing world to engage in development and control of new technologies, consequent exploitation of poor farmers, and generally inefficient and inequitable food distribution in the developing world, are frequently cited issues that must be addressed. And the results — hunger, disease, and death — are never very far removed from the popular media. The Hunger Site (a web site encouraging citizen- and consumer-engagement in food-poverty issues) claims that 24,000 people die every day from hunger or hunger-related causes, of which three-quarters are children under five years old.

In such circumstances, to whom do we look to identify and solve problems of food quality and availability in both the developed and the developing world? Typically — if we are to believe consumer polling conducted in industrialised countries — it is the campaign groups, the consumer organizations, food experts, media, international development agencies, and governments (Poppe & Kjærnes, 2003). And who is to blame for the problems? A quick tour of the popular titles in food policy reveals that the assumed culprits are invariably profit-driven multi-national corporations and their tame or corrupted counterparts in regulatory agencies.

Trenchant recent critiques of corporate involvement in agriculture and food production include *The Fatal Harvest Reader: The Tragedy of Industrial Agriculture* edited by Andrew Kimbrell (2002), and *Don't Worry, It's Safe to Eat* by Andrew Rowell (2003). Both advance wide-ranging criticisms of corporate involvement in food supply and distribution. *Fatal Harvest* also offers a vision for alternatives based on organic and sustainable forms of food production and consumption. Rowell's book rails against the U.K. government for its apparent failures to protect the public interest in the face of corporate influence and scientific hegemony — a criticism he extends to the U.S. and Canadian governments.

In *Stolen Harvest: The Hijacking of the Global Food Supply*, Indian social and environmental activist Vandana Shiva (2002) argues that small-scale agriculture using traditional seed varieties is superior in economic as well as social and ecological terms to intensive farming practices promoted by multi-national agrochemical and seed companies. She also provides powerful arguments for third-world farmers and governments not to co-operate with corporations promoting genetically engineered, patented seeds.

But is all this critical analysis of private sector food businesses realistic or fair? And indeed is it helpful if we are interested in designing an effective means of feeding a world population of 9 billion people?

There is no shortage of private sector food businesses to vilify. But are we to accept unquestioningly that McDonald's, KFC, and other fast-food chains must take primary responsibility for addressing childhood obesity in North America and Europe? Is Monsanto to be blamed for every issue arising from the promotion of genetically engineered seeds worldwide? Are Bayer,

Syngenta, and other pesticide manufacturers wholly responsible for incidents of worker and consumer poisoning through misuse of their products?

Have these companies and their technological advances in food production and safety contributed nothing to the common good?

And where are major North American food retailers like A&P, Costco, Giant, Loblaw, Safeway, Sobeys, and Wal-Mart on these issues? Have these companies, with their millions of employees and flexibility of food distribution and retailing, added absolutely nothing to our economic well-being and quality of life?

With these questions in mind, let us now turn to the role of private sector food businesses today, starting with an exploration of where the food business came from and why corporations now have to work so hard to establish their credentials for social responsibility and the protection of the public good.

THE PRIVATE SECTOR FOOD BUSINESS TODAY

Emerging from a History of Adulteration and Poisoning

One of the reasons why co-operative food production and distribution proved so popular in the nineteenth century was that the poor had long suffered at the hands of unscrupulous food producers and vendors who sold adulterated products to the direct detriment of the health and well-being of their customers. According to Professor Greg Tomso of Duke University, a widely read treatise on food adulteration authored by an early-nineteenth-century technologist, F. C. Accum, "created a storm of public interest in the issues of food purity and safety," leading to a "popular moral crusade" in London (Accum, 1820; Tomso, 1997).

Professor Anthony Wohl of Vassar College notes that the list of poisonous additives to other foods in Victorian England (apart from routine distribution of spoiled and microbiologically suspect grain and dairy produce) "reads like the stock list of some mad and malevolent chemist." The toxins routinely added to foods for purposes of preservation or colouration included strychnine in beer, lead chromate in mustard, mercury bisulphate in

ONE OF THE REASONS WHY CO-OPERATIVE FOOD PRODUCTION AND DISTRIBUTION PROVED SO POPULAR IN THE NINETEENTH CENTURY WAS THAT THE POOR HAD LONG SUFFERED AT THE HANDS OF UNSCRUPULOUS FOOD PRODUCERS AND VENDORS WHO SOLD ADULTERATED PRODUCTS TO THE DIRECT DETRIMENT OF THE HEALTH AND WELL-BEING OF THEIR CUSTOMERS.

confectionary and chocolate, and various other lead derivatives in wine, cider, and cheese. According to Professor Wohl, "as late as 1877 the UK Local Government Board found that approximately a quarter of the milk it examined contained excessive water or chalk, and ten per cent of all the butter, over eight per cent of the bread, and 50 per cent of the gin had copper in them to heighten the colour." Meanwhile, in 1862 the U.K. Privy Council estimated that "one-fifth of butcher's meat in England and Wales came from animals which were 'considerably diseased' or had died of pleuro-pneumonia, and anthacid or anthracoid diseases."

Small wonder, then, that by the end of the nineteenth century the co-operative production and retailing of wholesome food became so well established in Britain, or that a number of legislative measures, based on the application of the emerging fields of analytical chemistry and microbiology, were enacted to protect the public from food contamination.

If it was Victorian England that demonstrated the need for social innovation, co-operation, and eventually legislation to ensure wholesome food for the masses, it was in early twentieth-century America that the potential dangers of *corporate* control of food production and distribution were first given an airing. One landmark was the 1905 publication of Upton Sinclair's *The Jungle*, a novelistic exposé of the Chicago meat industry (Sinclair, 1971).

Responding to the scandal that followed publication of *The Jungle*, President Theodore Roosevelt met Sinclair and agreed that "radical action must be taken to do away with the efforts of arrogant and selfish greed on the part of the capitalist." In 1906 Roosevelt acted, passing into law the Pure Food and Drugs Act and the Meat Inspection Act.[5]

Despite these setbacks for the more cavalier elements of the American food industry, the rise of private sector food businesses in the U.S. and elsewhere was inexorable throughout the twentieth century.

Discovering the Business Opportunity

According to U.S. trade magazine *Supermarket Business*, by the end of the twentieth century total U.S. retail food sales stood at US$439 billion (Agriculture and Agri-Food Canada, 2004). ACNielsen estimates that Canadians spent CAN$34 billion on groceries in 2001. And according to the Canadian Department of Human Resources Development (2004), the Canadian agriculture and agri-food industry (farmers, suppliers, processors, transporters, grocers, and restaurant workers) accounts for one in seven jobs and 8 percent of GDP and exports $25 billion worth of products per annum.

In retrospect we can see how in the last century the corporate sector developed competencies and a growing presence in *every* element of the food chain in the industrialized world — from farm to plate. For the purpose of this chapter, six major areas of business opportunity are especially important to note because they all required (and continue to require) some level of technological and social innovation. The opportunities are set out below:

- *Technical Products Opportunities.* Fertiliser, pesticide, feed and seed companies became increasingly active in the provision of "essential" inputs to both farming and aquaculture industries. Multi-billion-dollar enterprises involved in producing such products include international corporations such as Bayer, Cargill, DuPont, Monsanto, Pfizer, and Syngenta.

- *Primary Production and Wholesale Opportunities.* With the exception of those agricultural and fishing people organized in co-operatives, primary food production shifted inexorably from small operators to corporate farmers and fishing fleets. Well-known Canadian companies involved in primary production and wholesaling include Gold Seal, High Liner, Maple Lodge Farms, and Maple Leaf Foods, and, internationally, Archer Daniels Midland (ADM), Cargill, ConAgra, International Multifoods, Nutreco, Tyson Foods, and Unilever.

- *Processing and Packaging Opportunities.* Economies of scale and the need for long shelf-lives dictated that processing, packaging, and sterilization or pasteurization technologies be centralized and often contracted out to specialist businesses. Leading corporations involved in processing and packaging include Alcan, Alcoa, Archer Daniels Midland (ADM), Cargill, ConAgra, DuPont, and TetraPak.

- *Distribution and Storage Opportunities.* The increasing diversity and distances involved in distributing and storing foods have led to enormous business opportunities for providers of national and international logistic services, in software, in transportation (road, rail, and air), and storage facilities (cold and regular). Large corporations with expertise in food logistics include Atlas Cold Storage, P&O Cold Logistics, Swire Group, Versacold Group, and the World Food Logistics Organization.

- *Retail and Consumption Opportunities.* Supermarket chains have outpaced small-scale grocery stores and fast-food outlets have challenged both home-cooking and conventional restaurants in the provision of readily available convenience food. Large corporate supermarket and fast-food chains around the world include retailers like A&P, Costco, Giant, Loblaw, Safeway, and Wal-Mart in North America, Lidl, Tesco, and Tenglemann in Europe, and fast-food giants like KFC, McDonald's, and Burger King almost everywhere.
- *Brand Control Opportunities.* Positioned at the centre of the web of corporate sector business opportunities, food manufacturers developed internationally recognized brands and distribution systems that connected production to powerful retail outlets supported by massive advertising budgets linked to technical, lifestyle, and other claims. The brand controllers include George Weston, Maple Leaf Foods, and Saputo in Canada, and Coca Cola, ConAgra, Danone, General Mills, Kraft, Kellogg, HJ Heinz, Mars, Nestlé, Parmalat, PepsiCo, Sara Lee, and Unilever globally (Higgins, 2002).

These opportunities — and their enablers — in the food production and distribution value chain are depicted in Figure 1 below. The centrality and influence of the brand controllers should be immediately evident.

In each of the business opportunity areas depicted in Figure 1, we can observe examples of private sector ingenuity and innovation. Some of the scientific, technological, and social innovations certainly brought great benefits to consumers: improved nutritional value, enhanced product diversity and convenience, lower cost, and longer shelf-lives. Others incurred a price and continue to have negative impacts — on food quality, on the environment, and on social equity. Especially interesting are the food brand controllers and owners (or "brand barons" as

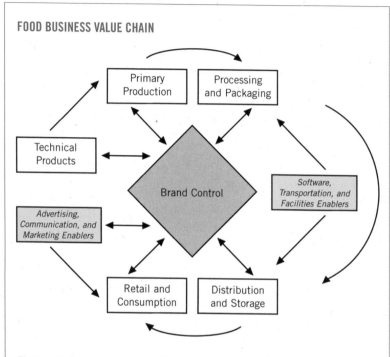

FOOD BUSINESS VALUE CHAIN

Primary Production

Processing and Packaging

Technical Products

Brand Control

Software, Transportation, and Facilities Enablers

Advertising, Communication, and Marketing Enablers

Retail and Consumption

Distribution and Storage

Figure 1. Major business opportunities and enablers in the food business "value chain" illustrating the centrality and influence of the brand controllers.

we shall call them). These players control much of the food value chain and they are the food businesses most attuned to consumer desires. Their marketing dollars persuade us where to buy, what to buy, and even when to buy. Below we describe the spectacular success of five such corporations: two American, one European, and two Canadian.

The Rise and Rise of the Food Brand Barons

The enormous growth of the brand barons is at the heart of what happened in the food industry during the twentieth century.

Employing tens or hundreds of thousands of workers and turning over billions of dollars, these brand-based enterprises now develop, produce, and channel most of the foods we trust and buy every day in supermarkets, grocery stores, and fast-food outlets.[6]

Starting just two years before the publication of *The Jungle*, Ontario-born James L. Kraft established a wholesale business in Chicago, selling reliable, branded cheese products to grocery stores. Today, in addition to a thriving cigarette business (Altria), Kraft has a stable of international food brands such as Jacobs and Maxwell House coffees, Toblerone chocolate, Planters peanuts, DiGiorno pizza, Nabisco cereals, and of course Kraft and Philadelphia cheese products. In 2003, international net revenues for Kraft's food products were US$31 billion and Kraft's food business employed a total of 109,000 people.

Pepsi-Cola was founded as a brand in 1898 by Caleb Bradham, a North Carolina pharmacist, who decided to name a carbonated soft drink he formulated for his drugstore's fountain

SOME OF THE SCIENTIFIC, TECHNOLOGICAL, AND SOCIAL INNOVATIONS CERTAINLY BROUGHT GREAT BENEFITS TO CONSUMERS: IMPROVED NUTRITIONAL VALUE, ENHANCED PRODUCT DIVERSITY AND CONVENIENCE, LOWER COST, AND LONGER SHELF-LIVES.

customers. After a catastrophic gamble on the price of sugar, Bradham's company and brand were purchased in 1923. Today Pepsi is part of the PepsiCo food and beverages empire, formed in 1965 through the merger of Pepsi-Cola and Frito-Lay. PepsiCo embraces the Pepsi, Gatorade, and Tropicana drinks brands together with the Frito-Lay and Quaker megabrands, comprising a bewilderingly wide variety of snacks and cereals products. Headquartered appropriately enough in Purchase, New

York, the company had worldwide revenues of US$27 billion in 2003 and employed 143,000 people.

Paris-based Danone is a European food and beverage giant with the mission to "help people around the world grow, live better and get more out of life through tastier, more varied and healthier food products every day." Formed through a series of mergers in the 1970s, Gervais Danone rapidly became France's leading food company. With aggressive international expansion since, Groupe Danone now claims to be "number one" in the world in fresh dairy products, packaged water (Evian), and cereal. In 2003 net sales were €13 billion. The company has 92,000 employees.

George Weston Limited is a Canadian food processing and distribution company founded in 1882 when Weston bought a bread route from his boss for $200. George's son Garfield expanded the company with a string of acquisitions between 1924 and 1972 in Canada and the U.K. Weston's food distribution division has been particularly successful. It includes the Loblaw chain of grocery stores, to which Weston introduced the President's Choice brand of specialty foods that now captures almost 25 percent of in-store sales. Other divisions focus on baking and dairy products, as well as fish farming and processing in North America and Chile. The Weston family has maintained majority ownership of the company throughout, and Galen Weston presently owns more than 60 percent of the company. In 2003 Weston accrued sales of over CAN$29 billion (with nearly 85 percent from Loblaw), and employed more than 145,000 people (Robin, 2003).

The Canadian Maple Leaf brand dates back to 1898, but the present-day Maple Leaf Foods Inc. was created in 1995 when the Ontario Teachers' Pension Plan Board and McCain Capital Corporation[7] acquired controlling interests in the company. The company became Canada's largest food processor in 1991 with the merger of Canada Packers Inc (a meat processing firm with a history dating back to the 1860s) and Maple Leaf

Mills Limited (with antecedents tracing back to 1836). Today, Maple Leaf sells meat, bread, and dairy products in eighty countries worldwide. The company is headquartered in Toronto and employs approximately 23,000 people in Canada, the U.S.A., Europe, and Asia, with sales of CAN$5.0 billion in 2003. Maple Leaf brands include Olivieri, Dempster's, and Olafson's bread, and Schneiders and Maple Leaf meat products.

These five stories help us understand the spectacular commercial success of many of the corporations that became involved in the various component parts of the food value chain during the last century — especially those that achieved dominant brand positions. Our key observations on the rise of the private sector food corporation during the twentieth century are:

- Private sector food businesses have long had to deal with a reputation for inadequate concern for consumer and environmental protection; they also have a more recent history of ensuring high levels of convenience and flexibility of choice for consumers, and some have achieved high levels of consumer trust on issues of food quality and safety.
- Private sector involvement now occurs at every point of the food value chain, frequently enabled by scientific and technological innovation, advertising, and communications. In most parts of the food value chain, the private sector is the dominant player; notably in the realm of brand ownership and control.

We will now turn to some contemporary examples of technological and social innovation in the food business that we believe provide insights for feeding the future. We will explore the six major areas of business opportunity identified above, dividing the opportunities into "upstream" — i.e., those associated with agricultural and fisheries production — and "downstream" — i.e., from food processing to consumption and retail. In many cases, innovation spans different elements of the food value chain.

THE TWENTY-FIRST-CENTURY FOOD BUSINESS:
INGENUITY IN SERVICE OF THE COMMON GOOD?

Ingenuity in Production

One of the most important drivers of technological innovation is the need to produce food efficiently *and intensively* if the world is to feed itself without encroaching too radically on the world's remaining biodiverse environments.

Progress has been made over the past two decades in reducing the number of undernourished people from 28 to 17 percent of the world's population. Unhappily, the proportion is not declining everywhere, and we see rising numbers in politically sensitive countries such as Afghanistan (from 58 to 70 percent between 1992 and 2001), Iraq (7 to 27 percent), Burundi (49 to 70 percent), and the Democratic Republic of Congo (31 to 75 percent). Moreover, the number of undernourished people in the world has risen in absolute terms since the early 1980s and now totals more than 842 million, 98.8 percent of whom live in developing or transition countries (FAO, 2004).

Meanwhile, the Earth's population is projected to surpass 9 billion by 2050 (WRI, 2002), and despite the likelihood that increasing numbers will live in absolute poverty, there will also be a growing middle class with increasing expectations of lifestyle and consumption patterns. As the global middle class grows, people will require more meat in their diets, placing further stress on land and water resources for food production. Animal farming demands both farms to keep the animals, as well as cropland to feed them, and 37 percent of worldwide grain production is for animal feed. Worldwide consumption of meat has more than tripled over the past forty years. China increased meat consumption thirteen-fold between 1961 and 1999 (WRI, 2002), and worldwide fish consumption doubled between 1973 and 1997 (Mann, 2004). These trends are expected to continue.

In response to the trends (and the desire by many conservationists to avoid the conversion of too much of the Earth's sensitive terrestrial and aquatic ecosystems to food production), some corporations have responded with strategies to enhance agricultural and aquacultural intensity and productivity through technological innovation. In the mid-late twentieth century, the catch phrase was the "green revolution" — a strategy based on seed variety selection, chemical pesticides, and fertilizers that would feed the industrialized world and provide self-sufficiency to the developing world with the same, or less, requirement for agricultural land. Today, it is the "gene revolution," based on genetic modification (GM) or genetic engineering (GE) — a food technology arising from the broader field of biotechnology.

Canada's food biotechnology industry is in its infancy, employing just 750 people in eighty-one companies (HRDC, 2004). The major players are based in the U.S. and Europe. One of the earliest proponents of agricultural innovation based on biotechnology and GE was U.S.-based Monsanto. Monsanto was one of the world's largest and longest established conventional chemical companies. In the mid 1990s, led by a charismatic CEO, Robert Shapiro, Monsanto radically reinvented itself as a biotechnology and life sciences company, and made an audacious attempt to persuade the world that genetically engineered crops were the answer to world hunger. Unfortunately for Monsanto, the world was not ready for such a strategy. A wide range of European environmental and consumer activists objecting to unlabelled GM food ingredients, and a coalition of third-world farmers resisting the company's dependency-creating seed and pesticide regimes, rejected Monsanto's vision.

Skepticism about GM foods in Europe now embraces a broad range of opinion, from the British royal family to governments, to large supermarket chains. European opinion-formers like Robin Bines, whom we interviewed for this chapter, described GM foods as "madness in the long term." Bines, who publishes *Natural Products News* and runs one of Europe's largest trade shows for organic food producers, compares GM technology to nuclear energy — dubious in principle and disastrous in application: "We would need a thousand years to figure out the risks. The biotech companies simply don't know what happens when they splice these genes."

One company with a sophisticated approach, but which still faces the challenge of persuading public opinion of the benefits of gene technology, is DuPont. While the company's re-invention as a life sciences and materials company is still unfolding, DuPont seems determined to move in pace with society, taking time to explore the benefits — and some of the social and technological challenges — of GM seed and crop commercialization. DuPont Canada has a special role to play because of its global leadership for DuPont on the Nutrition and Health file. We interviewed Canadian CEO Doug Muzyka for this chapter and we relate his story in the box below.

GENETIC MODIFICATION OF SEEDS AND CROPS — DUPONT PROCEEDING WITH EXTREME CAUTION

From a nineteenth-century American explosives company to a twentieth-century global chemical company, DuPont is now undergoing a twenty-first-century reinvention by adding biology to the core of its technology foundation.

Within DuPont's five main business areas, Agriculture and Nutrition is a US$5.5 billion growth platform that the company believes has the potential to double in size within six years. Agriculture and Nutrition comprises three main areas of activity: seeds (Pioneer is the world's largest seed company), agricultural

---

chemicals, and nutrition and health products. Its vision is to *"increase the quality, quantity and safety of the global food supply by leveraging DuPont strengths in biotechnology and our knowledge of the food chain"* (DuPont, 2004).

DuPont, which spends about US$500 million per year on agriculture and nutrition research and development, sees an opportunity in genetic engineering to reduce chemical inputs, increase crop yields, and enhance the nutritional value of food produced. They also acknowledge that producer and consumer acceptance of genetic engineering is variable. Traditionally, GE has impacted upstream food production (seeds, etc.), but DuPont hopes to add downstream value, such as elimination of trans fats or enhancement of nutritional value, thus directly connecting with consumers. *"It is all value-risk-reward balances for people so when people see that the reward outweighs their perceived risk, then I think we start to make progress"* (Muzyka, 2004).

Doug Muzyka, President and CEO of DuPont Canada, also has the lead for DuPont globally on Nutrition and Health. Recognizing the complexity of food issues, he feels that societal acceptance of GE technology is crucial: *"The richness of the technology I think is important if you want to achieve sustainable growth in the world — some people would say there is not a food production crisis in the world, that it is a food distribution crisis, and this may not be false. But it doesn't take away from the fact that with the projected growth in the world population we need to produce more food per less land area to sustain world population. So the alternative to bringing new technologies to bear for this is in fact to consume more of the world's arable land, which is by orders of magnitude, a greater negative environmental impact than any of the reasonable risks that you would associate with the new technologies. So this is an important thing, not just in the context of business enterprise, but it is an important thing in the context of a sustainable food supply for the world."*

The United Nations Food and Agriculture Organization projects the following trends to 2030 (FAO, 2002):

- World production, total consumption, food demand and per capita food consumption will increase over the next three decades; however, the rate of these increases will slow over time.
- World agriculture production is projected to stagnate, while world aquaculture production is projected to increase, albeit at a slower rate than in the past.
- In developed countries, consumption patterns will reflect demand for, and imports of, high-cost/high-value products.
- In developing countries, trade flows will reflect the export of high-cost/high-value products and the importation of low-cost/low-value products.

In exploring future trends in agriculture and aquaculture, it becomes clear that some major choices face businesses wanting to be part of a consumer- and environment-friendly future.

Agriculture is a land-intensive process, and, as noted above, there are strong conservationist and technological pressures for it to remain so. The World Resources Institute estimates that 28 percent of the Earth's land surface is devoted to agriculture, of which 31 percent is crops and 69 percent is pasture. However, with current intensive agricultural practices, 49 percent of agricultural land is either moderately or strongly degraded and therefore higher levels of chemical inputs and irrigation are required to produce the necessary yields (WRI 2002).

According to Jason Clay of the Center for Conservation Innovation at WWF, "Agriculture has had a larger environmental impact than any other human activity and today it threatens the very systems we need to meet our food and fiber needs" (Clay, 2004). Fertilizer consumption per hectare of cropland has increased since 1960 from 10 kilograms per hectare (kg/ha) to more than 50 kg/ha in 2000 (Earthtrends, 2003). One possible response to the problem of degradation is to significantly increase the amount of organic and biodynamic agriculture worldwide, although corporate actors like DuPont, and even leading conservationists, would express skepticism about the land use and productivity implications of a global food supply solution based on organic agriculture. According to Greenpeace founder Patrick Moore, "There's a misconception that it would be better to go back to more primitive methods of agriculture because chemicals are bad or genetics is bad. This is not true. We need to use the science and the technology we have developed in order to feed the world's population . . . and the more yield we get per acre of land, the less nature has to be destroyed" (Center for Global Food Issues, 2004).

Despite the strength of corporate interests and the skepticism of some conservationists, the worldwide retail market for organic-certified products is US$20 billion and growing at a rate of 10–30 percent annually in industrialized nations (WRI 2002). Organic production and distribution is often most associated with

DESPITE THE STRENGTH OF CORPORATE INTERESTS AND THE SKEPTICISM OF SOME CONSERVATIONISTS, THE WORLDWIDE RETAIL MARKET FOR ORGANIC-CERTIFIED PRODUCTS IS GROWING AT A RATE OF 10–30 PERCENT ANNUALLY IN INDUSTRIALIZED NATIONS.

the West Coast of the U.S. and northern Europe. However, in research for this chapter, one of the most interesting social innovations in organic agriculture we discovered was an Egyptian company called Sekem, which in 2003 employed no fewer than 2000 employees and enjoyed revenues of 100 million Egyptian pounds (approximately CAN$22 million). The Sekem story is told below.

ORGANIC PRODUCTION AND THE "ECONOMICS OF LOVE" IN EGYPT

The Sekem Group of companies is based in Egypt and was founded in 1977 by the present chairman, Dr. Ibrahim Abouleish. The company comprises three interrelated entities: the Sekem Holding Company, encompassing six companies, each contributing to the business value chain (from raw materials to processing to exporting, marketing, and retailing); the Egyptian Society for Cultural Development, responsible for all cultural aspects; and the Cooperative of Sekem Employees, responsible for human resource development. Together they form an alternative business model seeking to simultaneously add economic, social, and cultural value for their stakeholders.

Sekem was the first entity in Egypt to develop biodynamic farming methods. These methods are based on the premise that organic cultivation *improves* agro-biodiversity and does not produce any unusable waste. All products of the system can be either sold or re-used in cultivation, thereby creating a sustainable process. Their products include organic fruits, vegetables, and herbs; organic textiles; and organic foodstuffs for both domestic and export sales. They have also influenced and educated more than 800 other Egyptian farmers to adopt biodynamic agricultural techniques because of the successful results they have shown at Sekem farms.

In 2003, Sekem was chosen for the Right Livelihood Award, and cited as "a business model for the twenty-first century in which commercial success is integrated with, and promotes the social and cultural development of society through the 'economics of love.'" Current CEO Helmy Abouleish describes the company's approach to business: *"Sekem's competitive advantage lies in corporate social responsibility, which is demonstrated in the harmony it established between its economic, social, educational and cultural activities. Sekem focuses on human capital because investing in people leads to quality products and services which in turn contribute to increased productivity and a strong economy"* (www.rightlivelihood.se; www.sekem.com).

Interestingly, western-based corporations, including some of the brand barons, are jumping on the organic food bandwagon. In the U.S., Organic Valley Family of Farms, based in Wisconsin, is the only national organic dairy to remain independent. Other companies have been taken over by multinational companies. Stonyfield Farms, the largest organic yogurt producer in the world, was bought by Danone in 2001.

Fisheries is an important industry worldwide, valued at US$81 billion in 1997. However, fish stocks are declining: 48 percent are fully exploited, 16 percent overfished, and 9 percent depleted. In response, fish farming is on the rise, growing from 3.5 million to 42.8 million tonnes from 1970 to 1999 (WRI, 2002). Fish farming, or aquaculture, has compounded at an annual rate of 9.2 percent per year since 1970. In 2000, reported total aquaculture production (including aquatic plants) was 45.7 million tonnes by weight and US$56.5 billion by value (FAO, 2002).

More than 27 percent of all fish and shellfish production in 2000 was farmed, with an overwhelming proportion produced in China (estimated at 71 percent). Fish farming is not without its environmental and public health impacts. The David Suzuki Foundation estimates that it requires 3 to 5 kilograms of other fish as feed to produce one kilogram of farmed salmon. Similar inefficiencies are true for other carnivorous fish such as pollock and cod, which also represent a net loss of protein (David Suzuki Foundation 2004). Moreover, some studies have shown significantly higher levels of organochlorine chemicals in farmed salmon than in wild fish (Hites et al, 2004). Interestingly, this has a proportionally greater impact on human consumers as one-third of wild fish catch is used for animal feeds, while virtually 100 percent of farmed fish feeds humans.

Two examples of corporate ingenuity that address these issues are described below. The first relates to the harvesting of sustainable fish by Unilever, one of the world's largest food brand companies. The second is another example of the application of genetic engineering by U.S.-based AquaBounty in search of productivity and profits.

UNILEVER FISHING FOR GLOBAL SUSTAINABILITY

"In 1996 we ambitiously committed to source all our fish from sustainable stocks. As one of the world's largest fish buyers, we recognised the need to take the initiative and work with others to make fishing more sustainable and, of course, to secure our fish supplies for the future." Antony Burgmans & Niall FitzGerald, Joint Chairmen of Unilever (Unilever, 2003)

Unilever is a European food, home, and personal care products conglomerate established in 1932. The Anglo-Dutch firm is a significant brand baron and the company buys approximately 15 percent of the world's white fish catches. White fish makes up about 1.5 percent of all fish catches worldwide. Unilever's major processed fish brand is Birds Eye.

Since 1996, the company has taken a proactive approach to securing its fish product supply, and together with the World Wildlife Fund (WWF) helped establish the Marine Stewardship

---

Council (MSC), an independent certification program for sustainable fisheries. Since 1996 MSC has certified ten fisheries with twelve more working towards certification (MSC website). Fish caught from these fisheries can be labelled with the MSC logo, rewarding sustainable fisheries with product differentiation and granting consumers a sustainable choice for their purchase. In 1996, Unilever committed to buying all of their fish from sustainable sources by 2005. At the end of 2003, they surpassed 50 percent, and the company hope to achieve 75 percent by 2005.

FAST-TRACKING THE GENETICALLY MODIFIED FISH

In a venture that may be seen by many as one innovation too far, AquaBounty is raising the bar in aquaculture technology with its genetically engineered AquAdvantage salmon. (Scientists introduced an "antifreeze" protein from cold-water-dwelling ocean-pout into the salmon.) In the genetically engineered salmon, the pout antifreeze protein activates growth genes. Salmon naturally produce growth hormones in the summer only, so the genetically engineered salmon have two active growth hormone genes — the original, which works in the summer, and the introduced one, which induces growth the rest of the year, thus bringing fish to market in eighteen months, rather than three years.

AquaBounty, formed in 1994, is based in Waltham, MA, with offices in Newfoundland and Prince Edward Island. The company is currently seeking FDA approval for the AquAdvantage fish in the U.S.A., which, if granted, would make it the first genetically engineered fish for human consumption.

Interestingly, corporate domination of GE technology is already spawning contrarian biotechnology entrepreneurs. Operating from academic and public-interest laboratories, these scientists believe in a decentralized, democratic vision for GM crops and foods (Manning, 2004). Richard Jefferson, of the Center for the Application of Molecular Biology to International Agriculture in Australia, is an anti-corporate scientist with a big idea. He wants to develop crop plants that can reproduce themselves indefinitely, without pollination. This super-optimistic, Holy Grail–style endeavour is inspired by a desire to undermine the GE seed sale ambitions of the corporate players who, Jefferson believes, "have the morals of stoats." It remains to be seen whether such popular science will allow different risk-and-reward equations to emerge, or whether it will simply add to the complexity for ordinary consumers. Will today's anti-corporate biotech entrepreneurs become tomorrow's equivalent of Apple's challenge to IBM, or Linux's challenge to Microsoft, or will they go the way of the internet spammers, causing yet more confusion and uncertainty in the marketplace?

Ingenuity from Processing to Retail and Consumption

There is little question that advances in processing, packaging, and sterilization technologies over the last one hundred years have permitted the mass production, distribution, and consumption of an amazing array of nutritious and wholesome foods. But one of the most contentious issues in food policy relates to fast foods and convenience meals: the candies, burgers, pizzas, fries, snack foods, and sugar-based carbonated drinks that are at the centre of the growing controversy over childhood obesity. Convenience foods have seen high growth in retail food sales, increasingly displacing home cooking (AAFC, 2001). Increasing the sugar or salt content of foods reduces the danger of microbial spoilage and improves shelf life. It also creates a high demand for junk food among children.

It has been estimated that 33 percent of Canadian children aged between two and eleven were overweight in 1999, with the prevalence of obesity increasing threefold between 1981 and 1996 (Partridge, 2003, Clarke, 2003). In the U.K., child obesity has doubled since 1982 to 10 percent of six-year-olds and 20 percent of fifteen-year-olds (Van de Weyer, 2003). More than one in

THIRTY-THREE PERCENT OF CANADIAN CHILDREN AGED BETWEEN TWO AND ELEVEN WERE OVERWEIGHT IN 1999, WITH THE PREVALENCE OF OBESITY INCREASING THREEFOLD BETWEEN 1981 AND 1996.

seven (4.7 million) American children between the age of six and seventeen are now considered obese, largely as a result of a range of lifestyle, dietary, and hereditary factors (Smith, 1999).

There is no mistaking where food policy and medical commentators place the blame for such trends. Clearly some responsibility lies with schools and parents who do not encourage their children to exercise. Social class and genetic predisposition are also important factors. Nevertheless, a good deal of the critique is aimed at the corporate suppliers and retailers of processed, packaged convenience foods and beverages that contain too many fats and carbohydrates (especially sugars).

This critique is not unreasonable — especially in view of the demonstrated link between television advertising and children's dietary habits. A study by the Canadian Paediatric Society found that "children who watch a lot of television are less physically fit and more likely to eat high-fat and high-energy snack foods. TV viewing makes a substantial contribution to obesity because prime-time commercials promote unhealthy dietary practices" (Canadian Pediatric Society, 2003). Commenting on a study by the U.K. Food Standards Agency, which found that children's television food advertising is dominated by sugary breakfast cereals, soft drinks, sweets (candy), and salty snacks, the British medical journal *The Lancet* recommended a ban on sports and pop celebrity endorsements of junk food. The journal described such endorsements as "one of the most invidious techniques used by junk-food advertisers" (CBC, 2003).

In response to growing societal concerns, some of the most frequently accused corporate players, including Coca Cola, PepsiCo, Burger King, and McDonald's, have responded with changes and additions to their product lines and menus. McDonald's has also launched its "Bold Balanced Lifestyles Platform." This educational initiative, focusing on nutrition and exercise, aims to support the U.S. Department of Health and Human Services in determining the best way to communicate nutritional information to consumers. McDonald's serves 46 million customers every day through 30,000 company and franchised fast-food outlets in 119 countries, so there is no doubt the company could bring significant influence to bear should it decide to act in the common good.

Of course it remains to be seen whether these changes represent the beginnings of serious innovation or whether they are simply a creative but essentially low-cost, defensive response to growing societal disdain for junk food. In Canada there is increasing pressure in a number of provinces for the complete elimination of commercialization and promotion of junk food — particularly in schools. And this pressure is not just coming from concerned parents or public health professionals and activists; in British Columbia it is being led by the teaching profession and in Ontario by the provincial government itself (Mackie, 2004; BCTF, 2004).

Shaping America's Youth is a corporate social innovation that may evoke less skepticism than menu changes at McDonald's. A coalition of health associations and corporate sponsors endorsed by the U.S. Surgeon General, Shaping America's Youth (www.shapingamericasyouth.com) aims to create a one-stop shop for information and advice on healthy lifestyles and nutrition. Corporate sponsors include Nike and the Campbell Soup Company — both of whom have a commercial stake in the health and well-being of young people, but who may have a somewhat less controversial claim to be interested in the welfare of their customers.

These innovations — in menus and social partnerships — are of course very welcome. They demonstrate some hope for modifying consumer behaviour, using the broad and extensive reach of the fast-food corporations and major brands. However, it remains to be seen whether such measures result in significant reductions in the consumption of takeaway pizzas, burgers, and French fries, washed down with liberal quantities of soda. Ultimately, these products, which represent the best sources of revenue, are backed by multi-billion-dollar marketing and advertising budgets. So they are unlikely to be eschewed by corporations that depend on them for their commercial viability. We may need to look elsewhere for signs pointing to a radically different and altogether more ingenious future. And here the most interesting innovations seem to be very close to the values and concerns of increasing numbers of socially and environmentally aware end-consumers.

As public trust in food quality and safety decreases, the desire for individual consumers to feel more directly linked to the sources of their groceries and produce has increased. This trend can be coupled with the desire of many consumers for more convenient retail, home delivery, and internet-based shopping services, and for them to see a closer connection between what they eat and where it comes from. The result is a booming business opportunity for suppliers, distributors, and retailers of certified organic and fair-traded foods in both the developed and the developing world.

Worldwide there are about 23 million hectares of land under organic management, and in North America about 1.5 million hectares (0.25 percent of the total agricultural land). It may be noted that Austria has the highest percentage of organic arable land with 20,000 farms and 10 percent of total agricultural output organic. Worldwide sales of organic products are estimated at US$20 billion, mostly in the U.S., E.U., and Japan. Sales in the U.S. are now in excess of US$6 billion (Altieri & Nicholls 2004).

Canada has seen 20 percent annual growth in retail sales of organic products, and as of 2001 had 2,230 producers working on 340,000 hectares of land — just under one percent of the total number of farms in Canada. This level of growth is expected to continue for at least the next five years (AAFC, 2002). At the processing and retail level, British Columbia-based Nature's Path Foods has managed to carve out a CAN$100 million business in organic breakfast cereals, 60 percent of which are exported to the U.S.

One of the most interesting and commercially successful organic food retailers in the U.S.A. (and recently established in Canada) is Whole Foods. The Whole Foods story is one of significant social and commercial innovation and is set out in Box 5 below.

WHOLE FOODS: THE WORLD'S FIRST ORGANIC MEGA-CORPORATION

Whole Foods, started in 1980 by Craig Weller, Mark Skiles, and John Mackey in Austin, Texas, is now the world's largest natural-foods retailer. Mackey continues to serve as the president and CEO, and has clearly been highly successful with annual sales of US$3.1 billion in 2003. Through growth and acquisitions, it has risen to number 508 on Fortune's list of largest businesses in America, with impressive profit margins and shareholder returns. In 2004, the company operated in 158 stores in North America and the U.K.

Whole Foods does not carry any products with trans fats, artificial preservatives, sweeteners, or colours. They have branded the supermarket chain around customer trust for quality, unadulterated food. People are willing to pay a premium for their groceries as long as they feel confident that Whole Foods has done their "nutrition homework" for them. Traditionally, people associate natural foods stores with the alternative lifestyle crowd, but paradoxically, you are more likely to spot trendy yuppies than hippies at Whole Foods, which is gaining mainstream popularity, albeit with a more affluent set.

Values-based organizations can take a beating from their activist customers and suppliers who project their values on to the company. But Mackey doesn't feel pressure for Whole Foods to be anything other than what it is, and he unabashedly touts capitalism as the avenue for Whole Foods' success. *"It's interesting, that when an idea that began on the fringe hits the mainstream, it's no longer hip and cool, even if it preserves its integrity and values. America has a love affair with small business, the Jimmy Stewart, 'It's a Wonderful Life' kind of businesses. But when they get to be big, they're no longer good, they must be evil"* (quoted from Gertner, 2004). Mackey argues for a "stakeholder approach" to business where customers and employees come before shareholders, contending that with satisfied stakeholders, good returns will follow. He also takes a longer-term view than quarterly earnings targets, but it is tough to say whether shareholders would provide space for this without confidence in the company's ability to perform well in the market (Laing, 2004; Gertner, 2004; Whole Foods, 2004).

In Canada, grocery delivery services are gaining in popularity. Grocery Gateway in Ontario started in 1998, and by 2004 maintained a fleet of 140 trucks and 280,000 square feet (26,000 square metres) of warehouse space. Grocery Gateway carries a reasonable range of organic options within its mainstream grocery menu. In contrast, Vancouver-based Small Potatoes Urban Delivery (SPUD), is a highly innovative, *completely* organic grocery delivery service developed by David van Seters. We describe SPUD's contribution to food business ingenuity below in Box 6.

LOCAL ORGANIC FOOD DELIVERED DIRECT TO YOUR DOOR

David van Seters wanted to start a business to prove you can be profitable while simultaneously adding value to the community and the environment. So that is what he set out to do by creating Small Potatoes Urban Delivery (SPUD), an organic grocery delivery service based in Vancouver, BC. SPUD started with just nine customers in 1998, and has since grown to serve more than 5,000 in 2004.

SPUD sources as many products as possible locally, especially for the strictly organic produce they sell. This has been a process of building relationships with local farmers: starting with five farms, by 2004 SPUD had supply agreements with sixty-two farms, guaranteeing farmers a market for their crops. This process has been facilitated to a large extent by another Vancouver-based company called Discovery Organics. Discovery acts as a broker between the farmer and the buyers, thereby better matching supply with demand and ensuring that the farmers get a fair price for their crops.

SPUD's local sourcing policy stimulates the local economy, and also reduces fossil fuel emissions generated from shipping. They estimate that the average distance a SPUD item travels is 760 kilometres, compared with 2,500 kilometres at conventional grocery stores. Equally important to the business model is the fresh (and therefore more nutritious) produce that customers enjoy, never more than 24 hours from arrival in the warehouse to

---

shipment to the customer. Customers are educated along the way by SPUD's reporting of the "food miles" associated with each order's invoice. Finally, because of the pre-order nature of a delivery service (and therefore known demand for each product), wastage of produce at SPUD is around 1–2 percent compared with 10–20 percent at conventional grocery stores (van Seters, 2004; www.spud.ca).

Charles Mann has written extensively about the possibilities of marketing produce from self-reliant farmers and co-operatives in the developing world. In a report for the Ford Foundation, Mann (2004) describes how Mexican entrepreneur Ramírez Leyva opened a store called Itanoní ("maize flower"), selling tortillas made from traditional maize varieties grown in Oaxaca. Leyva was concerned about the near-disappearance of such varieties in Mexico's food outlets, and was determined to do something about it, describing the dangers of such genetic erosion as a "cultural tragedy." Mann explains how in gastronomic terms, it was "as if all the craft-baked bread in France had been replaced by packaged white bread." Leyva's long-term aspirations are to open a franchise business for traditional tortillas in Mexico, and then later in the rest of North America, as part of an aggressive, commercial claiming back of the gastronomic and nutritional space currently occupied by fast-food outlets across the industrialized world.

Mann sees five principal means by which agrodiversity projects can be supported: i) effective labelling; ii) crop improvement; iii) the removal of biodiversity-damaging incentives to agriculture; iv) the payment of small farmers for their services in biodiversity protection and enhancement; and v) the increase of social capital and strong networks among producers and promoters of foods produced in a socially and environmentally beneficial way. We believe that important as the structural and economic reforms may be over time, it is the marketing and social innovation that may be the most important factors in the short term.

Labelling has long been at the heart of the GM/GE versus organic debate. Should producers of GE crops be forced to label their produce even though there is evidence this will worry

IMPORTANT AS THE STRUCTURAL AND ECONOMIC REFORMS MAY BE OVER TIME, IT IS THE MARKETING AND SOCIAL INNOVATION THAT MAY BE THE MOST IMPORTANT FACTORS IN THE SHORT TERM.

"uninformed" consumers? Why should organic or fair-trade retailers have to pay for certifications and labels for differentiation purposes while the larger players remain quiet about their food ingredients?

Organic food labelling has been in existence for a relatively long time, and in some jurisdictions such as the European Union it is formally regulated. Fair-trade certification is a rather more recent innovation, starting in Europe in the late 1980s. But already it is proving to be successful. The Fairtrade Labelling Organizations International (FLO) sets worldwide fair-trade standards for certification and works with more than 800,000 producers and their dependents in more than forty countries to benefit from fair-trade labelling. FLO (www.fairtrade.net) helps consumers distinguish fairly traded products in the marketplace through the provision and monitoring of a logo or seal offered to traders who buy from registered co-operatives in developing countries and abide by fair-trade criteria. Food products that can be certified include coffee, tea, cocoa, honey, sugar, rice, fresh fruit, and juices.

According to FLO, worldwide purchases of fair-trade produce increased 42.3 percent between 2002 and 2003, with

83,000 tonnes of produce shipped. The highest market penetration is in Switzerland, where the population spent more than €10 per head on fair-traded produce in 2002. In Canada, the FLO affiliate is TransFair, whose logo guarantees consumers that their coffee, tea, cocoa, and sugar originate from a monitored supply chain in Latin America, Africa, and Asia (www.transfair.ca). Again, some of the brand barons are beginning to catch on to the trends. In April 2004, Giant Food announced a partnership with TransFair U.S.A. to sell five varieties of fair-traded coffee in all 199 Giant and Super G stores in the U.S.

These stories complete our tour of technological and social innovation in the "downstream" parts of the food value chain. As may be readily observed, some of the most interesting experiments are those featuring a high level of connectivity between producers and consumers united by a desire for nutritional, environmental, and social quality. In this regard, they echo some of the experiences and motivations of the early co-operative movement — the point at which we started our exploration of the role of ingenuity and innovation in the food business.

Let us now try to draw some general conclusions about where the food business may be headed, and what might be the opportunities for reconciling the competing needs of public and corporate interests in coming years.

CONCLUSIONS

At the beginning of this chapter we posed two important questions for the future of the food business.

- How can we ensure that technological and social ingenuity in food production and distribution promotes the common good: i.e., the interests of ordinary people and the natural environment?

- How can we strike the optimum balance between the common good and the need for private sector organizations to create economic value from food production and distribution?

Also, in the course of our exploration of the business case for feeding the future, we described a range of serious critiques of multi-national food businesses, and we have raised a number of issues surrounding the power and influence of the "brand barons" who dominate the fast-food and grocery businesses. There are no simple answers to the critiques. However shrill and simplistic they may appear, they do touch on profound and widely held concerns about the quality and availability of food today and in a future world of 9 billion people. They also relate to how we see the role of corporations in a globalized world. Opinions remain sharply divided on this broader political issue.

It is our belief that corporations and the people who run them are not inherently malevolent, but they do work with a framework that forces a certain style of decision-making: invariably to satisfy the very short-term needs of consumers and investors. And there is nothing shorter term driving the food business than the seemingly universal desire for individuals to get a candy fix, or a

TYPICALLY, THE MARKET DOES NOT REWARD COMPANIES THAT TAKE LONG-TERM, PRINCIPLED DECISIONS UNLESS THERE IS VERY CLEAR EVIDENCE OF LIKELY COMMERCIAL PAY-OFF.

fast-food fix. In contrast, there is nothing longer term than the painstaking process of educating and reinforcing the changed behaviours required for promoting wholesome food, healthy lifestyles, and a cleaner, safer environment for future generations.

Typically, the market does not reward companies that take long-term, principled decisions unless there is very clear evidence of likely commercial pay-off. Of course co-operatives, small companies, and privately held companies have more freedom in this regard, and that is why we may be seeing so many interesting innovations arising from such businesses.

So we return to the big questions, which speak to how we will achieve a generally better balance through technological *and social* ingenuity through businesses of all types in the future.

In terms of technological ingenuity, we have seen that a good deal of current research and development energy is being expended on genetically modified foods. This is occurring against a background of highly skeptical consumers, lukewarm retailers, and divergent views among producers and brand owners. These stakeholders — particularly consumers — are already highly sensitized to problems of food quality following the food scandals of recent years.

In contrast to this push for technological solutions to the world's growing need for nutritional and wholesome foods, we are seeing the emergence of social innovation in the production, distribution, and marketing of foods that are organic, fair traded, or otherwise nutritionally, environmentally, and socially wholesome.

The emergence of new value-based networks of like-minded producers and consumers may not yet represent a threat to the brand barons who dominate food sales through conventional supermarkets, grocery stores, and (increasingly) on-line retailers. Nevertheless, it is possible to conceive of growing opportunities for mainstream food corporations if they make appropriate adjustments to their practices. Here we may point to beacons like Unilever — a company that appears strategically committed to sustainable fisheries. And we may reference firms like DuPont and Danone that are treading extremely cautiously down the path of genetically modified produce and crops, seeking to take the public, and even the new networks of concerned producers and consumers, along with them.

Larger, more enlightened businesses — and we must hope some will be Canadian — may reconcile their desire to profit through technological innovation with the desire of consumers to connect more closely with the food they eat. Such a reconciliation will undoubtedly be based on new dialogues and new understandings between producers and consumers — in both the developed and the developing world. It may also be based on novel partnerships with the formal co-operative sector and organic, fair-trade, and other civil society organizations — like Unilever's with WWF. It may include myriad partnerships between development agencies and small farmers, small producer co-operatives, and

WILL CANADIAN CORPORATIONS BE LEADERS OR FOLLOWERS IN THE TWENTY-FIRST CENTURY'S FOOD BUSINESS?

other small self-reliant food businesses that will comprise a vital part of feeding the future, sustainably and equitably. Some corporations already know how to convene dialogues and build novel partnerships; others have yet to learn. Which companies can better adjust to this learning-curve may ultimately decide who profits most in the coming decades. Perhaps corporate food businesses can all learn something from Honey Care Africa, and from the history of the co-operative movement.

Enormous value can be gained from the nineteenth- and early-twentieth-century lessons. But we may have to go back to school to relearn some of those old lessons. To feed a world of

9 billion people will require a renewed spirit of institutional co-operation and partnership. We will need a global understanding of the common good. What risk levels will the future tolerate? Who will decide? And who will benefit from the decisions? Enlightened corporations will answer some of the questions posed in this chapter. But they are unlikely to provide all the answers without help from other actors. Social, rather than technological, innovations may in the end determine how we feed the future.

And will Canadian corporations be leaders or followers in the twenty-first century's food business? The stakes are undoubtedly high. In 2002, Canada's exports of fish and seafoods were worth CAN$4.7 billion; exports of grains, oilseeds, and related products were worth CAN$7.6 billion. It remains an open question whether these exports can be protected and enhanced through effective branding of Canadian agricultural and fisheries produce. The branding would have to be trustworthy in the fullest sense, certifying high-quality, wholesome foods produced with high standards of environmental and social care. The alternative to "full-trust branding" would be for the country and its leading agricultural and fisheries producers to slip into lowest cost or commodity status — a reputational niche from which it would be very difficult to escape. The time to choose the best brand position for Canada is now.

A HISTORY OF FOOD (CONTINUED)

1972 | Dr. Robert Atkins publishes his influential bestselling book *Dr. Atkins' Diet Revolution*, promoting his high-fat, low-carbohydrate weight-loss diet. A later edition of the book, *Dr. Atkins' New Diet Revolution*, will be published in the 1990s and be one of the fifty highest-selling books of all time, with sales in excess of 10 million copies.

1974 | The canola plant is invented by University of Manitoba scientist Baldur Stefansson, who breeds it from the ancient crop of rapeseed. His new plant is crucial to agricultural history because the high levels of erucic acid and glucosinates found in rapeseed are health hazards.

LATE 1970s | Danish scientists lead an expedition to Northern Greenland to compare the health effects of the diets of Greenland Inuit and Danes. They discover that, despite a very high fatty diet, Greenlanders have a much lower incidence of heart disease than Danes. They postulate that this reduction is linked to the high consumption of omega-3 fatty acids, found in the fish of the Greenlanders' diet. This is the first direct link between omega-3 fatty acids and beneficial health effects. Today, omega-3 is thought to have a wide range of beneficial health effects.

1981 | Bobby Sands, a jailed member of the Irish Republican Army, launches a hunger strike to protest his treatment in prison. In a test of wills with British Prime Minister Margaret Thatcher, Sands refuses to eat until five demands are met, including the right to wear civilian clothes rather than a prison uniform. Thatcher refuses to give in to the protest, and Sands dies after sixty days without food.

1982 | Former Black Sabbath front man John Michael Osbourne, a.k.a. Ozzy, bites a head off a bat that is thrown onstage at a concert in Des Moines, Iowa.

1984 | A poor harvest and civil war put over 6 million Ethiopians in danger of starvation. Although the impending disaster is widely reported, Western governments, suspicious of the country's Marxist rulers, are slow to provide aid, even though Europe experiences a bumper crop and has excess food in storage. Eventually, international attention to the looming disaster — spearheaded by singer Bob Geldof — prompts a wide-scale response and donations are sent. But these efforts are too late to save over one million Ethiopians from starvation.

▼ CONTINUED ON PAGE 258

BETWEEN FEAST AND FAMINE: FIXING GLOBAL TRADE

SYLVIA OSTRY

EDITORS' INTRODUCTION

There was a time when a meeting of the World Trade Organization (WTO) was not a reason for spontaneous protest. But that changed in November 1999, when somewhere between 30,000 and 60,000 protesters descended on Seattle, Washington.

Before the talks there began, it was clear that the Seattle meeting would feature friction between different visions of international trade. But no one, not even the protest organizers, predicted the sheer number of people who would show up to register their displeasure. The protesters represented a broad group of disaffected constituencies: labour, environmentalists, farmers, students. And some, a small minority, came for the sheer thrill of causing a ruckus.

The volume of dissent took Seattle police by surprise, who called in National Guardsmen. What resulted was a pitched battle with the protesters to control the Seattle downtown. Thousands of protesters spontaneously organized to "take" certain crucial blocks, using their numbers to cause congestion and force the WTO proceedings to grind virtually to a halt. The police fired tear gas and concussion grenades to clear the streets, but the waves of protesters were undeterred; some of the more prepared activists themselves donned gas masks and threw the tear-gas canisters back. Confusion reigned, with sixty-eight people arrested and 7-p.m.-to-dawn curfew three nights in a row.

The protests seemed to represent the genuine anger at organizations like the WTO and their power to enforce binding commitments on elected governments. One of the more articulate protesters, Paul Hawken, summarized the effect of the draft resolutions that were to be tabled at the WTO meeting:

> Farmers who have spent thousands of years growing crops in a valley in India could, within a decade, be required to pay for their water. They could also find that they would have to purchase seeds containing genetic traits their ancestors developed, from companies that have engineered the seeds not to reproduce unless the farmer annually buys expensive chemicals to restore seed viability.

The central role of agriculture and water in this dispute, and the view that the WTO represents the interests of the powerful few over the rights of the powerless many, is a common feature of protest today at most WTO meetings. But one aspect of that debate is rarely or inadequately discussed. And that is the role of agricultural trade subsidies, a potentially more distressing effect when viewed in terms of the human suffering that it has caused.

As Sylvia Ostry argues in this chapter, subsidies to farmers in developed countries have had a devastating impact on the developing world. Subsidized food is dumped into developing countries, undercutting the incomes of the poorest farmers, who in turn have no access to export into the protected markets of the developed world. The persistence of this trade imbalance, which has caused so much hardship and which has been so difficult to disentangle, is perhaps the greatest failing of the WTO. And few people are better qualified to explain the background than Sylvia Ostry, whose past experience has given her a unique window on trade relations. She was formerly Canada's Deputy Minister for International Trade as well as an Expert Adviser to the Commission on Transnational Corporations of the United Nations and a member of the Board of Distinguished Advisors for the Center for the Study of Central Banks.

INTRODUCTION

After the Second World War, the United States took the leading role in building a new trading system. Memories of the fierce protectionist battles of the 1930s, which had contributed to the Great Depression, the rise of the Nazis and fascism, and the war, were still vivid. Cordell Hull, Roosevelt's Secretary of State, was convinced that freer international trade was essential to prosperity and to the maintenance of world peace. Aided by the British, the Americans intended to create a trio of international institutions to govern the international economy: the International Monetary Fund (IMF), the International Bank for Reconstruction and Development (World Bank), and the International Trade Organization. The International Trade Organization was still-born, but a part of it — the General Agreement on Tariffs and Trade (GATT) — survived and thrived. GATT was launched in 1947, and signed by twenty-three "contracting parties." In the 1950s and 1960s, it oversaw successive rounds of negotiations aimed at reducing the border barriers of the 1930s. This ushered in the "golden age" of trade liberalization as trade fed growth and growth fed trade.

GATT was not based on a textbook model of *free trade* but on the promotion of *freer* trade over time. The negotiators made a number of compromises when writing the rules so there were many exceptions and exceptions to exceptions. Politicians certainly recognized that so-called free trade was not popular with the general public because the voice of the losers is always much louder than that of the larger and more diffuse winners in all trade deals. Also, over time, the compromises of the original GATT deal began to undermine the institution like termites in the basement.

The onset of a different mode of trade negotiations began in the 1970s with the Tokyo Round of negotiations. The mid-decade OPEC oil shock had produced a new economic malady, "stagflation," and a marked increase in "new protectionism," such as voluntary export restraints, as well as an explosion of subsidies to support declining industries, especially in Europe. The weak dispute settlement mechanism in GATT added to American frustration with the system. The Tokyo Round began to move the trade policy agenda inside the border, so that domestic policies with trade spillovers were on the table. But agriculture wasn't on the table yet. That had to wait until the Uruguay Round.

Agriculture was excluded for the first seven GATT negotiations. In the Uruguay Round — the eighth negotiation, which was launched in 1986 — agriculture was not only included but dominated the dynamic of the launch and almost torpedoed the agreement. And in the current negotiation — the Doha Development Round — it has nearly paralyzed the players and threatens to transform the rules of the game.

In this chapter I shall first deal with the background to the Uruguay Round and the results that transformed the global trading system, including the unintended consequences. I'll then turn to the Doha negotiations and the impact of the mid-term ministerial meeting in Cancun. I will conclude with an exploration of the main issues that should be covered in a ministerial agreement.

AGRICULTURE AND THE GATT PRE-URUGUAY

There are many "explanations" for why agriculture has been so difficult to reform and why it has remained protected for so long. The weather subjects farming to considerable variability, so governments respond by intervention. Agriculture is less adaptive than other industries because of income and price inelasticities, which also encourage intervention. Farmers are dispersed in most countries, so farm organizations each exert pressure on a wide range of political representatives. And the origins of our society may be traced to agriculture. Farmers and farming evoke a powerful nostalgia. These "explanations" are partly myth, partly reality. In any case, they have worked for a long time in rich countries. (Poverty-stricken, often starving, or landless farmers in poor countries are quite another matter that we'll get to later.)

The European Community (EC) best exemplifies the power of the agriculture lobby. In the 1957 Treaty of Rome, the clause on the adoption of a common agricultural policy (CAP) is so important that it comes right after the clauses establishing the customs union.[1] It is noteworthy that the second section of the CAP clause ensures "a fair standard of living for the agricultural community, in particular increasing the individual earnings of persons engaged in agriculture."

At the time of the Treaty of Rome, the agricultural work force was 30 percent of the total labour force of the six founder states (France, Germany, Italy, Belgium, the Netherlands, and Luxembourg).[2] But as farming became consolidated and productivity greatly improved (the CAP included a significant commitment to promoting technical progress), the number of smaller farmers diminished. Increasing production became a problem and efforts to reform the price supports failed.

France designed the CAP, and Germany was to provide the internal market to balance the German manufacturing advantage so feared by the French. But the German market did not suffice, so the European Community turned to exports. In 1979, the Community became a net exporter of temperate foodstuffs. But exports required subsidies because of oversupply engendered by high internal prices. And so by the 1980s, the Community's insulation from world trade ended. As one expert put it, "the moral obscenity of food mountains in the developed world, contrasting with shortages and famines in the developing world" became more and more apparent.[3] This helped to launch the Uruguay Round.

The Community was not alone in protecting agriculture. The GATT included looser rules for agriculture than other industries. But that hardly mattered. Countries found ways around them. As one legal expert has noted, "If governments lack the political will to obey the rules, the rules will not work, no matter how well they are crafted."[4] But even that was not enough. The United States secured a GATT waiver for its agricultural support schemes. Switzerland went one better: it exempted its agricultural sector through special arrangements in its Protocol of Accession.[5] And Japan just decided to ignore the GATT altogether in devising its wide range of restrictions.

But the honeymoon ended in the early 1980s. The Americans had tolerated the CAP in its early days but as its exports to the EC diminished and as EC exports flourished and, indeed, penetrated the American market, anger at the "unfair competition" of subsidized products exploded. Moreover, budget costs for agricultural support escalated. All these factors had one cause — or so the U.S. government decided: the CAP. The CAP had to be reformed. A multilateral trade negotiation was the answer.

Much easier said than done.

THE URUGUAY ROUND AND AFTER

The Uruguay Round was launched in Punta del Este in

September 1986 after the United States began calling for negotiations in 1981. The European Community was opposed, for one very clear reason: agriculture was to be a centrepiece of the Round. The Community dragged its feet with elaborate manoeuvres, not only in the GATT but also at the Organization for Economic Co-operation and Development (OECD) and the Economic Summits.[6] But the Community was not alone in trying to block negotiations. A group of developing countries, tagged the G10 hardliners, wanted to prevent a negotiation round, not because of agriculture (some of them, such as Brazil, were big agriculture exporters) but for quite unrelated reasons — the so-called "new issues."

The new issues were new in two fundamental ways. The original GATT covered only trade in goods and primary products. Trade in services would have been an oxymoron in 1947. And intellectual property, another of the new issues, was covered by the World Intellectual Property Organization, a U.N. institution. But the new issues — services, intellectual property, and investment — were also new in an even more fundamental sense: They would involve negotiations on what were traditionally considered *domestic* policies in GATT.

The Tokyo Round's tentative first steps became a marathon. The G10 hardliners were led by Brazil and India, both pursuing highly interventionist and protectionist industrial development policies. For the U.S.A., however, these issues were crucial in sustaining domestic support for the multilateral system. Their service sectors were world leaders, and the same was true in investment and technology. U.S. multinationals controlled over 40 percent of the world's stock of foreign investment at the outset of the 1980s. While every other OECD country was in deficit, the American technology balance of payments surplus reached well over $6 billion. The business advisory committees to the U.S. Trade Representative were very clear: Without the new issues they would prefer a bilateral or regional approach. And they didn't just talk the talk, they walked the walk. They organized business lobbies in a range of other countries to pressure their governments to support the inclusion of the new issues.[7] In Europe this probably helped to stop the Commission's foot-dragging. In any event, the Uruguay Round was launched with the inclusion of agriculture, services, trade-related intellectual property, and, though with a more restricted scope than the Americans desired, trade-related investment measures. It also included, of course, all the agenda items of traditional rounds, such as tariffs and trade rules.

The negotiations turned out to be as torturous as the launch. The Uruguay Round almost collapsed at a mid-term ministerial meeting in Montreal in 1988. It was supposed to be concluded by 1990 at a Brussels ministerial. It dragged on until December 1993 and the final agreement was signed in April 1994 at Marrakesh. The *Economist* headline was apt: "Can it be true?"[8] At the heart of the problem was the transatlantic divide over agriculture. By the onset of the 1990s, the G10 had disappeared, decimated by the debt crisis of the 1980s and chastened by the IMF and the World Bank. So the main players, the EC and the United States, were the key to an agreement for the Round as a whole. The French opposition to any reform of the CAP (a position supported by Germany) was finally overcome in Washington with the so-called Blair House Accord on agriculture between the EC and the U.S.A. at the end of 1992. That some countries were prepared to bring down the entire multilateral system for the shrinking population of farmers is evidence, once more, of agriculture's unique nature.

The Agreement on Agriculture (AOA) was mainly an agreement on rules. It was one step on the road to incorporating agriculture into the trading system. But the rule-making achievement was "balanced" by limited trade liberalization.

The AOA covered three domains: market access, export competition, and domestic support. Market access required countries to convert all existing nontariff measures into tariffs, bind these tariffs, and agree to a modest schedule of reduction. So OECD tariffs remained high, especially in several important

THAT SOME COUNTRIES WERE PREPARED TO BRING DOWN THE ENTIRE MULTILATERAL SYSTEM FOR THE SHRINKING POPULATION OF FARMERS IS EVIDENCE, ONCE MORE, OF AGRICULTURE'S UNIQUE NATURE.

sectors such as dairy, grains, sugar, and sweeteners. Non-OECD countries tend to have higher average tariffs, although often applied rates are lower than those bound. On the whole, it's fair to say that the Uruguay Round did not result in any significant liberalization.

In the export subsidies domain, the AOA prohibited any new export subsidies and any increase in other export assistance. But these curbs are trivial compared to existing expenditures. A recent estimate of the OECD states that the world's richest countries spent more than $257 billion in agricultural subsidies (including export and domestic) in 2002 — little changed from earlier years.[9] Most of the money was spent on dairy, beef, cereals, and sugar. The European Union (EU) is the big subsidy spender while the U.S.A. prefers export credits and other aids. But in 2002, although in the midst of the new Doha negotiations, the Americans passed a new farm bill that increased direct payments.

On domestic support, the AOA was very complex. It bears no resemblance to the subsidies agreement for industry. It created a quite new concept — the Aggregate Measure of Support (AMS) — and set bound limits of subsidies for each country. Reduction commitments for the AMS were minimal and applied to payments deemed trade distorting — the amber box. The blue box contained so-called decoupled payments that were considered not to encourage production and so were not required to be reduced, and the green box payments were completely exempt. Additional loopholes meant that a large part of expenditure on domestic programs remained virtually unconstrained by the rich countries.

While the AOA included a number of other rules, one in particular deserves mention here because it is emblematic of the broader thrust of the Uruguay Round mentioned earlier — the shift to domestic policy embedded in the new issues. The Sanitary and Phytosanitary measures (SPS) allow countries to block imports so as "to protect human, animal or plant life or health." The measure must be based on scientific principles and applied on a non-discriminatory basis. The SPS, in effect, spells out the procedural dimensions of the original GATT exceptions listed in Article XX. The agreement encourages the use of international standards, and, if stricter standards are used, scientific justification is required.

The SPS has generated a good deal of litigation and debate (on GMOs, for example), but the relevant point here is the shift to positive regulation and to legalization. The Southern countries often lack the technical, scientific, and legal capacities that are essential if they wish to overcome barriers to higher value-added products in food and agriculture.

But SPS is only one part of the broader transformation. The new issues have one common characteristic. They involve not the border barriers of the original GATT but domestic regulatory and legal systems embedded in the institutional infrastructure of the economy. Thus, for example, the barriers to access for service providers stem from laws, administrative actions or regulations that impede cross-border trade and investment. Intellectual property negotiations covered not only comprehensive standards for domestic laws but detailed provisions for enforcement.

So the Uruguay Round concluded with what I've called a North–South Grand Bargain. It was essentially an implicit deal: the reform and liberalization of OECD agriculture and textile and clothing markets for the inclusion of the new issues. Also, as virtually a last-minute piece of the deal, it created a new institution, the World Trade Organization (WTO), with the strongest dispute settlement mechanism in the history of international law but with virtually no executive or legislative authority. The evidentiary-intensive dispute system requires highly expert legal and technical human capital. More broadly, the South side of the deal requires major institutional and systemic upgrading and change in most Southern countries. These changes, even where they are feasible, will take time and cost lots of money. Implementation will thus involve considerable investment with uncertain medium-term results. A Grand Bargain or a Bum Deal?

The transformation of the system brought by the Uruguay Round had two significant unintended consequences. One is a serious North–South divide in the WTO. While the South is hardly homogeneous, there is a broad consensus that the system is profoundly asymmetrical and must be rebalanced — although there is as yet no consensus as to how this might be accomplished. Nonetheless the divide is amply evident. The debacle of Seattle in 1999 ended in the walkout of virtually all the developing countries. It's more than symbolic that the outcome of the 2001 ministerial meeting in Doha was termed the "Doha Development Agenda" (DDA). Both the EC and the U.S.A. visited Africa to woo ministers, and the declaration repeatedly refers to technical assistance and capacity-building. Pushed by the successful NGO campaign about AIDS in Africa, the Americans even seemed willing to antagonize Big Pharma and provide some leeway on generic drugs for developing countries. So Doha was unique in its focus on the South. But, of course, agriculture was on the agenda in addition to issues of competition, investment, government procurement, and trade facilitation — new, new issues, so to speak. The ambitious target date of January 1, 2005, for the DDA's completion underlined the fact that this was Doha not Seattle. And, finally, the Doha Declaration was a masterpiece of creative ambiguity, so the devil remained in the details of the negotiations. We'll cover that when we get to Cancun, the next ministerial meeting.

But before then it's important to note the second and equally unintended consequence of the Uruguay Round — the rise in profile of the multinational enterprises due to their crucial role in securing inclusion of the new issues into the trade regime. It made them and the WTO a magnet for what came to be called the anti-corporate globalization movement of NGOs. This is not the place for a review of the history and role of the NGOs in the trading system,[10] nor is there a homogeneous set of institutions called NGOs. But the most visible movement at the outset of the 1990s was what I've called the mobilization networks, for whom a major object is to rally dissent at a specific event such as a WTO ministerial meeting or a G8 summit. The NGOs have effectively utilized the Internet, and thus have made the market for policy ideas and policy agendas contestable. They were the activists on TV in Seattle and Genoa. But dissent attracts violence and extremists, and after Genoa, where one protester was killed, and then, of course, after 9/11, there was need for a new strategy. While no coherent approach has yet become apparent, a move from dissent to dialogue and debate is now evident.[11] The newly favoured name appears to be "the global justice movement" —in other words, anti-poverty. Moreover, and of great significance, is the spread of global civil society to the South.[12] So, adieu, Seattle, and bonjour, Cancun.

CANCUN: CAN DO AND CAN'T DO

The Doha negotiations went nowhere. All deadlines were missed. There was no progress on the core issues of agriculture.

Evidently the ambiguous drafting was too clever by half. And that brings us to Cancun.

I was at Cancun, and when the meeting ended so abruptly I was swept by a strong sense of déjà vu all over again. Cancun was a mid-term ministerial meeting as was Montreal in the Uruguay Round in 1988. On the last morning of the Montreal meeting, around 6 a.m., the bleary-eyed negotiators were waiting for the EC and U.S. warriors who had been up all night dealing with agriculture. They arrived to announce it was too bad they hadn't reached an agreement, but that we should tidy up the other agenda items and finish the communiqué. A group of Latin American countries, headed by Brazil, refused: no agreement on agriculture, no agreement on anything. It was a moment of shock (and maybe awe for some others), but we handled it with great finesse by announcing that the meeting was adjourned and would be reconvened shortly in Geneva. No big headlines ensued.

My déjà vu soon dissipated. The North–South divide had taken a different shape. There appeared to be an axial shift in the political economy of policy-making that would require a fundamental reorientation of the players and the game. Two new coalitions of Southern countries were formed at Cancun. One, termed the G20, led by Brazil and India as well as China (the Big Three) and South Africa, included a number of Latin American countries. Its main focus at Cancun was agriculture, catalyzed by an unacceptable draft proposal from the U.S.A. and EU. The G20 seemed an unlikely coalition since it included countries with varying views on economic policy and, indeed, on agriculture. But it didn't collapse under pressure at Cancun, and, despite losing members because of American bilateral pressure, it has survived thus far. Its leader, Brazil, has succeeded in challenging the Free Trade Agreement of the Americas, to the chagrin of the United States. And India and China are now exploring a free trade agreement, as are India and Mercosur, a South American trade group.

The G20 was very active at the UNCTAD XI meeting at Sao Paulo in June 2004, when a South–South Round of negotiations was launched under special provisions of the original GATT in which developing countries provide trade preferences for products from other developing countries. This was underlined as another example of the "new geography" of the trading system by UNCTAD head Rubens Ricupero and the Brazilian president Luiz Inacio Lula da Silva.[13]

Indeed, the new geography was evident at Cancun in the formation of another collation — the G90. This included the poorest developing countries, mainly from Africa. After failing to convince the U.S.A. to eliminate cotton subsidies to help the poverty-stricken African exporters and to persuade the EU to remove the Singapore issues from the agenda, the G90 terminated the negotiations. It's important to note that at Cancun NGOs played a prominent role with respect to the G90. African NGOs were included in many official delegations, and they provided ongoing information as well as research and policy analysis. They had regular briefing sessions from officials and ministers. They (plus some Northern NGOs) could be described as a virtual secretariat launched by the Internet. But unfortunately there's not enough information to explore this important development in more depth.

The formation of Southern coalitions will undoubtedly change the dynamics of the Doha negotiations, especially but not only on agriculture. But the outcome at present is shrouded in a fog of uncertainty. The G20 was actively engaged in the bargaining over a "framework" agreement (a broad outline with minimal detail) before the 2004 summer break. This would, it was hoped, allow the real negotiations to start after the U.S. election and be concluded just a year later than the target date set at Doha. But there won't be another Blair House deal by the Big Two without the Big Three and perhaps the G90 as well. Indeed, the rich countries encourage splits between the G90 and other developing countries. And another group called FIPS (Five Interested Parties), which included the EU, the U.S.A., Brazil, India, and Australia (for the Cairns Group), played the lead role in negotiating the framework agreement. The geography certainly makes trade policy more complex!

Let me first sketch out some of the components of a desirable agreement on agriculture. But a WTO agreement alone could not deal with the issue of poverty in developing countries, especially in Sub-Saharan Africa. So I will conclude with a proposal for a pilot project under the rubric of improved "coherence" in international economic policy — one of the original objectives of the Uruguay Round.

DOHA AND AGRICULTURE

The outcome of the Uruguay Round proved to be very disappointing to Southern countries. Much rests on the outcome of Doha. The inadequate liberalization and the continuing impact of export subsidies and domestic support in the rich countries have greatly increased the pressure for reform. Of course, at the same time, the agricultural lobby has not gone away as the Farm Bill of 2002 in the United States so clearly demonstrates. Congress was hardly fixated on the WTO, and the Doha negotiations as domestic subsidies were increased.

As noted above, the failure at Cancun demonstrated that an accord of the Big Two will be difficult and the role of the Big Three will be significant. What is not clear is whether or how the poorest countries (the G90) can be integrated into the negotiations and the outcome so that the trading system will serve to reduce poverty and the marginalization of the poorest countries.

The EU's offer to eliminate all export subsidies would require what Pascal Lamy calls "parallelism" by others. This would involve American programs such as export credit and food aid, or Canadian institutions such as the Wheat Board (State Trading Enterprise).

Not on the table in Geneva is the issue of agriculture dumping. While the elimination of visible export subsidies would help, other forms of government intervention distort market

THE OUTCOME OF THE URUGUAY ROUND PROVED TO BE VERY DISAPPOINTING TO SOUTHERN COUNTRIES.

prices, as do the policies of the agribusiness oligopolies that dominate agricultural markets. These closed, often vertically integrated, markets are subject to no price competition or transparency. The impact on poor countries has been devastating. Some recent policy papers provide a number of proposals for consideration. What's not clear, however, is how they could be incorporated into the WTO.[14] The issue should be tackled by some of the injured countries, perhaps the G20. And it should be discussed as soon as possible since dumping continues to inflict damage. A related issue concerns low and falling commodity prices, especially of primary commodities. Past efforts to regulate prices failed dismally. But given the major structural changes in markets, a proposal at UNCTAD XI to establish a global task force on commodities suggests the issue has been revived.

In the area of domestic support (the amber, blue, and green boxes), a wide range of studies demonstrate that "box shifting" is ongoing. Indeed, some critics call this game "play boxes." Moreover, decoupling or direct income support can lead to more production. It is not the magic bullet the reformists assumed it to be at the end of the Uruguay Round.[15] Redesigning domestic support will be extremely contentious because it will significantly impact not only the configuration of the rural population, especially in Europe, but also other concerns, including the environment.

Since subsidies, export or domestic, are for the most part a luxury only rich countries can afford, it is the Southern countries that are the applicants. But market access, the third pillar of the AOA, is of interest to all participants. The OECD countries have argued strongly and cogently that liberalization of Southern markets is a key part of the Doha Round. Essential for an acceptable "balance of benefits," it is also of considerable benefit to the middle-income countries such as the G20.[16] There is general agreement that the poorest countries will not be required to provide reciprocal access. Market access is traditional trade territory, so one might assume that, after long and tough negotiations, a reasonably balanced agreement could be achieved. Considering the record of agricultural protectionism, that may be too optimistic. Certain commodities — sugar in the U.S.A. and Europe, for example — appear to be sacrosanct. And in countries like Japan, the entire political and social system is allegedly at stake. Some deals involving trade-offs between agriculture and other agenda items may be possible.

Market access includes tariffs and non-tariff barriers such as tariff rate quotas. And a very important potential import barrier for developing countries is the SPS. The fastest-growing markets for developing countries are high-value commodities such as fruits and vegetables and livestock products. The need for adequate technical and scientific resources to satisfy developed country regulatory standards is essential if these markets are to be tapped. This will require technical assistance as well as aid for institution-building in the poor countries. While there has been some modest increase in the WTO's resources for technical assistance and capacity building, an enormous gap remains between what is needed and what is available. More broadly, and more importantly, if the poorest marginalized countries are to be integrated into the trading system, a comprehensive program of rural development would be required. Let me conclude, then, with a brief account of a proposal to deal with poverty and agriculture.

CONCLUSION: A PILOT PROJECT FOR COHERENCE

It is usually forgotten that one of the goals of the Uruguay Round was to improve the coherence of international policies by establishing better linkages between the GATT, the World Bank, and the International Monetary Fund. After more than seven years' negotiations, the result was the largely rhetorical *Ministerial Declaration on the Contribution of the World Trade Organization to Achieving Greater Coherence in Global Economic Policymaking*. The declaration achieved little of any consequence.

This is hardly surprising. The origin of the coherence proposal was the serious current account imbalances of the first half of the 1980s and the rise of the American dollar that fanned the flames of protectionism in the U.S. Congress. "Coherence" was essentially a euphemism for curbing extreme swings in exchange rates, and the phrase "greater exchange rate stability" is highlighted in the ministerial declaration, although other examples of cooperation, for example developing countries' structural adjustment, were also mentioned.

Nothing need preclude the initiation of a joint WTO–World Bank pilot project on Sub-Saharan African agriculture: project as process, as it were. The case to be made for such a project is stark and clear: "Sub-Saharan Africa is the only region in the world where hunger and poverty will get worse if present trends continue."[17] Nearly 90 percent of Africa's poor work in agriculture. So there cannot be significant poverty reduction without a significant rise in agricultural productivity and growth.

Trade policy alone is not enough to enhance agricultural productivity in these countries. What is needed is a combination of trade policy and a comprehensive rural development policy that would vary from country to country, depending on domestic and local conditions. A recent OECD study, *Agriculture, Trade and Poverty*, notes, "To achieve the objectives of agricultural development and poverty alleviation, developing countries must design adequate domestic policies and investment programs in human capital, infrastructure, technology, regulation and expansion of land ownership by small producers and landless workers, and, in general promote the adequate functioning of product, factor, input and financial markets."[18] This is clear. But nothing can be done without the essential technical and financial aid.

While there are many poor farmers in many developing countries, the most marginalized countries in the world are African. The project would serve not just to provide a living laboratory but also analytical capital for policy innovation that could provide benchmarking for other countries. Private industry uses benchmarking for innovation, and so should governments. Policy innovation should be a crucial component for dealing with the complex and little-understood problem of African poverty. Economists today talk a great deal about the need for key institutions in the "third generation reform." But if we don't really understand how they were formed, we surely don't know how to transform them. It will be experimental — as is incremental innovation. And often the trial will create errors. Weak and corrupt state institutions, and elites with little interest in reform, present formidable challenges. The institutional economists stress "path dependency," in other words, the idea that over time there is a co-evolution of institutions, economic structures, and elite interests that define the path of development.[19] A new growth path will have to be created. Elites will have to be convinced that it is in their long-term interest.

The pilot project should include the WTO (and would require increased analytical research capability), the World Bank, and the new institution NEPAD (New Partnership for Africa's Development), established in 2001. It has received enthusiastic support from OECD countries and the G8 Summit. Prime Minister Blair, host of next year's summit, has promised to put Africa at the heart of the agenda. While NEPAD requires some institutional and legal strengthening,[20] it represents a new (for Africa) development outlook that supports international trade and investment as key engines of growth. And it accepts the new World Bank view of "ownership," that is, that development must be owned and managed by Africans in partnership with other agents. Finally, and most importantly, in the current context, NEPAD gives primary importance to agriculture. It states that "improvement in agricultural performance is a prerequisite of economic development on the continent."[21] Sounds just right. All that's needed is leadership from the other two partners.

A HISTORY OF FOOD (CONTINUED)

1986   In response to the plummeting numbers of whales due to overfishing, the International Whaling Commission bans all commercial whaling. Countries such as Japan continue to hunt whales, using a clause in the agreement that allows hunting whales for "scientific purposes."

1993   Dr. Robert Atkins dies in New York from head trauma after slipping on a sheet of ice and hitting his head on the pavement. Following his death, the *Wall Street Journal* prints a controversial story based on an autopsy report that claims the famous dietician weighed over 110 kilograms (250 pounds) at the time of his death — which at his height would have made him technically obese. It also reports that he suffered from high cholesterol, heart attacks, and heart disease. His widow, Veronica Atkins, calls those who leaked the report to the *Journal* "extremists," and claims that his weight and heart disease were not related to the Atkins diet.

1996   Monsanto Corporation begins the development of "Roundup Ready" canola, which is genetically modified to withstand the effects of the company's herbicide Roundup. In 2002, Monsanto will follow up with Roundup Ready wheat.

2000   Millions of cattle are slaughtered in Britain as an epidemic of mad cow disease (BSE) results in the deaths of over seventy people. The British government institutes a range of measures to prevent the further spread of BSE. The reforms include regulations to prevent cow and sheep carcasses from being fed to other cows.

2002   The red colobus becomes the first primate to be hunted to extinction for its meat. Given the rapid decline in numbers of African primates, it is likely not to be the last, however, as many of the primates in central and western Africa are threatened by the bush meat trade, a business that is worth over $500 million annually. Scientists warn that both gorillas and chimpanzees are likely to be extinct by 2020 if the bush meat trade is not significantly curtailed.

2003   Twenty percent of all adults in the United States over the age of twenty are obese. * Following increased awareness of the negative health consequences of trans fats, numerous large food companies move to eliminate these fats from their processed foods.

2004   McDonald's phases out its "supersized" meals.

REVITALIZING THE RANCH: A MEXICAN FARM STORY

MARK JUHASZ

EDITORS' INTRODUCTION

A good place to go to see the true effect of global trade policies is Lake Chapala, the largest lake in Mexico, in an area that throws into high relief the problems facing today's agricultural communities, including water scarcities, soil degradation, and poverty. But when Mark Juhasz, an environmental student at York University, travelled there to study these problems, he found to his surprise that the area was also a hotbed of innovative solutions.

Like many people, Juhasz knew the intellectual arguments about trade policies and agriculture that Sylvia Ostry outlines in the previous chapter. He knew that in Africa, trade policies have been blamed for keeping millions in poverty, causing peasant farmers' produce to compete with unnaturally low-priced food from developed countries. But to Juhasz, and to many of us, these arguments remained dry, statistical. He wanted to meet the people who had actually been affected by these trade policies, to see for himself what effects the global food market was having on farmers and how they chose to deal with them. So Juhasz decided to put a face on the food crisis. And he found that face in Mexico.

Mexican food production is integrally tied to its American and Canadian partners, so it's a very good place to see the immediate impact of global trade policies. Trade imbalances are, however, only one of the problems that Mexican farmers face on a daily basis. The growing influence of the agri-food companies and disputes over ever-decreasing quantities of water are also part of the changing landscape of Mexican agriculture. And those factors brought Juhasz to Lake Chapala and a place called the SEVA ranch.

Faced with every possible obstacle in a very unlikely place, he discovered that the SEVA ranch is a testament to ingenuity in action. Not only had the managers disavowed conventional farming techniques in favour of organic farming methods, but they were also finding innovative means for farmers to better manage their dwindling water supply. The farm has become a microcosm of various ingenious strategies to resist — or at least to regain control of — the changes that are being forced on small farmers around the world.

CHANGE HAPPENS in the most unlikely places. This time it's unfolding in the west-central region of Mexico, near Lake Chapala. The biggest natural body of water in the country, the lake lies at the heart of the state of Jalisco. The car I'm in bumps along a dusty road beside the lakeshore before turning on to a man-made ridge developed in the middle of the twentieth century to separate Lake Chapala from the agricultural plots of land that its waters fertilized. Now, however, the ridge is completely redundant. There's no water on either side of it because Lake Chapala has receded by over ten kilometres. Like so many things in this once fertile region, the lake is drying up.

This is not a small tragedy. Lake Chapala, and the Lerma River that feeds it, form the most important drainage basin in the country. One of Mexico's major agricultural regions, the river basin supports tens of millions of people. If you looked on a map, you would find Mexico City to the southeast and Guadalajara within the basin. Both these major cities are supported by the Chapala-Lerma watershed. However, the pressures of development are straining the quality and quantity of water, for human use as for the ecosystem at large. Large quantities of agrochemicals and industrial effluent flow into the lake from the Lerma River, threatening local fish and wildlife and endangering the agricultural industries in areas immediately surrounding the lake.

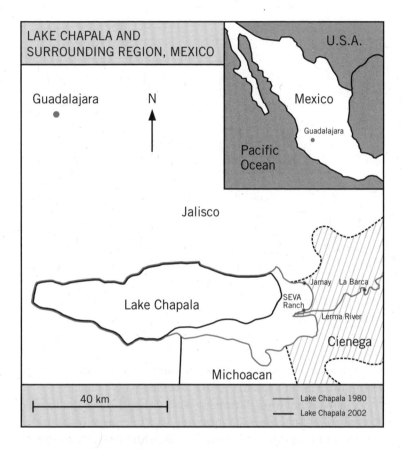

I had spent some time learning about these conditions before coming to this place, but being here turns prior thoughts into hard reality. As we pass the ejido (a small-holding) of Maltarana, I notice an old hacienda — a large, nineteenth-century Mexican ranch — that evokes the drama of Mexico's agrarian past. The crumbling yet still ornate remains of the building contrasts with the more modest homes in the town. The hacienda was built at the turn of the twentieth century, during the Porfiriato, the dictatorship of Porfirio Diaz, when the lands around here were dedicated to producing agricultural products for the large cities and for export. Today, the hacienda has been locked up against looters and curious children. Its immediate vicinity has been taken over by cows lazing in the afternoon sun and the field plots of small landholders, known as ejidatarios. There is little money to be made from small-scale ranching in these parts.

The road I'm on takes a sharp turn because the Lerma River fans out into a delta between the states of Jalisco and Michoacan. This region is generally referred to as the Cienega de Chapala. (Cienega means wetland in Spanish.) For centuries, the Cienega was a much larger area, covered by water and marshland. But like the lake itself, it too is shrinking. Advertising billboards mark the farmers' fields, promoting transnational companies like Monsanto and DuPont and their products. Around here, they're usually selling corn seed — typically, the latest generation of hybrids.

Finally I see the gates of the SEVA ranch, where a not-so-quiet agricultural revolution is taking place in Mexico.

I am here with a group of researchers from various countries to meet with the founders of this unique ranch in order to find out how they are coping with the monumental challenges facing the Chapala-Lerma region. The ranch is right at the end of the Lerma River, and the SEVA people view it as a microcosm of the various tensions, conflicts, and emerging solutions to the agricultural, water, and environmental crises paralleled in many parts of Mexico and the world. I find out later that SEVA is a Sanskrit word for "service without personal reward, but for social and ecological benefit"; however, for government registration purposes, SEVA officially stands for "Servicios Ecologicas Voluntarios Autonomous," which translates as Autonomous Voluntary Ecological Services.

In front of a large sprawling bungalow on the ranch there is a diverse garden of plants, rock formations, and rows of vegetables.

Raul Medina de Wit, a tall, gentle, yet intense man sporting a ponytail, comes out to greet us. His suntanned face shows that he spends a lot of time outside.

Raul explains the ranch's mandate to us. It was founded in 1986 to develop an alternative relationship with the land and with the region's health, agricultural, and educational systems — and

THE RANCH IS RIGHT AT THE END OF THE LERMA RIVER, AND THE SEVA PEOPLE VIEW IT AS A MICROCOSM OF THE VARIOUS TENSIONS, CONFLICTS, AND EMERGING SOLUTIONS TO THE AGRICULTURAL, WATER, AND ENVIRONMENTAL CRISES PARALLELED IN MANY PARTS OF MEXICO AND THE WORLD.

the local food markets. For starters, that means no pesticides and no artificial fertilizers. Theirs is an organic ranch. Raul explains that it covers more than a hundred hectares, with a central home property, the plots immediately in front dedicated to growing a broad variety of organic crops. Over the years, they've grown everything here from varieties of corn (including red, purple, blue, deep yellow, and white types), to garbanzo beans, safflower, sorghum, cucumber, lettuce, onions, Swiss chard, tomatoes, zucchini, wheat, pumpernickel, and, most recently, organic soya. Raul also notes that growing each crop organically poses a new set of challenges, challenges that we will all come to know in much greater detail.

In a sense, the ranch itself emerged organically. In the early 1980s, Lionel, a Cuban expatriate musician, met another musician named Michael in New York. In 1982, both came to Guadalajara, Mexico, about two hours from the SEVA ranch. Here they organized meditation classes and started developing the idea of an association dedicated to addressing health-related social and environmental issues. As more people attended their classes, a loose association formed, and eventually some members began to run a vegetarian restaurant in Guadalajara. Raul was the restaurant's administrator. Around the mid-1980s, a woman named Margarita met the group and was so impressed by their philosophy that she offered her family property in Maltarana, in the town of Jamay, as a home base. By 1986, this property became the SEVA ranch.

As the ranch grew, Raul learned as much as possible about farming, permaculture, and organic agriculture. He enrolled in courses to find out how to grow crops without the intensive agrochemicals that were standard in the area.[1] For example, the SEVA ranchers avoid burning cornhusks at harvest. Rather, they turn the cornhusks into mulch and then reapply it the field. One of their many innovations, this increases compost and soil fertility.

Raul admits that their organic ambitions — and finding new markets for their produce — were confounded by lack of experience and, more importantly, by resistance from government authorities. For example, when SEVA established a store in a neighbouring town to sell organic fertilizers derived primarily from garlic, the federal agricultural regulatory commission decided to label their product "toxic." For three years SEVA was unable to sell their organic fertilizers. Raul interpreted this as a sign that the regulatory commission was protecting the agrochemical industry from competition. Eventually, SEVA overcame the regulations and now sells their fertilizer. But Raul explains how every innovation meets up with these obstacles.

Relating his various stories, Raul leads us to SEVA's main house and its courtyard. A feast for the senses, it has a fountain in the centre, trickling with clean, refreshing water. There are numerous exotic plants, and two notable pets, a very proud and large Great Dane spread out on the veranda, and near to him, a colorful macaw studies the new faces. The main dining area and inner courtyard contain an enormous wall of books, spanning topics from arts to agriculture and zoology. There are also archaeological pieces, as well as paintings and sculptures throughout the main area of the house. The dinner we are served adds to our sensual pleasure: blue and purple tamales, calabaza flower soup, an avocado and mango layered torte, and juices from tamarind, melon, and lime fruits.

Given this cornucopia, it is hard not to think of the problems facing the region as a whole. Change has come to the Cienega over the past few decades, gradual and steady — but sometimes disruptive. Big agribusiness has forced many small farmers into other sectors of the economy. Economies of scale require large plots to make farming profitable. In the town of Jamay, where the SEVA ranch is located, many have left farming for work in the United States. Younger generations find agriculture less attractive than opportunities in the city. As a result, it becomes difficult to maintain a broad range of farms that can grow a diversity of crops.

Larger farms aim their crop cycles to the demands of international markets. The growing presence of exporting farms amongst producers still catering towards regional and national markets has resulted in increased competition for water. As a result, since the 1990s, farming communities throughout the Cienega have become acutely aware of the new importance of dealing with water in a much more organized way. This has led to a movement to protect and revitalize both the Lerma River and Lake Chapala.

EFFORTS TO MANAGE WATER

The Cienega and the town of Jamay form the delta of the Lerma River. This river is the main source of water for Lake Chapala. After decades of economic development, including expanding industrial, urban and agricultural infrastructure, the Cienega's watershed has diminished drastically and has become much more polluted.

Throughout the entire Lerma river watershed there are numerous sources of water extraction. The vast majority of this water is used for agro-industry. This is particularly true in the state of Guanajuato. Located within the watershed, the state is the traditional heartland of Mexican agriculture known as "El Bajio." This rich agricultural land has fermented everything from the War of Independence from Spain to parts of the Mexican revolution. The recent election of Guanajuato governor and rancher Vicente Fox marked the end of over seventy years of one-party rule in Mexico. More recently, Guanajuato has continued on the path towards agricultural modernization in a state known for its independent spirit and well-organized, powerful agricultural groups.

As the export agro-industry has grown in Guanajuato during the past thirty years, so has water demand. This is topped off with an intensively chemical agricultural model. The result is less water for the lower river basin states of Michoacan and Jalisco, and more chemically saturated water.

But there is another problem. Since the Mexican revolution, water in Mexico has been considered public property, which has made it much more difficult to regulate. Although the government has established groups such as The National Water Commission (NWC) — which has the unenviable responsibility of trying to manage the various conflicting interests of everyone who uses and needs water in Mexico — this has been a largely uphill battle. In the past, water was used extravagantly. And only recently has water pollution been taken seriously.

But as the water crisis in the Cienega continues, changes in attitude and behaviour are beginning. In some cases, these have good effects, such as innovations in efficiency, drip irrigation, and soil humidity retention technologies. However, the growing trend towards illegal extraction of water from underground aquifers is a major cause for concern.

SEVA has been working on ways to improve the water situation since the early 1990s — when water resources became particularly scarce in the Cienega region. Raul Medina and the rest of SEVA set out to discover ways to use their water more efficiently in agriculture. At the time, they were growing wheat on the ranch. But after research into the water requirements of wheat, SEVA decided to find other crops that use scarce water resources more efficiently. And so in 1992 they switched their crop base from wheat to crops like barley, garbanzo, and oilseeds, which require much less water to grow.

This experience in dealing with water issues on their own property put the SEVA collective in a good position to apply their learning to the region. By 1999, as the water crisis approached its height, Raul Medina had become spokesman for the agricultural users of the Lerma Watershed Council — a government-created regulatory and policy advisory body. Medina was also instrumental in the creation of GTEPAI (Grupo de Trabajo Especializado en Planeacion Agricola Integral), or Specialized Work Group on Integrated Agricultural Planning, which was founded in December 2000. Formed out of active agriculturalists from across the Lerma watershed, the group included representatives from the area around Lake Chapala and the Cienega. Their aim was to help solve the water and ecological problems in the river basin. Some of the initial questions that the group developed included: how can we make more efficient use of water? How can evaporation be reduced? How can organic matter and soil quality be improved? And, where can organic agriculture be applied?

To avoid an impending crisis, the group decided it was imperative to stop the seeding of over 200,000 hectares of land for one autumn-winter cycle. The other major challenge was to convert 80,000 hectares of land from water-hungry crops such as wheat to more water-efficient crops, just as SEVA itself had done years earlier. As Raul Medina proudly tells it, "We arranged for the planting of barley for the Mexican brewery industry, and found industrial counterparts to buy these 'new' crops from our farmers."[2] This was accomplished through a series of eight workshops in the states of Jalisco, Michoacan, and Guanajuato, where the majority of the agricultural users are located. Invitations were also sent out to numerous farmers' organizations and regulators to introduce them to water-conservation techniques. The various state governments also provided financial assistance to farmers to make the change required in machinery and logistics as they switched from one crop to another. Ultimately, the effort succeeded. A major shift in collective planning reduced the water requirements in the watershed. The planning helped economic survival, distributed water more efficiently, and thus slightly replenished Lake Chapala.

The GTEPAI continues to innovate and promote increasing efficiency in agricultural planning at the watershed level. But as Raul Medina sees it, creating change like this still must be a slow and deliberate process: "If you introduce changes and taxes quickly, you could have a social revolution, especially over water controls."[3]

CROP DIVERSITY, BIOTECHNOLOGY, AND THE SEED COMPANIES

In the struggle for resource-control, water is only one major factor in a matrix of changing variables. In the Cienega, as in most parts of Mexico and the world, seed design and engineering has penetrated local economies. In communities such as Jamay, successful farmers are usually those who buy and plant hybrid seeds. These farmers often have the largest crop returns, as well as fancy new trucks, a major status symbol amongst Mexican farmers.

Since Mexico has become an integral part of the North American food-production chain, it has also come under the influence of the large-scale agribusiness companies. The five largest companies — Astra-Zeneca, DuPont, Monsanto, Novartis, and

SINCE MEXICO HAS BECOME AN INTEGRAL PART OF THE NORTH AMERICAN FOOD-PRODUCTION CHAIN, IT HAS ALSO COME UNDER THE INFLUENCE OF THE LARGE-SCALE AGRIBUSINESS COMPANIES.

Aventis — are all active throughout the Cienega de Chapala region. They not only sell the seeds, they also vertically integrate their production by buying back the harvest from the same farmers. This allows the seed companies to monitor the seeds that were most productive under certain regional growing conditions.

The impact of this intensive form of agriculture that now dominates the Cienega is most evident at seeding time. During my field work in the town of Jamay, I took the opportunity to go out to the fields with Javier Jimenez, a successful local farmer and former mayor of Jamay. Jimenez is that rare breed of farmer who has met with consistent success by diversifing his production to include vegetables along with more standard cash crops such as corn.

Under the high, intense blaze of the sun, we arrive at the Jimenez plot in his shiny, black truck. Jimenez's crewmen are busy opening antiseptic, white bags, weighing about fifty pounds each. These bags contain two types of corn, manufactured by Pioneer (a subsidiary of Monsanto) and AsGrow (a subsidiary of DuPont). Inside the bags, instead of the generally expected yellowy-white corn kernels, I see that the corn kernels are coated in a fluorescent pink powder, a fungicide or herbicide I presume. From another container beside the seed-holder, a crewman pours out an insecticide powder that smells oddly of garlic. The side of the bag bears the internationally recognized skull-and-crossbones symbol for poison, but this does not seem to bother the crewman who gets a nose full of the powder when the wind blows it towards him. Finally, in yet another compartment, the crewmen place tiny, white hail-like nuggets of fertilizer. This chemical process prepares the corn for combat in a region plagued by the "nestiquil," an indigenous white maggot-like creature that loves to feast on the corn plant's roots.

I am told that this initial shock of agrochemicals must be followed by regular spraying of insecticide to ensure the crop's continued growth. Jimenez says this agrochemical bombardment is the new norm in a North American market where corn products and the distribution networks sprawl across the entire continent. "I buy the *improved* seeds from these seed companies because we can get up to fifteen tonnes per hectare," he hesitantly explains to me. "For economic purposes, to have higher yields, there is nothing better than *improved* seeds. In the past, farmers with four hectares could obtain seventeen tonnes of corn. Now with the hybrid seeds they can get generally ten tonnes for one hectare."[4]

INTERNATIONAL TRADE AND ITS EFFECT ON MEXICAN AGRICULTURE

The pressure to increase yields is itself a response to the demands of the international market economy in the agricultural sector. Farmers realize that the supply and demand of key cash crops such as corn and oil-based seeds relate to regional supply and demand as well as international trade in these crops. The Chicago Stock Exchange has a major effect on the fluctuation of basic grain prices, establishing prices for the all-important American market. And today a farmer in Jamay in the Cienega could just as easily be competing with a corn farmer from the state of Puebla in central Mexico, as he could with a farmer from the mid-western United States.

New for Mexico, this competitive market has really developed only over the last fifteen or so years. Following the Mexican revolution, which generally ended towards the beginning of the 1920s, the rural sector and the government, ruled by the PRI (the Institutional Revolutionary Party), established an informal social contract. Smallholders, or ejidatarios and their agricultural organizations would support the government in elections in return for rural support programs. This loose agreement, with all its corruption, scandals and increasing poverty, continued throughout much of the twentieth century until the 1980s, when international market pressures, and agricultural inefficiencies in the Mexican countryside became untenable for the national and regional leadership. Domestic and foreign pressures would fundamentally alter the social contract during the *sexenio* (the six years of a Mexican presidency) of Carlos Salinas de Gortari from 1988 to 1994. In Salinas's eyes, Mexico was ready to join the first world. He felt that the Mexican economy had the capacity to compete under its comparative advantages with leading world economies, and his administration introduced sweeping market principles that culminated in his signing of the North American Free Trade Agreement.

Another of the Salinas administration's most far-reaching legislative acts was amending Article 27 of the Mexican Constitution. This article related to the allocation of land, in an attempt to create and secure ejidos for Mexican small-scale farmers. The revolution had been fought over land rights, and the constitution aimed at securing smallholdings for those previously dispossessed. With the amendment made during the Salinas administration, lands, and more specifically ejidos, could be sold or rented by ejidatarios. Many modernizers in Mexico saw this as securing greater efficiency and more land productive utilization. However, the rural poor saw it as a threat to the one aspect of the constitution that protected land ownership. Apart from the elaborate details and complexity of the issue, the reaction to these reforms contributed to the violent uprising in Chiapas in January 1994, when the Zapatistas and their now-famous, hooded leader, Subcommandante Marcos, came on the world-scene to criticize the Mexican government and the steady slide towards extreme poverty in southern Mexico.

Industrialized agriculture's high demands have again tended to concentrate profitable farming into fewer hands in the Cienega and Mexico at large. During the transitional period from centralized, command-style agriculture to the free market, many farmers bought into the idea that they could secure the technologies and machinery on credit, and that this would allow smallholders to join the competition. This backfired when larger numbers of farmers were not able to meet their payments and fell deeper into debt with the Mexican rural development banks.

The government abandoned indebted farmers to the ravages of the new market economy. Meanwhile, Mexican policies allowed imported food products from the United States and elsewhere to flood the country just when farmers most needed help. In the resulting confrontation known as "El Barzon," indebted farmers developed a nationwide campaign to address the rural financial crisis.

All of these new challenges facing the Mexican farmer are compounded by the enormous financial support given to farmers in developed countries. For example, the 2002 U.S. Farm Bill assigned $190 billion for ten years through subsidies directly benefiting the 150,000 families of the largest producers in the United States.[5] This level of agricultural subsidization in advanced industrial countries has inevitably led to overproduction, which in turn gets exported to Mexico to compete with Mexican produce. In 2002, the United States produced 245 million tonnes of maize (a staple in the Mexican diet). Exporting 52.7 million tonnes, the

U.S.A. maintained a reserve of 33 million tonnes. SAGARPA (the Mexican Agricultural Ministry) statistics show that Mexico produces 16 million tonnes and imports 18 million tonnes, mostly from the United States.[6]

As a result of this increasingly competitive environment, agricultural production in Mexico has concentrated on mono-

ALL OF THESE NEW CHALLENGES FACING THE MEXICAN FARMER ARE COMPOUNDED BY THE ENORMOUS FINANCIAL SUPPORT GIVEN TO FARMERS IN DEVELOPED COUNTRIES.

cropping of key cash crops. In turn, the increased scale of production with its heavy use of agrochemicals has disrupted the ecological balance. SEVA is working with farmers to break their chemical dependency. The aim is to develop management tools that can produce healthy crops with less money and fewer fertilizers. The organization is also trying to break dependence on international food markets, and to reinforce local food production and consumption patterns. A growing educational tenet of SEVA is that people will eat healthier the closer their food is consumed to its source. However, in the Mexican diet, current eating habits include a marked increase in bottled, canned and processed foods, and a 100 percent increase in the consumption of foreign meat since NAFTA.[7]

To find out how SEVA, and those who share the organization's aims, have dealt with current realities, I talked to one of Mexico's most experienced agricultural experts.

DEVELOPING ALTERNATIVE FORMS OF SUSTAINABLE AGRICULTURE

I first met Ingeniero (Engineer) Jesus Lomeli at his office in La Barca, Jalisco, the neighbouring town to Jamay in the Cienega. He had been for many years the regional coordinator on agrarian affairs for the federal agricultural ministry. His charisma and booming laughter must have charmed and calmed many troubled and worried farmers. Lomeli would almost always finish his serious commentaries with humorous anecdotes about some unfortunate farmer, field animal, or mythical character from Mexican history. This great storyteller commanded the attention of the large groups of farmers we met at the various stops we made to meet the people of the Cienega.

Aside from his gifts as a communicator, Jesus Lomeli also has an uncanny ability to discover practical solutions to the agricultural problems he sees around him. As I mentioned above, in the Cienega, as in many parts of the Lerma watershed and across Mexico, a pest known as *nestiquil* causes millions of dollars of agricultural damage annually. A solution, Lomeli and a few others felt, was the practice of zero-tillage. This countered the chemical prescriptions of heavy-handed central planners who promoted highly toxic insecticides to kill the pest, which, by the way, proved incredibly adaptable to new chemical "solutions."

Zero-tillage farming is a technique that leaves the land fallow after harvest. The land is not turned over with machinery, but rather the plant's roots remain in the soil, and the leaves are left to rot into the fall season. With Lomeli, I visited a farmer in the region who had been practising zero-tillage agriculture since 1988. According to the farmer, his soil fertility had increased considerably. Its humidity and organic matter had improved, and the agrochemical requirements for his crops were greatly reduced. Over the years, Lomeli has held series after series of workshops to promote zero-tillage agriculture.

The result has been improved water retention, reduced agro-chemical costs and improved health for the farming community in the Cienega.

Lomeli's excellent rapport with the region's farmers has also increased SEVA's credibility. When Jesus Lomeli and Raul Medina met in 1996, they immediately recognized that they shared a similar approach to agriculture. Diminishing water and soil quality especially concerned both men, as did the increasing use of agrochemicals to combat pests. Although Lomeli at first questioned SEVA's ability to introduce organics to the region, he soon recognized the significance of the organization's growing education, outreach, and knowledge networks. And Lomeli's prestige and influence has helped convince other farmers of the importance of SEVA's mission.

SEVA'S USE OF ORGANIZATION, MEDIA, AND EDUCATION PROGRAMS

Part of building an alternative organic agricultural base requires a network of seed providers. SEVA members and other farmers have considered developing a germ plasma bank of various indigenous crops. It would revitalize the biodiversity of available food products, guarding them against the patented hybridized seeds that dominate the region.[8] As another stage in economic sustainability, SEVA has been able to sell vegetables and food products year-round. They have established contracts with buyers in Guadalajara, and are looking to expand production by growing and harvesting a series of indigenous medicinal herbs for regional markets.

To promote their success, and to spread the word to other farmers in the Cienega, SEVA produces a weekly radio show broadcast throughout the region. The show is called, "The Hour of the Agriculturalist." SEVA, which ran a cultural-affairs show from 1987 to 1992, already had some experience with radio. In those days, SEVA members were in contact with the Canadian

Foundation for World Development, which trained them how to develop a radio show. With some additional help from "Red de Radio Rural de los Paises en Desarrollo" (Rural Radio Network of Developing Countries), they aired programs on everything from food nutrition, to conservation, to sustainable farming. The show also features dramas re-enacting traditional stories, myths, and legends. The station's hundred-kilometre range reaches all communities in the Cienega and around Lake Chapala.

To add to their community-outreach efforts in the Cienega, the SEVA ranch is building a research and educational centre with four classrooms. Courses for children, youth, and adults will begin in the fall of 2004. The centre will provide classes in English, computer programming, cooking, nutrition, visual arts, and dramatic arts. With financial support from the National Educational Institute for Adults, enrolled adults can obtain credits towards their primary and secondary school diplomas recognized by the Federal Education Secretariat.[9]

SEVA AND THE CIENEGA: ALTERING PERSPECTIVES

SEVA represents a unique, active, principled source of conscience and action within a highly contested region of Mexico. For me, SEVA's work in the Cienega underlines many regional and global issues: the conflict of the local producer with large international trading systems; water rights in a world where water is becoming an increasingly valuable and scarce commodity; the influence of agribusiness on food systems worldwide. Concentrated at the Lerma river delta around the SEVA ranch, these issues test everyone's problem-solving skills.

Groups like SEVA are important for their ability to look at problems systemically, and to suggest new — sometimes radically new — solutions. There are certainly those who feel that SEVA's work is too fringe, too esoteric, too experimental to face the harsh, competitive market realities in which the Cienega and Mexico at large find themselves today. But SEVA can bridge the distance between small producers and market realities. New ideas can be incorporated into the mainstream. SEVA has also raised the level of debate and awareness about a range of agricultural, environmental, water-usage, and trade issues. And finally — perhaps most importantly — SEVA has built a living, caring community where these ideas and issues can continue to be worked on, developed, and enhanced.

AFTERWORD

TO GET TO TED ZETTEL'S FARM you have to take a journey that is, to a certain degree, both a trip back into the past and a trip into the future. Leaving Toronto, you fight the congestion on the Gardiner Expressway with such concentration that you forget that Lake Ontario, that under-appreciated miracle, glistens like a mirror to the south. Cutting up to the airport, you get on Highway 401 Westbound, a highway lined by gas stations linked at the hip to fast-food restaurants ready to provide cheap, unhealthy fuel. The sprawling industrial views eventually give way to glimpses of the grand Canadian cut-away of the Niagara Escarpment. Finally, near the town of Guelph, farm country takes over. Not so many years ago, you think, these rolling hills and corn fields lay just a few minutes outside of the city, but developers long ago bulldozed that memory.

As you drive you will see the road signs change. From celebrations of McDonald's and Wendy's you start to see freshly painted barns proudly proclaiming "Henderson Farms. Home of Penny & William Henderson." No matter how fast you drive through this part of the country, you still feel time slow, shift back to its more seasonal pace. Past Elora, with its century-old refurbished brick buildings, you might see a horse-drawn carriage driven by black-clad Amish farmers coming to town to sell their produce. And before you know it, you're driving up small laneway beside a river, and parking outside Ted Zettel's farmhouse.

When you step inside, Ted will welcome you and offer you a lemonade or a coffee. To describe Ted you could mention his short brown hair or his clean-shaven, tanned face, or the lean, muscular frame of someone who works outside. But what strikes you most deeply is his demeanour. He conveys an almost antiquated sense of quiet confidence and honesty, so that by the time he introduces you to his wife, Christine, and leads you out the back door of his farmhouse, past his huge Newfoundland dog, to sit on the back porch, you already feel like you've made a friend.

In the mid-1980s Ted and his family — he and his wife have six children, all of whom have worked on the farm — transformed his farm and became one of the "early adopters" of organic farming. At the time it was a dangerous move. There were no markets for his "organic milk," and no proven ways to grow commercial produce without pesticide. Despite these challenges, Ted says he was taken by the logic of organic agriculture, how it works as a system in which all inputs and outputs must be considered in relation to the whole. So he made the jump.

Organic farming, Ted explains, entails a different way of seeing the land. Take weeds, for instance. To most farmers, weeds are simply a pest, and chemical companies make millions of dollars selling herbicides to get rid of them. Ted, however, sees weeds a little differently from most farmers. According to him, they can be useful as an information source; they tell him about the health and properties of his soil. Since certain weeds only grow in certain soil conditions, Ted can "read" the weeds on his property to understand what is going on beneath ground, and then, instead of resorting to the chemical sprayer, he can address the problem by growing a different crop, one more suitable to the soil.

Soil fertility is another fundamental problem an organic farmer like Ted faces. After years of farming, all fields eventually develop a phosphorous deficiency. If left unchecked, declining phosphorous levels result in declining nitrogen levels that can cause real problems for the farm. Conventional farmers deal with this quite easily by applying a synthetic chemical called super-phosphate. This product is not allowed by the Organic Crop Producers and Processors, the body that certifies all organic foods. So at great expense Ted must import from Florida a mined rock high in phosphorous, and then apply it to his fields.

The next step in Ted's process is to develop markets that will compensate farmers willing to incur the additional cost and time needed to farm organically. Before Ted helped to start OntarBio — he was the first president of what is now the country's largest organic food co-operative — organic farmers in Ontario had trouble finding anyone who would pay premium prices for organic foods. Ted had to sell his organic milk into the conventional dairy pool at the same price as everyone else. Now — thanks in part to OntarBio and their popular "Organic Meadow" brand of organic milk[1] — consumers are willing to pay more for Ted's milk. He receives an average 15–18 percent more than conventional farmers for his dairy. As Ted says, so many consumers are now questioning what goes into in their food that it is now the conventional farmer, not the organic one, who is on thin ice. Ted is happy to work harder for a product that people want and will pay a little more for.

Despite his quiet optimism, Ted Zettel knows he is still in the minority. He is striving to build a community of farmers to share the learned intelligence about new and different agricultural practices. Ironically, that used to be the government's job, but as large agricultural companies became more aggressive in their marketing, and their sales staff began acting as "consultants" to farmers, the government simply backed away. Of course salesmen of the large agrochemical businesses don't come calling on Ted, which is why he helped start the Ecological Farmers Association of Ontario.

It is somewhat bizarre to see that, after a century of advanced technological development, we are now faced with relearning how to farm without chemical enhancements. And some consumers are paying for the education. If at one time Ted Zettel was a renegade, he's more and more coming into a new mainstream. The market for organic foods in North America has been growing at a rate of more than 20 percent a year for almost twenty years straight, and food chains like Whole Foods are doing a booming business capitalizing on this fact.

Whether this trend is based on solid scientific evidence, as the Lappés argue in their chapter of this book, or if it is rather an expression of a misplaced ideology and bad science, as Bill Atkinson asserts in his chapter, there is no doubt that the public appetite for information about their food has undergone a profound change. Well-publicized food and water scandals about *E. coli*, salmonella, mad cow, GMOs, and trans fats have changed the way consumers view their food. Long gone are the days when no one read the label, or even demanded a label. Farms, slaughterhouses, and fishing vessels are all undergoing much closer scrutiny, and if the public is not comfortable with current practices — and it is clear that the public is not — then change will come. It's already happening all over the world. Every month sees new laws about beef safety, fish safety, the uses of pesticides, and fat-content labelling.

Despite these changes, however, the paradox of food remains. While most people still expect their food system to represent a certain set of idealistic values, they also want it to remain cheap and plentiful all year around. Which is why the person who buys bacon in the morning does not imagine that his breakfast quite likely came from a pig who lived a short, miserable life in an overcrowded pen, feeding on a diet dosed with antibiotics and growth hormones (and where the hog waste may have run off into rivers and polluted the water table), before being shipped in an open truck along freezing highways to be slaughtered, packed, and processed by an underpaid worker. The industrial farm is far from the agrarian ideal lodged in the consumer's mind. Instead, the consumer prefers to think of that pig — if he thinks of it at all — as roaming an idealized barn, perhaps like the barn in *Charlotte's Web*, before the farmer magically transformed the pig into that nice, friendly packaged strip of meat that somehow ends up in the grocery refrigerator. As the urban population around the world increases, the disconnect between farm and fork grows wider, and remains one of the greatest barriers to change.

But the obstacles go deeper than lack of knowledge. As marketers well understand, urban consumers sometimes don't *want* to know where their food comes from. Even the most avid supporter of industrial farming and GMO foods would not have the audacity to use a label such as "grown with the help of pesticides, herbicides, and genetic modification." That simply does not appeal to anyone. Instead, our food is sold using ancient symbols of sun, rain, and flowing fields, reinforcing the stereotype of the old-world family farm. The power of marketing in this regard is impossible to overestimate, and so to find new ways of seeing efficiencies within the agricultural production cycle — like Ted Zettel has done — is a difficult job indeed.

For all of his innovation, Ted Zettel is the last person to set himself up as having all the answers. Still, there has been so much popular interest in the merits of organic farming, and such growth in this market sector, that champions of industrial agricultural techniques have become publicly defensive. To someone like Norman Borlaug, the father of the Green Revolution, portraying synthetic chemicals, pesticides, and genetically modified foods as the "enemy" — as he believes the media do all too frequently — is a dangerous position. His story is also worth knowing.

Born in 1914 in Iowa, Norman Borlaug is a food business legend. As a young geneticist and plant pathologist, Borlaug joined the Rockefeller Foundation on their 1944 project in Mexico to research new strains of wheat. After twenty years of work, Borlaug successfully bred high-yield, disease-resistant wheat that dramatically increased Mexico's ability to feed its exploding population.

That experience led Borlaug to believe that farm mechanization, new forms of irrigation, new pesticides, genetic plant breeding, and use of fertilizers could save the world from what he called the "population monster" to avert mass starvation. In 1968, the director of the U.S. Agency for International Development, William Gaud, coined the term "Green Revolution" to describe this approach. With huge support from the Rockefeller and Ford foundations, Borlaug took his Green Revolution to India, Pakistan, and Latin America, where his results were nothing short of miraculous. He not only increased crop yields and food outputs, he trained thousands of young scientists in his new, more efficient agricultural techniques. In India, for example, Borlaug encouraged strategies such as double-cropping existing fields by using water derived from new dams and irrigation systems, and using genetically altered seeds of dwarf wheat, millet, rice, and corn. Between 1947 and 1979, yield per unit of farmland in India increased a startling 30 percent, a transformation that allowed the country, once on the verge of starvation, to become one of the giants of world agriculture. By the 1990s, almost three-quarters of all the rice in Asia, and half the wheat and corn in Africa and Latin America, came from farms using Borlaug's Green Revolution techniques. Borlaug was awarded the Nobel Prize for his work.

But as the Lappés observed in their chapter, tremendous controversy surrounds Borlaug's work. Reports about the negative consequences of the Green Revolution — the poisoning of farm workers in India from pesticide use, the salination of water tables from over-irrigation, the increasing costs of industrial farming — have put Borlaug and his legions of Green Revolution fans on the defensive. "Science is under attack in affluent nations, where anti-biotech activists claim consumers are being poisoned by inorganic fertilizers and synthetic pesticides," Borlaug wrote in the *Wall Street Journal* on December 6, 2000. "They also claim that newer genetic engineering technologies decrease biodiversity and degrade the environment. Neither claim is true, but fear-mongering could be disastrous for less-developed nations." Fears about herbicides and genetics, Borlaug argues, are not only overblown and unproven, they pander to rich North American consumers who have never experienced the scarcities common in the developing world. Borlaug argues that not only has the Green Revolution staved off starvation in the developing world, but that its dramatic increase of yields per acre has actually saved millions of acres of wildlife habitat from being transformed into farmland. "In 1960 in the U.S., the production of the 17 most important food, feed, and fiber crops was 252 million tons," Borlaug writes. "By 1999 it had increased to 700 million tons. It is important to note that the 1999 harvest was produced on 10 million fewer acres than were cultivated in 1960. If we had tried to produce the harvest of 1999 with the technology of 1960, we would have had to increase the cultivated area by about 460 million acres of land of the same quality — which we didn't have." In other words, according to Borlaug, one way to save wildlife habitat is to promote industrial farming.

Borlaug's challenge raises some difficult questions. Organic farming is taking hold in the developing world as a return to a purer form of food production. Yet Borlaug insists it's all wrong, that we need to move in the opposite direction. How do we reconcile these two positions?

Perhaps one way is to see the merits in both positions. This makes sense, if we stop trying to find a magical cure and instead look for a range of solutions to a variety of different problems. While it is tempting to pick a side in the food debate — organics versus industrial — the choice is faulty. The two sides are not, as Borlaug likes to cast them, mutually opposed.

The reality is that both may offer valid solutions — to different problems. In North America and Europe, for example, the consumer is faced with bad food, and too much of it. Obesity costs the U.S. health care system an estimated $93 billion annually,[2] or almost 10 percent of American health care costs. Organic farmers like Ted Zettel offer an interesting solution to this problem by providing an arguably higher quality food product to a part of the world where food scarcity is no longer the primary concern.

Meanwhile, large swaths of the globe are still facing food scarcities. Bread for the World Institute estimates that 842 million people in the world are currently malnourished, and 6 million children under age five die every year from starvation.[3] And solving this problem may require different solutions.

It is unrealistic to assume that one grand plan — one magic bullet — will solve all the world's food problems. Each person, each region, each country, will have a different set of circumstances to consider when choosing the direction they wish to follow. Today, the beauty is that choices are available, to farmers, governments, and consumers. Today, we have options that we never had before.

So how do we make the best choices among all the available options? The first way is to become more educated about our food and where it comes from. We must see through the food industry's marketing façade to recognize the infrastructure behind it. We must become more knowledgeable about the choices, and what they mean to us, our families, and our environment.

And to help us do this, it is useful to return to a thinker we mentioned at the beginning of this book, University of Manitoba professor and scientist Vaclav Smil. In his brilliant book *Feeding the World*, Smil provides an excellent way to help frame our education, and to close the intellectual gap between our different available options. He does so by focusing on the concept of efficiency. "Our response to higher demand should not be primarily the quest for higher supply through increased inputs," Smil writes, "but rather the pursuit of higher efficiency."[4] Before we choose a radical new vision for our food future, Smil says we should first discover the many ways to make our current system function at a more sophisticated level — how we produce food and what we consume, how we farm and what we farm. Dietary choices are crucial to Smil's understanding of efficiency; they make his discussion much broader than most. For example, he claims we must come to terms with the fact that over 30 percent of all food energy in developed countries comes from animals, a percentage difficult to duplicate around the globe. Smil argues that we need to examine the whole complex chain of associations between the consumer, supplier, distributor, and producer of food to understand the most efficient and best way of feeding the future.

Inherent in Smil's concept of food efficiency is a willingness to look into the complicated interactions between the participants in the food chain. This higher level of awareness offers a way forward, and a model for us to follow. First and foremost, of course, change is consumer-driven. The consumer wants to know what's on the plate, how it got there, and its true costs. A full cost-accounting model, which includes how much it costs to grow a product as well as environmental and community clean-up costs, is leaching into the public mind. When consumers begin to ask how much packaging their food requires, how much energy has gone into growing and transporting it, how sustainable and healthy are the fish and mammalian species they eat, then these questions will mark the first important step towards a more authentic and healthy food system. In short, when people see through the food industry's stories, the world will be ready for a broad transformative change.

Not all farmers will be like Ted Zettel, and not all consumers will choose to eat only organic foods. Nor should they. Our point is not to advocate one position. But Ted Zettel is just one farmer who has taken the time to examine the links of our food chain, to be concerned about every part of it, and to try to find new and different farming techniques that are both sustainable and profitable. Zettel offers a ray of hope in the possibility of choice. We have many options arrayed before us, from GMOs, to new crop strains, to organics. Our problem is not to eliminate choices for ideological motives, but to examine the merits of each new development. To make better choices, we must ask better questions — and be mindful of the unintended consequences of every new innovation.

According to an old Byzantine proverb, "A man who has enough food has many problems, a man who has no food only has one problem." We have many problems in our current food system, no doubt about it. But to solve these dilemmas, to feed our future, our only option is to eat with greater interest, curiosity, and intelligence. That is the recipe of hope.

BIOGRAPHIES

ABOUT THE CONTRIBUTORS

WILLIAM ILLSEY ATKINSON writes for the *Globe and Mail*. His first book, *Prototype: How Canadian Technology Is Shaping the Future*, was a finalist for the 2002 National Business Book Award. In 2003, he delivered the William A. Stewart Memorial Lecture to Ontario's Advanced Agriculture Leadership Program and was named the first Leaf Initiative Innovation Champion by the Toronto Technology Alliance. In 2004, his second book, *Nanocosm*, was shortlisted for the Canadian Science Writers Association *Science in Society* Award. He lives in North Vancouver.

DR. KELLY D. BROWNELL is an internationally known expert on eating disorders, obesity, and body weight regulation. He is professor and chair of the Department of Psychology at Yale University, where he is also professor of Epidemiology and Public Health and the director of the Yale Center for Eating and Weight Disorders. He has been president of several U.S. organizations, including the Society of Behavioral Medicine, the Association for the Advancement of Behavior Therapy, and the Division of Health Psychology of the American Psychological Association. He has received numerous awards and honours for his work, including the James McKeen Cattell Award from the New York Academy of Sciences and the award for Outstanding Contribution to Health Psychology from the American Psychological Association. Dr. Brownell has written eleven books, including 2004's *Food Fight*, and more than 200 scientific articles and chapters.

CARRIE BROWNSTEIN is the research and outreach coordinator for the Blue Ocean Institute (BOI), a non-profit marine conservation organization based in New York. With BOI's From Sea to Table project, Ms. Brownstein works to change the way consumers and food service professionals select seafood. She is now preparing to work with supermarket chains and culinary schools to guide purchasing decisions toward more sustainably caught and farmed seafood. She has authored articles about fisheries and seafood and has been interviewed in national U.S. media. Ms. Brownstein has also worked as a seafood specialist with Audubon's Living Oceans Program, and has taught environmental and art education in Vermont, Philadelphia, Belize, and the British Virgin Islands. She has a Master's degree in Environmental Management from Duke University, where she focused on interactions between marine mammals and fisheries.

MARK JUHASZ is an environmental consultant with specialization in the agricultural and agri-food industry. In 2001, he completed a master's degree in the Faculty of Environmental Studies at York University, with a focus on the environmental and technological results of agricultural modernization as a consequence of the NAFTA agreement. Following studies at York, under a joint Canada–Mexico government scholarship he worked at a research centre in Guadalajara, Mexico, with a project group on the emerging agricultural challenges and innovations in the largest watershed in Mexico, the Cuenca Lerma-Chapala. During the summer of 2002, part of his field work involved close contact and collaboration with SEVA. The experience of working with this organization and understanding its regeneration efforts formed the basis of his final report.

STUART LAIDLAW is a business reporter at the *Toronto Star*, where he served on the editorial board for three years. He has led the paper's coverage of food and agricultural issues as well as covering the World Trade Organization. Before joining the *Star*, he was a senior news editor with the *Financial Post* and a reporter for the Canadian Press, where he also covered agriculture and world trade talks. He first got to know Canada's farming community early in his career as a reporter for several small-town papers. His coverage of food, agriculture, and trade has taken him across North America and to Europe and introduced him to farmers, activists, scientists, and business people from around the world. His book, *Secret Ingredients: The Brave New World of Industrial Farming*, was based on that experience.

ANNA LAPPÉ is the co-author, with Frances Moore Lappé, of *Hope's Edge: The Next Diet for a Small Planet*. A regular public speaker and commentator on food politics, globalization, and the media, Anna Lappé's articles have been widely published in the United States and Canada, appearing in the *Washington Post, San Francisco Chronicle, Los Angeles Times,* and *Globe and Mail*, among others. She is currently a Food and Society Policy Fellow of the Kellogg Foundation and is working on her second book, *Grub: Ideas for an Urban, Organic Kitchen*, with Bryant Terry.

FRANCES MOORE LAPPÉ is author or co-author of fourteen books, including the three-million-copy bestseller *Diet for a Small Planet*. Her books have been used in hundreds of colleges and in more than fifty countries and have been translated into over a dozen languages. She lectures widely and has received seventeen honorary doctorates from distinguished universities. In 1975, she co-founded one of the U.S.A.'s most respected food think tanks, the Institute for Food and Development Policy (Food First). She co-founded the Center for Living Democracy (1990–2000) to bring to light democratic innovations in which regular citizens contribute to problem-solving in their communities, and she served as founding editor of the Center's American News Service. In 1987 she received the Right Livelihood Award in Sweden, considered the "alternative Nobel." Her most recent book is *You Have the Power: Choosing Courage in a Culture of Fear.*

IAN MacLACHLAN is an Associate Professor in the Department of Geography at the University of Lethbridge but his contribution to this collection was written while he was on leave at the Centre for Canadian Studies at the University of Edinburgh. His book, *Kill and Chill: Restructuring Canada's Beef Commodity Chain,* describes the locational dynamics of Canada's cattle and meat-packing industries during the twentieth century. His current research is on livestock slaughter in nineteenth-century Britain.

DR. SYLVIA OSTRY is the Distinguished Research Fellow at the Centre for International Studies, University of Toronto. She has a doctorate in economics from McGill University and Cambridge University. Dr. Ostry has held many positions in the Canadian federal government, including chief statistician, deputy minister of Consumer and Corporate Affairs, chairman of the Economic Council of Canada, deputy minister of International Trade, and ambassador for Multilateral Trade Negotiations. From 1979 to 1983 she headed the Economics and Statistics Department of the OECD in Paris. She is a member of the Inter-American Dialogue, the Advisory Board of the Institute of International Economics, and the Group of Thirty, and a founding member of the Pacific Council on International Policy. Her most recent publications include "The World Trading System: In Dire Need of Reform." She has received numerous honorary degrees and awards and is a Companion of the Order of Canada and a Fellow of the Royal Society of Canada.

DR. CARL SAFINA grew up loving the ocean and its creatures. He now works to highlight, explain, and solve problems facing the oceans' wildlife. Dr. Safina is author of more than a hundred publications, including the books *Song for the Blue Ocean: Encounters Along the World's Coasts and Beneath the Seas* and *Eye of the Albatross: Visions of Hope and Survival.* He also co-authored the *Seafood Lover's Almanac.* His conservation work has been profiled in the *New York Times,* on *Nightline,* and in the Bill Moyers television special "Earth on Edge." He is a recipient of the Pew Scholar's Award in Conservation and the Environment, a World Wildlife Fund Senior Fellowship, the Lannan Literary Award for nonfiction, the John Burroughs Writer's Medal, and a MacArthur Prize. He is now president of the Blue Ocean Institute, a nonprofit organization he co-founded in 2003 which seeks to inspire a closer relationship with the sea.

ERIC SCHLOSSER is an award-winning journalist who serves as a correspondent for the *Atlantic Monthly* and is the author of the books *Fast Food Nation* and *Reefer Madness.* He is currently at work on a book about the American prison system.

JANE THOMSON, P.Eng., is a Research Fellow at the Institute for Research and Innovation in Sustainability at York University in Toronto, where she earned a master's degree in Environmental Studies, specializing in Business and Sustainability, and is a sustainability consultant. Her research background spans capital markets and sustainability investing, sustainability of the energy sector, human capital management, the role of business and sustainability in developing countries, and business strategies for sustainability. Ms. Thomson has worked with organizations such as the Canadian International Development Agency, Canada's National Roundtable on the Environment and the Economy, Enbridge Gas Distribution, and the Greater Vancouver Regional District. She has several years of experience as a mechanical engineering consultant, responsible for design and project management for numerous clients in Canada and internationally.

DR. FLORENCE MURINGI WAMBUGU is the founder and CEO of Africa Harvest Biotech Foundation International and is also an agricultural plant pathologist. Under her leadership, the Biotech Tissue Banana Project in Kenya won the World Bank Global Development Network Award. She is a member of the Private Sector Committee of the Consultative Group on International Agricultural Research, DuPont Biotech Advisory Panel-USA, and Board of Trustees of the International Plant Genetic Resources Institute, and is the vice-chair of the African Biotechnology Stakeholders Forum. She also participates in the Bill & Melinda Gates Foundation as well as the United Nations Hunger Task Force. Dr. Wambugu has participated in many international forums and authored or co-authored about sixty papers. She is also the author of the book *Modifying Africa: How Biotechnology Can Benefit the Poor and the Hungry: A Case Study from Kenya.*

DR. DAVID WHEELER is the founding director of the York Institute for Research and Innovation in Sustainability at Toronto's York University, where he is also the director and Erivan K. Haub Professor in Business and Sustainability at the Schulich School of Business. Dr. Wheeler has advised the governments of Canada and the U.K. as well as governments in Africa and Latin America and has worked with a wide variety of international organizations and businesses. In 2003 he received the Corporate Knights award for External Impact as a faculty pioneer in Canadian business schools. He is Visiting Professor in Sustainable Enterprise at Kingston University Business School (U.K.) and is a member of the boards of the Laidlaw Foundation and the European Foundation for Business and the advisory councils of DuPont Canada, Real Assets and SustainAbility. He has authored more than sixty articles and book chapters.

ABOUT THE EDITORS

ANDREW HEINTZMAN is president of Investeco Capital Corp, a company that provides capital and expertise to private environmental businesses. He is also currently a director of The Sustainability Network, an organization that develops capacity building for Canadian environmental not-for-profit organizations, and the Foundation for Ontario Nature. He was the co-founder and publisher of *Shift* magazine and a founder of consulting company d~Code.

EVAN SOLOMON is the host of CBC Newsworld's *Hot Type* and co-host of the current affairs show *CBC News: Sunday*. He co-founded and was the editor-in-chief of *Shift* magazine and is the author of the novel *Crossing the Distance*. He has hosted many award-winning television series about the impact of technology on society, including CBC's *FutureWorld* and *ChangeMakers* and PBS's *Masters of Technology*. He contributes regularly to newspapers and magazines around the country and sits on McGill University's Arts Advisory Board.

NOTES AND ACKNOWLEDGEMENTS

Introduction

1. Yet one more example of the light and dark sides of science: Haber's synthetic ammonia is needed to make nitric acid, the fundamental ingredient in high explosives. When the First World War broke out, the British promptly blockaded access to Chile's saltpetre mines in an effort to suffocate the German munitions industry. Haber's process allowed Germany to keep producing explosives, and to continue fighting a war that would cost millions of lives.

Chapter 1
SAVING AGRICULTURE FROM ITSELF

1. As cited in *Beyond Factory Farming: Corporate Hog Barns and the Threat to Public Health, the Environment and Rural Communities*, ed. Alexander Ervin et al., Centre for Canadian Policy Alternatives, 2003.
2. Wendell Berry, *What are People For?* (New York: North Point Press, 1990), 123.
3. Richard Manning, *Against the Grain: How Agriculture has Hijacked Civilization* (New York: North Point Press, 2004), 89–91.
4. Stuart Laidlaw, *Secret Ingredients: The Brave New World of Industrial Agriculture* (Toronto: McClelland & Stewart, 2003), 129.
5. Manning, *Against the Grain*.
6. Bob Stirling, "Work, Knowledge and the Direction of Farm Life" in *Writing Off the Rural West: Globalization, Governments and the Transformation of Rural Communities* (University of Alberta Press: Edmonton, 2001), 257.
7. Leo Horrigan, Robert Lawrence, and Polly Walker, "How Sustainable Agriculture Can Address the Environmental and Human Health Harms of Industrial Agriculture," *Environmental Health Perspectives* 110, no. 5 (May 2002): 445.
8. National Farmers Union, *The Farm Crisis, Bigger Farms, and the Myths of "Competition" and "Efficiency,"* November 2003.
9. First recounted in Laidlaw, *Secret Ingredients*, 81–82.

10. Horrigan, Lawrence, and Walker, *Sustainable Agriculture*, 446.
11. Interview, January 29, 2004.
12. Manning, *Against the Grain*.
13. David Tilman et al., "Agricultural Sustainability and Intensive Production Practices," *Nature* 418 (August 8, 2002): 671–77.
14. Horrigan, Lawrence, and Walker, *Sustainable Agriculture*, 446.
15. Laidlaw, *Secret Ingredients*, 66.
16. Ibid., 63–81.
17. Bill Weida, "The ILO and Depopulation of Rural Agricultural Areas: Implications for Rural Economies in Canada and the U.S.," in *Beyond Factory Farming*, 114–16.
18. Ibid., 136.
19. Ibid., 129.
20. Ibid., 127.
21. Richard Manning, "The Oil We Eat," *Harper's Magazine*, February 2004.
22. Brian Halweil, *Home Grown: The Case for Local Food in a Global Market*, WorldWatch Institute Paper no. 163 (November 2002).
23. Manning, "The Oil We Eat." Energy statistics also taken from Tilman, et al., "Agricultural Sustainability."
24. Michael Pollan, "When a Crop Becomes King," *New York Times*, July 19, 2002.
25. Manning, "The Oil We Eat."
26. Vandana Shiva, *Stolen Harvest: The Hijacking of the Global Food Supply* (Cambridge, MA: South End Press), 62.
27. Michael Pollan, "Power Steer," *New York Times Magazine*, March 31, 2002.
28. Taken from transcript prepared by Van Acker. Talk given October 29, 2003, in Dauphin, MB.
29. Halweil, *Home Grown*.
30. Russell Shorto, "A Short Order Revolutionary," *New York Times Magazine*, January 11, 2004.
31. Ibid.
32. Interview, March 18, 2004.
33. Interview, March 30, 2004.
34. Interview, March 18, 2004.
35. Interview, April 14, 2004.
36. Taken from transcript prepared by Van Acker. Talk given October 29, 2003, in Dauphin, MB.
37. http://www.organicvalley.coop/ (accessed June 23, 2004).
38. Telephone interview, June 24, 2004.
39. Quotes taken from transcript prepared by Van Acker. Talk given October 29, 2003, in Dauphin, MB.
40. Telephone interview, June 24, 2004.

Chapter 2
BETTING THE FARM: FOOD SAFETY AND THE BEEF COMMODITY CHAIN

1. Verna Mitura and Lina de Piétro, *Canada's Beef Cattle Sector and the Impact of BSE on Farm Family Income 2000–2003*, Statistics Canada Agriculture Division Working Paper no. 69 (Ottawa, June 2004): 5.
2. Statistics Canada, Census of Agriculture, 2001.
3. Statistics Canada, Agriculture Division, special tabulations from "Cattle Statistics" Catalogue, July 2003, 23–012.
4. Temple Grandin, "Conveyor Restrainer," http://www.grandin.com/restrain/new.conv.rest.html.
5. Experimentation showed that material from tuberculous lesions in the viscera (notably in the lungs, lymphatic glands, and liver) could contaminate otherwise wholesome meat by the hands, knives, and clothes of the butcher during the processes of flaying and dressing the carcass. See *Royal Commission Appointed to Inquire into the Effect of Food Derived from Tuberculous Animals on Human Health*, P.P. 1895, xxxv, 14.
6. The Honourable Donald H. Oliver, Q.C., Chairman, Senate of Canada, The Standing Committee on Agriculture and Forestry, *The BSE Crisis — Lessons for the Future*, Interim Report (April 2004): 10.
7. Canadian Food Inspection Agency, "Transmissible Spongiform Encephalopathies (TSEs) Questions and Answers," February 5, 2001, http://www.inspection.gc.ca/english/anima/heasan/disemala/spong/tse_e.shtml.
8. Kevin Grier and Larry Martin, *Cattle Pricing and Other Contentious Industry Issues*, Special Report (Guelph: George Morris Centre, 2004), http://www.georgemorris.org/PDF%20Files/GMCSpecialReport-BeefPricing031604.pdf.
9. Anthony S. Wohl, *Endangered Lives: Public Health in Victorian Britain* (London: Dent, 1983), 130.
10. Keir Waddington, "The Science of Cows," *History of Science* 39 (2001): 355–81.
11. Barry Wilson, "Eliminating Bovine TB Said Next to Impossible," *The Western Producer*, March 10 2003, http://www.producer.com/registered/articles/2003/0306/livestock/20030306ls05.html; and Canada House of Commons Standing Committee on Agriculture and AgriFood, *Bovine Tuberculosis in the Immediate Area of Riding Mountain National Park in Manitoba* (April 2003), http://www.parl.gc.ca/InfoComDoc/37/2/AGRI/Studies/Reports/agrirp01-e.htm.
12. F. D. Menzies and S. D. Neill, "Cattle-to-Cattle Transmission of Bovine Tuberculosis," *The Veterinary Journal* 160 (2000): 92–106.
13. Nobel e-Museum, "Stanley Prusiner," http://www.nobel.se/medicine/laureates/1997/prusiner-autobio.html.
14. Variant CJD (vCJD) is a rare degenerative brain disease that is invariably fatal with no known treatment. It is associated with the consumption of tissue contaminated by the active agent that causes BSE in cattle. The vast majority of cases have been in the United Kingdom and the average age at mortality is under 30. Classic Creutzfeldt-Jakob disease (CJD) is an invariably fatal degenerative brain disease of the elderly and is endemic worldwide. See http://www.hc-sc.gc.ca/english/diseases/cjd/bg4.html and http://www.cdc.gov/ncidod/diseases/cjd/cjd_fact_sheet.htm.

15. Patrick Van Zwanenberg and Erik Millstone, "BSE: A Paradigm of Policy Failure," *The Political Quarterly* 74 (2003): 30.
16. United Kingdom, *The BSE Inquiry Report*, vol. 6, chap. 7, 740–742, http://www.bseinquiry.gov.uk/index.htm.
17. National Creutzfeldt-Jakob Disease Surveillance Unit, University of Edinburgh, CJD Statistics, http://www.cjd.ed.ac.uk/figures.htm.
18. Health Canada, *First Canadian Case of vCJD* (May 2003), http://www.hc-sc.gc.ca/english/diseases/cjd/index.html.
19. Merle Jacob and Tomas Hellström, "Policy Understanding of Science, Public Trust and the BSE–CJD Crisis," *Journal of Hazardous Materials* 78 (2000): 309.
20. Keir Waddington, "Safe Meat and Healthy Animals: BSE and Bovine TB," *History and Policy*, http://www.historyandpolicy.org/archive/policy-paper-04.html.
21. Oliver, *The BSE Crisis*, 14.
22. Health Canada Food Directorate, *Policy on Specified Risk Materials (SRM) in the Food Supply* (2003), http://www.hc-sc.gc.ca/food-aliment/fpi-ipa/e_policy_srm.html.
23. Canadian Food Inspection Agency, "Risk Assessment on Bovine Spongiform Encephalopathy in Cattle in Canada, Part C: Risk Estimation," Section 3.1 Probability that the Imported Bovine Animal is BSE-Infected, December 2002, http://www.inspection.gc.ca/english/sci/ahra/bseris/bserisc1e.shtml#Cfig2.
24. Ibid., Section 6.1 Risk Estimate, http://www.inspection.gc.ca/english/sci/ahra/bseris/bserisc2e.shtml#Cfig5.
25. William Leiss, "A Closer Look at CFIA's BSE Risk Estimation," BSE Risk in Canada, Part 4, 2004, http://www.leiss.ca/bse/155?download.
26. Health Canada Food Directorate, *Policy on Specified Risk Materials (SRM) in the Food Supply* (2003), http://www.hc-sc.gc.ca/food-aliment/fpi-ipa/e_policy_srm.html.
27. Canadian Food Inspection Agency, "Canada: A Minimal BSE Risk Country," December 2003, http://www.inspection.gc.ca/english/anima/heasan/disemala/bseesb/minrisexece.shtml.
28. In Canada the term "specified risk materials" (SRM) is now used to denote an expanded list of bovine by-products that contain the infective agent of BSE and are restricted from entering the human food supply. SRM include skull, brain, trigeminal ganglia of the skull, eyes, tonsils, spinal cord, and dorsal root ganglia of the spine from cattle aged 30 months or older; and the distal ileum (the end of the small intestine) from cattle of all ages. Because complete removal of the dorsal root ganglia is impractical, the Meat Inspection Regulations require removal and disposal of the vertebral column from all cattle aged 30 months or older and it cannot be used in the preparation of mechanically separated meat or finely textured meat. To ensure the complete removal of the distal ileum, the entire small intestine of all cattle, regardless of age, must be removed and disposed of as inedible product. See Health Canada, "Regulations Amending the Food and Drug Regulations," July 2003, http://www.hc-sc.gc.ca/food-aliment/friia-raaii/food_drugs-aliments_drogues/part-partie_11/e_1389.html; and Canadian Food Inspection Agency "Report on Actions Taken by Canada in Response to the

Confirmation of a Case of Indigenous BSE, http://www.inspection.gc.ca/english/anima/heasan/disemala/bseesb/internate.shtml ." In the U.K., specified bovine offal (SBO) was defined differently in 1989. See United Kingdom, *The BSE Inquiry Report*, vol. 6, chap. 3, 77–91; vol. 13, chap. 3, 38–44, http://www.bseinquiry.gov.uk/index.htm.

29. Gary Little, "BSE Surveillance in Canada," *CAHNet Bulletin*, Canadian Animal Health Network Edition 8, (Winter 2003): 3; and Alberta Auditor General, *Report of the Auditor General on the Alberta Government's BSE-Related Assistance Programs* (July 27, 2004): 49.

30. "Farmers Not Meeting BSE Test Quotas," *Lethbridge Herald*, August 5, 2004, 1.

31. Alberta Auditor General, *Report on Alberta Government's BSE-Related Assistance Programs*, 48.

32. Upton Sinclair, *The Jungle*. (New York: Bantam Books, 1906; Bantam Classics Edition, 1981). For an account of the effect of Sinclair's novel in Canada, see Ian MacLachlan, *Kill and Chill: Restructuring Canada's Beef Commodity Chain* (Toronto: University of Toronto Press, 2001), 128–31.

33. U.K. Food Standards Agency, *Report on the Review of Scientific Committees* (2002), http://www.food.gov.uk/multimedia/pdfs/CommitteesReview.pdf.

34. Anne Hardy, "Animals, Disease and Man," *Perspectives in Biology and Medicine* 46 (2003): 200–15.

35. D. S. Edwards, A. M. Johnston, and G. C. Mead, "Meat Inspection: An Overview of Present Practices and Future Trends," *The Veterinary Journal* 154 (1997): 136.

36. Ibid., 136, 138.

37. Ibid., 135–36.

38. Tag is manure that has caked-up in a thick layer and becomes matted in the hide.

39. Canadian Cattle Identification Program, http://www.canadaid.com/.

40. Canadian Cattlemen's Association, "Quality Starts Here," http://www.cattle.ca/QSH/.

41. John Spriggs, Jill Hobbs, and Andrew Fearne, "Beef Producers Attitudes to Coordination and Quality Assurance in Canada and the U.K.," *International Journal of Food and Agribusiness Management Review* 3 (2000): 98; and Farm Assured British Beef and Lamb, http://www.fabbl.co.uk/.

42. Eunice Taylor and Joanne Zaida Taylor, "Perceptions of 'the Bureaucratic Nightmare' of HACCP," *British Food Journal* 106 (2004): 65–72.

43. Reported slaughter for federally and provincially inspected plants does not include unreported domestic slaughter on-the-farm. Agriculture and Agri-Food Canada, Annual Livestock and Meat Report, 2003, http://www.agr.gc.ca/misb/aisd/redmeat/almr2003.htm.

44. Saskatchewan, *Final Report of the Live Stock Commission of the Province of Saskatchewan*, (Regina: King's Printer, 1918): 20.

45. Temple Grandin, *Report on Handling and Stunning Practices in Canadian Meat Packing Plants*, prepared for Agriculture Canada, Canadian Federation of Humane Societies, Canadian Meat Council and Canadian Poultry and Egg Processor's Council, (Fort Collins, CO: Grandin Livestock Handling Systems, 1995).

46. Gordon Doonan, Martin Appelt, and Alena Corbin, "Nonambulatory Livestock

Transport: The Need for Consensus," *Canadian Veterinary Journal* (August 2003), http://www.inspection.gc.ca/english/anima/heasan/transport/consensuse.shtml.

47. Canadian Food Inspection Agency, "Interim BSE Export Restriction," January 2003, http://www.inspection.gc.ca/english/anima/meavia/commun/20040113come.shtml.

48. Grandin, *Report on Handling and Stunning Practices*, 13.

49. Ontario Office of the Provincial Auditor, 2001 Annual Report, chap. 3.01, http://www.auditor.on.ca/english/reports/en01/301e01.pdf.

50. Deadstock refers to any food animal that has died due to disease or accident sometime prior to processing. In Ontario, it is illegal to sell or process meat from dead animals for human consumption. For details of the various allegations involving Aylmer Meat Packers, see Canadian Food Inspection Agency, "Update — Health Hazard Alert," September 2003, http://www.inspection.gc.ca/english/corpaffr/recarapp/2003/20030916e.shtml, and The Honourable Roland J. Haines, *Farm to Fork: A Strategy for Meat Safety in Ontario*, Report of the Meat Regulatory and Inspection Review (Toronto, 2004): Appendix B.

51. Haines, *Farm to Fork*, 247–51.

52. The notable exception is Quebec, which recently established the *Centre québécois d'inspection des aliments et santé animale*, which enjoys a level of independence similar to the CFIA.

53. Haines, *Farm to Fork*, 245.

54. Ontario Ministry of Agriculture and Food Inspection Programs, June 2004, http://www.gov.on.ca/OMAFRA/english/food/inspection/.

55. Anthony Giddens, "Risk, Lecture 2," *BBC Reith Lectures*, 1999, http://www.lse.ac.uk/Giddens/reith_99/week2/week2.htm; Anthony Giddens, *The Third Way and its Critics* (Cambridge: Polity Press, 2000), 135–39; and Michael Jacobs, "Environment, Modernity and the Thirds Way," in *The Global Third Way Debate*, ed. Anthony Giddens (Cambridge: Polity Press, 2001), 325–26.

56. United Nations Conference on Environment and Development, "Rio Declaration on Environment and Development," Principle 15, 1992, http://www.un.org/documents/ga/conf151/aconf15126-1annex1.htm.

57. Tony Van der Haegen, "EU View of Precautionary Principle in Food Safety," European Union in the U.S., October 2003, http://www.eurunion.org/news/speeches/2003/031023tvdh.htm.

58. Canada Privy Council Office, "Framework for the Application of Precaution in Science-Based Decision Making About Risk," July 2003, http://www.pco-bcp.gc.ca/default.asp?Language=E&Page=publications&Sub=precaution&Doc=precaution_e.htm#1.0.

59. William Leiss, "BSE Risk in Canada: Finally the Penny Drops," July 22, 2003, 14–15, http://www.leiss.ca/chronicles/125.

Chapter 3
FISH OR CUT BAIT: SOLUTIONS FOR OUR SEAS

1. Fred (Fritz) Goldstein, personal communication, May 2004.
2. Ibid.
3. Ibid.
4. Carl Safina, *Song for the Blue Ocean* (New York: Henry Holt, 1998).
5. Food and Agriculture Organization of the United Nations (FAO), "The State of World Fisheries and Aquaculture," 2002.
6. Ibid.
7. Ibid.
8. Ibid.
9. Reg Watson and Daniel Pauly, "Systematic Distortions in World Fisheries Catch Trends," *Nature* 414 (November 2001): 29.
10. Dayton L. Alverson et al., Food and Agriculture Organization of the United Nations, *A Global Assessment of Fisheries By Catch and Discards*, FAO Fisheries Technical Paper no. 339, (Rome, 1996), http://www.fao.org/docrep/003/t4890e/t4890e00.htm.
11. Dayton L. Alverson, personal communication to Mercedes Lee, Blue Ocean Institute, 2004.
12. Inter-American Tropical Tuna Commission (IATTC), *Annual Report of the Inter-American Tropical Tuna Commission 2001* (2002), ISSN: 0074-1000.
13. Lance E. Morgan and Ratana Chuenpagde, *Shifting Gears: Addressing the Collateral Impacts of Fishing Methods in U.S. Waters*, Pew Science Series (Washington, DC: Island Press, 2003).
14. Larry B. Crowder and Ransom A. Myers, *A Comprehensive Study of the Ecological Impacts of the Worldwide Pelagic Longline Industry*, First Annual Report to the Pew Charitable Trusts (2001).
15. National Marine Fisheries Service (NMFS), "Stock Assessment and Fishery Evaluation for Atlantic Highly Migratory Species," 2003, http://www.nmfs.noaa.gov/sfa/hms/.
16. Western Pacific Fishery Management Council (WPFMC), "Western Pacific Council Announces Opening of Model Swordfish Fishery," 2004, http://www.wpcouncil.org/press/pressreleasemodelswordfishfishery.pdf.
17. Dayton L. Alverson et al., Food and Agriculture Organization of the United Nations, *A Global Assessment of Fisheries By Catch and Discards*.
18. Environmental Justice Foundation, "Squandering the Seas: How Shrimp Trawling Is Threatening Ecological Integrity and Food Security Around the World," London, U.K., 2003.
19. Randall Arauz, Sea Turtle Restoration Project, personal communication, 2004.
20. Ransom A. Myers and Boris Worm, "Rapid Worldwide Depletion of Predatory Fish Communities," *Nature* 423 (May 15, 2003): 280–83.
21. Ibid.
22. Daniel Pauly et al., "Fishing Down Marine Food Webs," *Science* 279 (February 6, 1998): 860–63.

23. Daniel Pauly et al., "Towards Sustainability in World Fisheries," *Nature* 418 (August 8, 2002): 689–95.
24. Ibid.
25. "No Seafood Grille, 2050," *Hollywood Ocean Night: A Town Hall for the Oceans*, DVD, produced and directed by Randy Olsen (2004; The Groundlings).
26. Food and Agriculture Organization of the United Nations (FAO), "The State of World Fisheries and Aquaculture," 2002.
27. Fred (Fritz) Goldstein, personal communication, May 2004.
28. Rebecca J. Goldburg, Matt S. Elliot, and Rosamond L. Naylor, *Marine Aquaculture in the United States*, prepared for the Pew Oceans Commission (2001).
29. Food and Agriculture Organization of the United Nations (FAO), "The State of World Fisheries and Aquaculture," 2002.
30. Carrie Brownstein, Mercedes Lee, and Carl Safina, "Harnessing Consumer Power for Conservation," *Conservation in Practice*, Fall 2003.
31. Carl Safina, "What's a Fish Lover to Eat? The Audubon Guide to Seafood," *Audubon* 100 (1998): 63–66.
32. Carrie Brownstein, Mercedes Lee, and Carl Safina, "Harnessing Consumer Power for Conservation."
33. Julian R. Ashford et al., "Seabird Interactions with Longlining Operations for *Dissostichus Eleginoides* at the South Sandwich Islands and South Georgia," CCAMLR *Science* 1 (1994): 143–53.
34. Susan Boa, Seaweb, personal communication, 2003.
35. International Commission for the Conservation of Atlantic Tunas, *Report of the Standing Committee on Research and Statistics*, (Madrid, Spain: SCRS, 2002).
36. Matthew Scully, "The Last Gasps of the Fur Trade," *Humane Society of the United States News*, Fall 1998.
37. Andrea Cimino, Humane Society of the United States, personal communication, 2004.
38. Matthew Scully, "The Last Gasps of the Fur Trade."
39. Aldo Leopold, *Sand County Almanac* (New York: Ballantine Books, 1966).
40. Neil A. Campbell, *Biology*, third ed. (New York: The Benjamin/Cummings Publishing Company, Inc.).
41. NOAA Fisheries, *The Status of U.S. Fisheries*, 2002 Report to Congress (May 2003).
42. National Research Council, *Sustaining Marine Fisheries* (Washington, DC: National Academy Press, 1999).
43. Larry B. Crowder and Ransom A. Myers, *A Comprehensive Study of the Ecological Impacts of the Worldwide Pelagic Longline Industry*.
44. Australian Government, Great Barrier Reef Marine Park Authority, "Explanatory Statement for Great Barrier Reef Marine Park Zoning Plan 2003," 2003, http://www.reefed.edu.au/rap/.
45. Pew Oceans Commission, *America's Living Oceans, Charting a Course for Sea Change* (2003).

Chapter 5
DIET FOR A SMALLER PLANET: REAL SOURCES OF ABUNDANCE

1. See Frances Moore Lappé and Anna Lappé, "Maps of the Mind," in *Hope's Edge: The Next Diet for a Small Planet* (New York: Tarcher/Penguin, 2002). Statistics from United Nations FAO.
2. According to Food Research and Action Center. For more information visit http://www.frac.org.
3. Malnutrition in India statistics from the World Bank Group.
4. See Lappé and Lappé, "Seeding Annapoorna," in *Hope's Edge*. Quote from Shanta Kumar, then minister of Consumer Affairs and Public distribution.
5. Estimates of the percent of world grain fed to livestock vary. We are relying here on Vaclav Smil, *Feeding the World: A Challenge for the Twenty-first Century* (Cambridge, MA: The MIT Press, 2000). After considerable research he arrives at 45 percent but cautions that it is impossible to know precisely.
6. Data supplied by the Economic Research Service, Department of Agriculture, and correspondence, December 2000. See also Frances Moore Lappé and Anna Lappé, *Diet for a Small Planet* (Ballantine Books, 1971, 1991), 445n13.
7. For more information see http://www.rprogess.org. Other alternative indicators include the United Nations Human Development Index (UNHDI), http://www.un.org; the Gross Sustainable Development Product (GSDP) developed by the Global Community Assessment Center and the Society for World Sustainable Development in the U.K.; and the Calvert-Henderson Quality of Life indicators, http://www.calvert-henderson.com.
8. See Gary Gardner and Brian Halweil, *Underfed and Overfed: The Global Epidemic of Malnutrition*, WorldWatch Institute Paper no. 150 (March 2000).
9. See, for example, Eric A. Finkelstein, Ian C. Fiebelkorn, and Guijing Wang, "State-Level Estimates of Annual Medical Expenditures Attributable to Obesity," *Obesity Research* 12, no. 1 (2004): 18–24; and Eric Finkelstein, Ian Fiebelkorn, and Guijing Wang, of the U.S. Centers for Disease Control and Prevention, "National Medical Spending Attributable to Overweight and Obesity: How Much, and Who's Paying?" *Health Affairs*, http://www.healthaffairs.org.
10. Centre Europe-Tiers Monde (CETIM), http://www.cetim.ch.
11. CETIM, "Land Concentration in Brazil: A Politics of Poverty," *Human Rights Sub-Commission 1999.*
12. Statistic from the Brazilian Embassy.
13. Export figures based on statistics from the U.S. Economic Research Service.
14. Brazilian Constitution, 1988, "Chapter III Agricultural and Land Policy and Agrarian Reform, Article 184." The full text reads: "It is within the power of the Union to expropriate on account of social interest, for purposes of agrarian reform, the rural property which is not performing its social function, against prior and fair compensation in agrarian debt bonds with a clause providing for maintenance of the real value, redeemable within a period of up to twenty years computed as from the second year of issue, and the use of which shall be defined in the law."
15. See Lappé and Lappé, "The Battle for Human Nature," in *Hope's Edge*, 67.

16. Ibid., 80.
17. Ibid., 89.
18. See the Community Environmental Legal Defense Fund, http://www.celdf.org.
19. Dr. C. Robert Taylor, Auburn University, personal communication.
20. Environmental Working Group Farm Subsidy Database, http://www.ewg.org/farm.
21. National Campaign for Sustainable Agriculture, Update, June 2001.
22. For more information see http://www.etcgroup.org.
23. Hope Shand, ETC Group, personal communication.
24. For more information see http://www.primalseeds.org.
25. See ETC Group, "Globalization, Inc. Concentration in Corporate Power: The Unmentioned Agenda," no. 71, July/August, 2001.
26. Ibid.
27. See, for example, John Tuxill, *Nature's Cornucopia: Our Stake in Plant Diversity*, WorldWatch Institute Paper no. 148 (September 1999).
28. Cary Fowler and Patrick Mooney, *Shattering: Food, Politics, and the Loss of Genetic Diversity* (Tucson, Arizona: University of Arizona Press, 1990).
29. See Jeffrey Smith, *Seeds of Deception: Exposing Industry and Government Lies About the Safety of Genetically Engineered Foods*, (Fairfield, Iowa: Yes! Books, 2003).
30. The International Service for the Acquisition of Agri-biotech Applications publishes these statistics and others on the global production of GMOs, http://www.isaaa.org.
31. See Clive James, ISAAA Board of Directors "Global Status of Commercialized Transgenic Crops: 2003," http://www.isaaa.org.
32. A. F. Jeu, "Organic Agriculture Can Save the World," *Well Being Journal* 13, no. 2 (March/April 2004).
33. UNFAO, *The State of Food and Agriculture 2004*, (United Nations: May 2004).
34. Smith, *Seeds of Deception*.
35. Margaret Mellon and Jane Rissler, *Gone to Seed: Transgenic Contaminants in the Traditional Seed Supply* (Cambridge, MA: Union of Concerned Scientists, 2004).
36. Definition of hybrid seeds can be found at Genetics Resources Action International (GRAIN), http://www.grain.org.
37. Norman Borlaug (lecture, Earth Institute at Columbia University, 2003).
38. Lappé and Lappé, "Seeding Annapoorna," in *Hope's Edge*, 143.
39. Ibid., 156.
40. See Third World Network, http://www.twnside.org.sg.
41. Lappé and Lappé, *Hope's Edge*, 161–62.
42. Jules Pretty and Rachel Hine, "Empirical Findings of SAFE-World Project," in *Reducing Food Poverty with Sustainable Agriculture*, Center for Environment and Society (University of Essex, U.K., February 2001).
43. Pretty and Hine, see "Empirical Findings," in *Reducing Food Poverty*.
44. Lappé and Lappé, *Hope's Edge*, 286.
45. Margot Roosevelt, "The Coffee Clash," *Time* Online Edition, March 1, 2004.
46. For more information see TransFair USA, http://www.transfairusa.org.
47. For studies on the productivity of sustainable agriculture, see, for example, Pretty

and Hine, *Reducing Food Poverty*; Jeu, "Organic Agriculture"; and Nicholas Parrott and Terry Marsden, Department of City and Regional Planning, Cardiff University, "The Real Green Revolution" (Greenpeace Environmental Trust, February 2002). See in particular Table 4.1 — Examples of yield increases attributable to adoption of OAA.

48. Jules Pretty quotes in *New Scientist*, "An Ordinary Miracle: Bigger harvests, without pesticides or genetically modified crops? Farmers can make it happen by letting weeds do the work" (February 3, 2001).

49. Quoted in Jeu, "Organic Agriculture." From Remarks by the President at the Bio 2003 Convention Center and Exhibition, Washington Convention Center, Washington, DC, June 2003.

Chapter 6
OVERFEEDING THE FUTURE

1. Shengxu Li et al., "Childhood Cardiovascular Risk Factors and Carotid Vascular Changes in Adulthood: The Bogalusa Heart Study," *JAMA* 290 (2003): 2271–76.

2. World Health Organization, *Obesity: Preventing and Managing the Global Epidemic* (Geneva, Switzerland: World Health Organization, 1998).

3. World Health Organization, "Global Strategy on Diet, Physical Activity and Health," http://www.who.int/dietphysicalactivity/publications/facts/obesity/en/ (accessed July 14, 2004).

4. R. Sturm, "The Effects of Obesity, Smoking, and Problem Drinking on Chronic Medical Problems and Health Care Costs," *Health Affairs* 21 (2002): 245–53; and R. Sturm and K. B. Wells, "Does Obesity Contribute as Much to Morbidity as Poverty or Smoking?" *Public Health* 115 (2001): 229–95.

5. Table adapted from information on American Obesity Association website, http://www.obesity.org/subs/fastfacts/Health_Effects.shtml (accessed July 17, 2004).

6. Eric A. Finkelstein, Ian C. Fiebelkorn, and Guijing Wang, "State-Level Estimates of Annual Medical Expenditures Attributable to Obesity," *Obesity Research* 12, no. 1 (2004): 18–24.

7. S. Musich et al., "Association of Additional Health Risks on Medical Charges and Prevalence of Diabetes Within Body Mass Index Categories," *American Journal of Health Promotion* 18 (2004): 264–68.

8. Rebecca Puhl and Kelly D. Brownell, "Bias, Discrimination, and Obesity," *Obesity Research* 9, no. 12 (2001): 788–805.

9. S. A. Richardson et al., "Cultural Uniformity in Reaction to Physical Disabilities," *American Sociological Review* (1961): 241–47.

10. Janet D. Latner and Albert J. Stunkard, "Getting Worse: The Stigmatization of Obese Children," *Obesity Research* 11, no. 3 (2003): 452–56.

11. Adapted from Kelly D. Brownell and Katherine Battle Horgen, *Food Fight: The Inside Story of the Food Industry, America's Obesity Crisis, and What We Can Do About It* (New York: McGraw-Hill/Contemporary Books, 2004).

12. Barry M. Popkin, "An Overview on the Nutrition Transition and its Health Implications: The Bellagio Meeting," *Public Health Nutrition* 5 (2002): 93–103; Barry M. Popkin, "The Nutrition Transition and Obesity in the Developing World," *Journal of Nutrition* 131, no. 3 (2001): 871S–73S; and A. Drewnowski and Barry M. Popkin, "The Nutrition Transition: New Trends in the Global Diet," *Nutrition Reviews* 55 (1997): 31–43.

13. See M. J. Friedrich, "Epidemic of Obesity Expands its Spread to Developing Countries," *JAMA* 287, no. 11 (2002): 1382–86.

14. Michael Pollan, "This Steer's Life," *New York Times Magazine*, March 31, 2002.

15. Saritha Rai, "Protests in India Deplore Soda Makers' Water Use," *New York Times*, May 21, 2003.

16. Table adapted from Michael Browner and Warren Leon, *The Consumer's Guide to Effective Environmental Choices: Practical Advice from the Union of Concerned Scientists* (New York: Three Rivers Press, 1999).

17. M. Story and S. French, "Food Advertising and Marketing Directed at Children and Adolescents in the U.S.," *International Journal of Behavioral Nutrition and Physical Activity* 1, no. 3 (2004): 3–20; Kaiser Family Foundation, "The Role of Media in Childhood Obesity," publication no. 7030, http://www.kff.org/entmedia/7030.cfm (accessed July 12, 2004); American Psychological Association Taskforce, "Television Advertising Leads to Unhealthy Habits in Children," February 23, 2004, http://www.apa.org/releases/childrenads_summary.pdf (accessed July 12, 2004); Brownell and Horgen, *Food Fight*; and World Health Organization, "Marketing Food to Children: The Global Regulatory Environment," http://www.who.int/dietphysicalactivity/publications/en/ (accessed July 14, 2004).

18. P. Rozin et al., "The Ecology of Eating: Smaller Portion Sizes in France than in the United States Help Explain the French Paradox," *Psychological Science* 14, no. 5 (2003): 450–54.

19. Barbara J. Rolls et al., "Increasing the Portion Size of a Packaged Snack Increases Energy Intake in Men and Women," *Appetite* 42 (2004): 63–69; and Barbara J. Rolls, Erin L. Morris, and Liane S. Roe, "Portion Size of Food Affects Energy Intake in Normal-Weight and Overweight Men and Women," *American Journal of Clinical Nutrition* 76, no. 6 (2002): 1207–13.

20. Marion Nestle, *Food Politics: How the Food Industry Influences Nutrition and Health* (Berkeley: University of California Press, 2002).

21. Kelly D. Brownell and Marion Nestle, "The Sweet and Lowdown on Sugar" (OpEd) *New York Times*, January 23, 2004, A23.

22. David A. Kessler, *A Question of Intent: A Great American Battle with a Deadly Industry* (New York: Public Affairs, 2002).

23. K. D. Brownell and K. E. Warner, *The Perils of Ignoring History: Big Tobacco Played Dirty and Millions Died; How Similar is Big Food?* Paper submitted for publication.

24. Courtney Kane, "TV and Movie Characters Sell Children Snacks," *New York Times*, December 8, 2003.

25. World Health Organization, "Marketing Food to Children," http://www.who.int/dietphysicalactivity/publications/en/ (accessed July 14, 2004).

26. American Psychological Association, *Psychological Issues in the Increasing*

Commercialization of Childhood, report of the APA Task Force on Advertising and Children, http://www.apa.org/releases/childrenads_summary.pdf (accessed July 14, 2004).

27. American Academy of Pediatrics, "Prevention of Pediatric Overweight and Obesity," *Pediatrics* 112 (2003): 424–30.

28. Kaiser Family Foundation, "The Role of Media," http://www.kff.org/entmedia/entmedia022404pkg.cfm (accessed July 14, 2004).

29. Story and French, "Food Advertising and Marketing," 3–20.

30. Comments of William McLeod at public meeting of the Kaiser Family Foundation on food advertising directed at children, http://www.kaisernetwork.org/health_cast/uploaded_files/022404_Media_and_Obesity1.pdf (accessed July 14, 2004).

31. Comments of Shelley Rosen of McDonald's in response to a *Reveries Magazine* survey, http://www.reveries.com/reverb/revolver/obesity_marketing/ (accessed July 14, 2004).

32. David S. Ludwig, Karen E. Peterson, and Steven L. Gortmaker, "Relation Between Consumption of Sugar-Sweetened Drinks and Childhood Obesity: A Prospective, Observational Analysis," *Lancet* 357, no. 9255 (2001): 505–08.

33. George A. Bray, Samara Joy Nielsen, and Barry M. Popkin, "Consumption of High Fructose Corn Syrup in Beverages May Play a Role in the Epidemic of Obesity," *American Journal of Clinical Nutrition* 79, no. 4 (2004): 537–43.

34. S. Nielsen and B. M. Popkin, "Changes in Beverage Intake Between 1977–2001," *American Journal of Preventive Medicine*, 2004, in press.

35. National Soft Drink Association, http://www.nsda.org/softdrinks/CSDHealth/Nutrition/NutritionPR/Consumption43.html (accessed July 14, 2004).

36. K. Severson, "L.A. Schools to Stop Soda Sales: District Takes Cue from Oakland Ban," *San Francisco Chronicle*, August 28, 2002, A1.

37. Brownell and Nestle, "The Sweet and Lowdown," A23.

38. Report on letter for William Steiger from the U.S. Department of Health and Human Services to the World Health Organization, http://bmj.bmjjournals.com/cgi/reprint/328/7433/185-a.pdf (accessed July 14, 2004).

39. T. J. Muris, "Don't Blame TV," *Wall Street Journal*, June 25, 2004, A10.

40. Kelly D. Brownell and Marion Nestle, "Are You Responsible for Your Own Weight?" *Time*, June 7, 2004.

41. Brownell and Horgen, *Food Fight*.

42. Brownell and Warner, *The Perils of Ignoring History*.

43. M. F. Jacobson and K. D. Brownell, "Small Taxes on Soft Drinks and Snack Foods to Promote Health," *American Journal of Public Health* 90, no. 6 (2000): 854–57.

44. Brownell and Horgen, *Food Fight*.

45. Frances Moore Lappé and Anna Lappé, A. *Hope's Edge: The Next Diet for a Small Planet* (New York: Tarcher/Penguin, 2002); David Suzuki Foundation, "The Nature Challenge," http://www.davidsuzuki.org/WOL/Challenge/Meals.asp (accessed July 12, 2004); Browner and Leon, *Consumer's Guide to Effective Environmental Choices*; and Cary Fowler and Pat Mooney, *Shattering: Food, Politics, and the Loss of Genetic Diversity* (Tucson: University of Arizona Press, 1996).

Chapter 7
BRAND BARONS AND THE BUSINESS OF FOOD

1. The ICA now has more than 230 member organizations from over 100 countries, representing the livelihoods of more than 760 million individuals worldwide (International Co-operative Alliance, 2004).
2. The ICAO was founded in 1951 and represents agricultural co-operatives and farmers under 47 umbrella agricultural co-operative organizations in 38 countries (International Co-operative Agricultural Organization, 2004).
3. The IFCO was established as an independent entity in 1976 and has 27 member organizations in 23 countries (International Co-operative Fisheries Organization, 2004).
4. According to the UN Food and Agriculture Organization, world population will increase to as many as 8.85 billion people by 2030.
5. Using the Sherman Anti-trust Act and other measures, Roosevelt went on to earn a solid reputation for "trust busting," breaking monopolistic capital enterprises in a number of industry sectors (Wheeler & Sillanpää, 1997).
6. Anglo-Dutch consumer goods conglomerate Unilever employs around a quarter of a million employees worldwide and has a turnover in excess of €42 billion.
7. The McCain Capital Corporation represents the family interests of Wallace McCain, whose New Brunswick family firm McCain Foods manufactures and sells one third of the world's frozen French fries, and has CAN$6 billion in sales and 13,000 employees around the world. Wallace McCain formed McCain Foods with his brother Harrison (dec'd) in 1956. They were estranged in 1994 and never reconciled.

References
F. C. Accum, *A Treatise on Adulterations of Food, and Culinary Poisons: Exhibiting the Fraudulent Sophistications of Bread, Beer, Wine, Spirits, Spirituous Liquors, Tea, Coffee, Cream, Confectionery, Vinegar, Mustard, Pepper, Cheese, Olive Oil, Pickles, and Other Articles Employed in Domestic Economy and Methods of Detecting Them* (London: J. Mallett, 1820).
Agriculture and Agri-Food Canada, *Canada's Organic Industry* (Ottawa: AAFC, 2002), http://ats.agr.ca (accessed June 12, 2003).
Agriculture and Agri-Food Canada, *What's Hot and What's Not in the US Food Market* (Ottawa: AAFC, 2001), http://www.agr.gc.ca/misb/fb/food/industryinfo/data/retail/trends_e.html (accessed June 12, 2004).
M. Altieri and C. Nicholls, "Returning Organic Farming to its Roots," *In Business*, January/February 2004.
BCTF, "Selling our Public Spaces: Teachers Host Seminar on Commercialization of Schools," British Columbia Teachers Federation News Release, May 5, 2004, http://www.bctf.ca/publications/newsreleases/archive/2004/2004-05-05.html.
J. Birchall, *Co-Op. The People's Business* (Manchester: Manchester University Press, 1994).
L. R. Brown, "World Food Security Deteriorating," Earth Policy News, 2004, http://www.earth-policy.org/Updates/Update40.htm (accessed May 6, 2004).

Canadian Paediatric Society, "Impact of Media Use on Children and Youth," *Paediatrics and Child Health* 8, no. 5 (2003): 301–306.

CBC, "Medical Journal Condemns Junk Food," CBC News Online, 2003, http://www.cbc.ca/stories/2003/11/13/Consumers/lancet_junkfood031113 (accessed June 17, 2004).

Center for Global Food Issues, "High-Yield Conservation Protects Biodiversity," Center for Global Food Issues web site (accessed June 12, 2004).

J. Clay, *World Agriculture and the Environment* (2004).

David Suzuki Foundation, 2004, http://www.davidsuzuki.org/Oceans/Fish_Farming/Salmon/.

DuPont, Annual Review, 2004, http://www1.dupont.com/dupontglobal/corp/documents/US/en_US/news/publications/dupfinancial/2003review.pdf (accessed June 14, 2004).

Earthtrends, *Agriculture and Food — Canada* (Washington DC: WRI, 2003), http://www.wri.org (accessed June 6, 2004).

FAO, *The State of World Fisheries and Aquaculture 2002* (Rome: FAO, 2002).

Farmcare, Farmcare web site, 2004, http://www.co-opfarmcare.com/index2.htm (accessed June 12, 2004).

FCPMC, *Submission to the Standing Committee on Health*, April 11, 2002.

K. Higgin, "The World's Top 100 Food and Beverage Companies," *Food Engineering*, October 2002, http://www.foodengineeringmag.com/CDA/ArticleInformation/coverstory/BNPCoverStoryItem/0,6326,96622,00.html (accessed June 20, 2004).

R. Hites et al., "Global Assessment of Organic Contaminants in Farmed Salmon" *Science* 303 (January 9, 2004): 226–229.

K. Holmes, *Carnivorous Cravings: Charting the World's Protein Shift* (Washington, DC: WRI, 2001).

HRDC, "Biotechnology in Agriculture," HRDC website, 2004, http://www24.hrdc-drhc.gc.ca (accessed June 11, 2004).

International Co-operative Agricultural Organization, ICAO website, 2004, http://www.agricoop.org/about/about.htm (accessed June 12, 2004).

International Co-operative Alliance, ICA website, 2004, http://www.ica.coop/ica/ica/ica-intro.html (accessed June 12, 2004).

International Co-operative Fisheries Organization, ICFO website, 2004, http://www.coop.org/ica/ica/sb/fish.html (accessed June 12, 2004).

International Co-operative Information Centre, ICIC website, 1994, http://www.wisc.edu/uwcc/icic/def-hist/history/1994.html (accessed June 12, 2004).

ISNAR, *Biotechnology and Sustainable Livelihoods — Findings and Recommendations of an International Consultation*, Briefing Paper 54, The Hague, International Service for National Agricultural Research, 2002.

A. Kimbrell, *The Fatal Harvest Reader: The Tragedy of Industrial Agriculture* (Gabriola Island BC: Island Press, 2002).

J. Laing, "Letter from Los Angeles," *Fashion*, Summer 2004, 34.

R. Mackie, "Ontario Zeroing in on Smoking, Junk Food" *Globe and Mail*, April 9, 2004, http://www.theglobeandmail.com/servlet/ArticleNews/TPStory/LAC/20040409/ONTARIO09/TPHealth/.

C. C. Mann, "The Bluewater Revolution," *Wired* 05 (2004).

C. C. Mann, *Diversity on the Farm*, Political Economy Research Unit (New York: University of Massachusetts and Ford Foundation, 2004).

R. Manning, "Superorganics," *Wired* (May 2004): 178-180, 215.

K. Partridge, "Read the Cold Hard Facts about Childhood Obesity and Inactivity," *Today's Parent*, November 2003.

Pew Initiative on Food and Biotechnology, *Feeding the World. A Look at Biotechnology and World Hunger* (Washington: Pew, 2004).

C. Poppe and U. Kjærnes, *Trust in Food in Europe: A Comparative Analysis* (Oslo: National Institute for Food Research, 2003), http://www.trustinfood.org/SEARCH/BASIS/tif0/all/publics/DDD/24.pdf (accessed June 21, 2004).

P. Pringle, *Food Inc. Mendel to Monsanto — The Promises and Perils of the Biotech Harvest* (New York: Simon & Schuster, 2003).

J. Rifkin, *The Biotech Century* (New York: Jeremy P Tarcher/Putnam, 1998).

J. Rifkin, "A Precautionary Tale," *The Guardian*, May 12, 2004.

Raizel Robin, "5. George Weston Ltd.," *Canadian Business Top 75 Companies*, 2003, http://www.canadianbusiness75.com/05.htm (accessed June 14, 2004).

A. Rowell, *Don't Worry, It's Safe to Eat: The True Story of GM Food, BSE and Foot and Mouth* (London: Earthscan, 2003).

M. Schwartz, *How the Cows Turned Mad* (Berkeley: University of California Press, 2003).

V. Shiva, *Stolen Harvest: The Hijacking of the Global Food Supply* (Cambridge: South End Press, 2002).

U. Sinclair, *The Jungle* (Cambridge: Bentley Publishers, 1971).

J. C. Smith, *Understanding Childhood Obesity* (Jackson: University of Mississippi Press, 1999).

G. Tomso, "Death in the Pot. Victorian Food Adulteration, Food Analysis and Analytical Chemistry. An Annotated Bibliography," 1997, http://www.duke.edu/~sedgwic/textures/deathpot.htm

Unilever, *Annual Reports and Accounts and Form 20-F 2003* (London: Unilever, 2004).

Unilever, *Fishing for the Future II: Unilever's Fish Sustainability Initiative* (London: Unilever, 2003).

C. Van de Weyer, "Child Obesity — An Epidemic of Inequality," *New Statesman* 20 (October 2003).

D. Wheeler and M. Sillanpää, *The Stakeholder Corporation* (London: Pitman, 1997).

M. L. Winston, *Travels in the Genetically Modified Zone* (Cambridge: Harvard University Press, 2002).

A. S. Wohl, *Endangered Lives: Public Health in Victorian and Edwardian England* (Cambridge: Harvard University Press, 1983).

WRI et al., *Tomorrow's Markets* (Washington DC: WRI, 2002).

The authors would like to thank all the social entrepreneurs who contributed to our thinking on this topic: especially Hany Abouleish, Robin Bines, Doug Muzyka, Jan Kees Vis, Farouk Jiwa, and David van Seters.

Chapter 8
BETWEEN FEAST AND FAMINE: FIXING GLOBAL TRADE

1. Brian E. Hill, *The Common Agricultural Policy: Past, Present and Future* (London, 1984), 19.
2. François Duchene, Edward Szczepanik, and Wilfrid Legg, *New Limits on European Agriculture: Politics and the Common Agricultural Policy* (London, 1985), 25.
3. David Harvey, "The Production Entitlement Guarantee (PEG) Option," in *The Common Agricultural Policy and the World Economy: Essays in Honour of John Ashton*, ed. Christopher Ritson and David Harvey (Wallingford, U.K.: CAB International, 1991), 312.
4. Stefan Tangerman, "Agriculture on the Way to Firm International Trading Rules," in *The Political Economy of International Trade Law: Essays in Honor of Robert E. Hudec*, ed. Daniel L. M. Kennedy and James D. Southwick, (Cambridge: Cambridge University Press, 2002), 254.
5. Patrick Low, *Trading Free: The GATT and U.S. Trade Policy*, (New York: Century Foundation Press, 1995), 24.
6. Sylvia Ostry, "Summitry and Trade: What Could Sea Island Do for Doha?" in *Security, Prosperity and Freedom: Why America Needs the G8* (Indiana: Indiana University, June 2004).
7. Sylvia Ostry, *Governments and Corporations in a Shrinking World: Trade and Innovation Policies in the United States, Europe and Japan* (New York: Council on Foreign Relations, 1990), 18–25.
8. John Croome, Reshaping *the World Trading System: A History of the Uruguay Round* (Geneva, Switzerland: World Trade Organization, 1995), 386.
9. UN Wire 11-06, Friday June 11, 2004.
10. Sylvia Ostry, "Dissent.Com: How NGOs are Re-Making the WTO," *Policy Options*, (June 2001).
11. Ostry, "Summitry and Trade."
12. *Global Civil Society, 2003*, ed. Mary Kaldor, Helmut Anheier, and Marlies Glasius, Part IV, (London: Oxford, 2003); and *Global Civil Society, 2002*, Part IV.
13. See TWN Info Services on WTO Issues, June 11, 2004; June 12, 2004; June, 17 2004; June 19, 2004; Third World Network, http://www.twnside.org.sg.
14. Institute for Agriculture and Trade Policy, *United States Dumping on World Agricultural Markets* (Minneapolis, 2004).
15. Joachim von Braun, Ashok Gulati, and David Orden, "Making Agricultural Trade Policy Work for the Poor," address delivered at the WTO Public Symposium *Multilateralism at a Crossroads*, Geneva, May 25, 2004.
16. Ibid.
17. David Orden and Michael Taylor, "Global Agricultural Policy Reform: Venues and Issues," Resources for the Future and International Food Policy Research Institute, contact IFPRI, copyright@cigar.org. Quote from Per Pinstrup-Andersen, 24.
18. Eugenio Diaz-Bonilla, Marcelle Thomas, and Sherman Robinson, "Trade, Food Security and WTO Negotiations: Some Reflections on Boxes," in OECD, *Agricultural Trade and Poverty: Making Policy Analysis Count* (Paris, 2003), 85; For a

recent review of literature on trade and growth see A. Winters, N. McCulloch, and A. McKay, "Trade Liberalization and Poverty: The Evidence so Far," *Journal of Economic Literature* (2004): 72–115. There is no consensus on the link nor on the relationship with poverty.

19. See D. C. North, "The New Institutional Economic and Third World Development," ed. J. Harriss, J. Hunter, and C. Lewis, *The New Institutional Economics and Third World Development*, (New York: Taylor & Francis Books, 1995), 17–26.

20. Victor Masoti, "The New Partnership for Africa's Development: Institutional and Legal Challenges of Investment Promotion," *San Diego International Law Journal* 5, no. 1 (2004): 1–36.

21. Ibid., 21. Masoti points out that there is already an ongoing project on agriculture but nothing has been implemented, 22–24.

Chapter 9
REVITALIZING THE RANCH: A MEXICAN FARM STORY

1. Interview with Raul Medina, July, 2004.
2. Interview with Raul Medina, May, 2004.
3. Interview with Teodoro Silva, Hydrologist, IPN-CIIDIR, October 4, 2002, Jiquilpan, Michoacan.
4. Interview with Javier Jimenez, July, 2002, Jamay, Jalisco.
5. Herb Barbolet, "Bringing Food Back Home: Factory Farms, Food as Commodity and the Politics of Selfishness," *Shared Vision* 168 (Vancouver, BC, August, 2002): 19; also see Mayrand et al., "The Economic and Environmental Impacts of Agricultural Subsidies: An Assessment of the 2002 U.S. Farm Bill and Doha Round," Unisfera International Centre, Montreal, January 2003.
6. Naveli Cortes, "El PRI elabora esquema de reconversion agricola," *Publico* 21 (Monday, August 12, 2002): 21.
7. Matilde Perez y Patricia Muñoz, "Llego a su etapa final la proteccion del capitulo agropecuario en el TLCAN," *La Jornada* (July 8, 2002): 8.
8. Interview with Raul Medina, May, 2004.
9. Interview with Raul Medina, July, 2004.

Afterword

1. Through Investeco Capital Corp., Andrew Heintzman has a financial interest in Organic Meadow Inc.
2. See http://my.webmd.com/content/article/64/72524.htm.
3. See (http://www.worldhungeryear.org/info_center/just_facts.asp).
4. Vaclav Smil, *Feeding the World: A Challenge for the Twenty-first Century* (Cambridge, MA: The MIT Press, 2000), xxv.

EDITORS' ACKNOWLEDGEMENTS

The Ingenuity Project, more than most endeavours of this sort, is a group effort. It would not happen without the input, dedication, friendship, and sage advice of many people. Most important, of course, are the contributors to the book: William I. Atkinson, Kelly Brownell, Carrie Brownstein, Mark Juhasz, Stuart Laidlaw, Anna Lappé, Frances Lappé, Ian MacLachlan, Sylvia Ostry, Carl Safina, Jane Thomson, Florence Wambugu, and David Wheeler. Thanks also to Eric Schlosser, whose work partly helped to inspire this book, for penning the foreword.

We would especially like to thank Kevin Siu, who was absolutely central in creating this book. We have now worked with Kevin on a number of projects, starting back in our days at *Shift* magazine. His good-natured style is mixed with effectiveness, insight, and intelligence. Kevin is responsible for pulling together many of the chapters in this collection. Without him this book would not have happened; simple as that. Kevin is now editing the back-of-the-book section for *Report on Business*, where we are sure his editorial abilities will continue to be well received by readers and colleagues alike. We hope that he will continue to be involved in the Ingenuity Project for many years to come. Thank you sincerely, Kevin.

Another person we would like to thank is another Kevin: Kevin Linder, the managing editor at House of Anansi Press. Kevin Linder's great editorial judgement and his dedication to this series have been invaluable to us. He is professional, smart, and a pleasure to work with.

Other important contributors from Anansi include Martha Sharpe, the publisher, Sarah MacLachlan, the president, Laura Repas, the publicity manager, and Scott Griffin, chairman and owner. The commitment of these good people to this series shows in the level of quality of production and promotion they have put into this project.

The Ingenuity Project is more than a book, and we must note out other multimedia partners, who include Anthony Wilson-Smith and his team at *Maclean's* magazine, Stuart Coxe, Heaton Dyer, Janet Thompson, Alice Hopton, and Dana Glassman at CBC *Newsworld*, and the wonderful Pam Bertrand and the team at *The Current* at CBC Radio One.

Thanks also go to John Hall, Cammilla Leigh, and the visionary team at McGill university.

Finally, and most importantly, our gratitude goes to our families. To our wives, Tammy and Roz, whose patience, insight, and support are so crucial and at times so tested. And to Maizie, Molly, Theodore, and the newly arrived Gideon, our children, who are why any and all of this make sense. We love you more than one book can explain.